Ravine East of Funchal.

A WINTER
IN
MADEIRA:
AND
A SUMMER
IN
SPAIN AND FLORENCE.

BY JOHN A. DIX.

SECOND EDITION.

NEW YORK:
PUBLISHED BY WILLIAM HOLDREDGE,
140 FULTON STREET.
1851.

BANER AND PALMER, STEREOTYPERS,
201 William, corner of Frankfort street, New York.

PREFACE.

THE following pages were the fruit, not so much of deliberate design as of a long-settled habit, on the part of the writer, of devoting a portion of every day to some steady employment. During his absence from his native country, for want of his usual occupations of business, he found the continuance of this practice in some degree essential to his comfort. In attempting to delineate the objects by which he was surrounded, and the scenes into which he was thrown, many an hour, which would otherwise have hung heavily on his hands, was beguiled, and, at least, rendered agreeable to himself. If the sketches he has drawn, or the opinions he has advanced, shall prove in any degree interesting or useful to others, he will enjoy a still higher gratification than that which the occupation afforded him. In the lighter portions of the work he has written down every thing he saw precisely as it presented itself; in the graver, his sole aim has been to state facts with accuracy, and in a plain and intelligible shape. If he has succeeded in this respect, he will have accomplished all the expectation he has ventured to indulge in entering, for the first time, and probably the last, the field of authorship. Those who read these sketches will acquit him of all over-anxiety to make them public, when they perceive, as the dates show, that they have been for seven years unused, and especially when he states that they are given up now to oblige a friend, and to furnish as full a response as he is able to give to inquiries frequently addressed to him for information respecting Madeira, by persons designing to visit that island. He will only add, that the lapse of time has not detracted materially from the value of his notes, if any value they have. The Madeira of 1843 is the Madeira of 1850. The changes in New York in a single year are greater than those in Madeira in half a century. He is aware that the sketches in Spain and Italy, which he has appended to those in Madeira, will have less novelty for most readers; but they were written in connection with each other, and are, therefore, published together.

NEW YORK, *October*, 1850.

CONTENTS.

CHAPTER I.

THE VOYAGE.

CHAPTER II.

FIRST IMPRESSIONS OF MADEIRA.

CHAPTER III.

THE CITY OF FUNCHAL AND ITS ENVIRONS.

CHAPTER IV.

CITY OF FUNCHAL.

CHAPTER V.

CITY OF FUNCHAL.

CHAPTER VI.

CITY OF FUNCHAL.

CHAPTER VII.

CITY OF FUNCHAL.

CHAPTER VIII.

CLIMATE OF FUNCHAL.

CHAPTER IX.

GOVERNMENT OF PORTUGAL.

CHAPTER X.

LOCAL GOVERNMENT OF MADEIRA.

CHAPTER XI.

MADEIRA.

CHAPTER XII.

VOYAGE TO CADIZ.

CHAPTER XIII.

CITY OF CADIZ.

CHAPTER XIV.

CITY OF SEVILLE.

CHAPTER XV.

CITY OF SEVILLE.

CHAPTER XVI.

GIBRALTAR.

CHAPTER XVII.

EASTERN COAST OF SPAIN.

CHAPTER XVIII.

VOYAGE TO LEGHORN.

CHAPTER XIX.

JOURNEY TO FLORENCE.

CHAPTER XX.

FLORENCE.

WINTER IN MADEIRA.

CHAPTER I.

THE VOYAGE.

The Departure.—The Ship and Captain.—A Storm.—The Planets and the Sea at Night.—The Azores, or Western Islands.—A Sailor's Life.—The two Mates.—Charley, the Raw Hand.—Termination of the Voyage.

At four o'clock in the afternoon of the 16th of October, 1842, the pilot left the ship Mexican at the Narrows, and as the sun went down over the highlands of Neversink, these last vestiges of American soil were fast fading upon the sight. Five days have not yet elapsed since our berths were engaged. In this brief space of time our arrangements for an absence of months, possibly years, have been made; business has been settled as well as it could be; a hasty adieu has been exchanged with the friends immediately around us, and others more remote have been left to learn our departure from the shipping list, and to wonder at the unceremonious manner in which we have separated ourselves from them and our native land. Nothing but the sternest necessity would have reconciled us to the numberless embarrassments, annoyances, and sacrifices inseparable from so precipitate a movement. The hope of restoring to health one of our number suddenly stricken with disease, and the conviction that an immediate change of climate alone could accomplish an object so near the hearts of all, outweighed every consideration of convenience; and if in the healing air of Madeira, to which our good ship is destined, it shall be our happiness to find "the priceless pearl" we seek, these few hurried days of preparation, painful as they have been, will be remembered as among the brightest of our lives.

We found seven passengers, besides our own party, embarked with us, making thirteen in all, for we numbered six. Of these seven, four were invalids, leaving the country in pursuit of health. The lunch at noon found us all united at table. We were still in the smooth waters of the harbor, and our ship was running on before a fine westerly breeze as gently as though she was wholly without motion. As usual, the first meal on board ship was best attended. All were in the highest spirits. The wind was fair. We were sure, as the sailors have it, of making a good offing. Though we were past the middle of October, a fine, warm sun was pouring his beams down upon us; and even the invalids were cheered and renovated by the favorable auspices under which we commenced our voyage. In a few hours more we were on the broad bosom of the ocean, riding over its long, swelling surges; and when dinner was announced, the captain and two of our fellow-passengers were all that could be mustered in the cabin "fit for duty." The rest had crawled into their berths, trying to get rid of the motion of the vessel by shutting their eyes against it; or, in despair of relief from that resource, preparing for the worst, and looking unutterable things over basins. For five days the wind with which we started not only continued to blow from the same quarter, but constantly with increasing strength. On the fifth it became violent, until at last the ship was entirely stripped of her canvas, with the exception of a close-reefed fore-topsail; and thus we ran for twenty-four hours before the gale, with two men at the wheel, our decks washed incessantly by the sea, but hurrying on toward our destined haven with a speed which the most impatient could not well have wished greater. At the end of the six days we were nearly 1200 miles from New York. Two fifths of our entire voyage were completed. The sea itself did not run as high as our hopes. "We shall have a short passage," was the general exclamation. But all these expectations and prophecies were to be dissipated by the inconstant winds. A calm succeeded, then head-winds, and at the end of six days more we had scarcely added 200 miles to the distance we had run during the first six.

I know nothing more idle for a landsman than the time spent at sea, unless he is adding to his stock of health. Any thing like systematic application is out of the question. At least, I have always found it so. The utmost one can hope to compass is to make time pass away agreeably; and this is usually a matter of no small difficulty. In the larger packets or in the steamers, which are now traversing the Atlantic, the resources for amusement and occupation are far more numerous than in small vessels like ours. Our burden is only 300 tons; but in a gale, commend me to one of these little craft instead of the overgrown sea structures of modern times, which have always seemed to me to decrease in strength and facility of management as they increase in size and weight, just as a man loses his muscular power and activity as he adds to his bulk. This may be a prejudice of ours, which experience will correct. If it be, it has a legitimate origin; for we have thrice at sea ridden out violent gales in vessels of the tonnage of this, when every larger one we encountered had sustained severe injuries. We labor under some disadvantages it is true. We are only about 25 feet in width and something less than 100 in length—scarcely the size of a New York building lot—and unless we go down into the hold or up into the rigging we can only make two passable stories out of our sea house. For all that, we have snug sleeping apartments, an excellent dining-room, and in calm weather we have a comfortable parlor on deck, though a dash of salt water will sometimes come over us when we are sitting up in state under heaven's broad canopy, and cheating the voyage of something of its tedium by reading the last novel, or, if we are more studiously inclined, Liebig's "Organic Chemistry," in the ample pages of the "New World" or the "Boston Notion."

Next to a good ship (for no skill in seamanship will compensate for a bad one) the thing most to be desired is a good captain. We were singularly fortunate in this respect. A better seaman or a more prudent and careful navigator than Captain Deming, it would not be easy to find. What is more, this was his seventy-third voyage to Madeira. Nobody knows the way there better than himself. And let it not be supposed that this is an idle fancy of ours. The ocean has its paths as well as the land. In the passage from New York to Madeira there is the Gulf-stream on one side and the trade-winds on the other; and the direction to be taken to secure the greatest aggregate number of chances of catching the prevailing currents of air in different portions of the course, at different seasons of the year, is a matter requiring experience and good judgment. In the autumn, westerly winds are the most frequent on the American coast—on the European, northeasterly. The captain, therefore, ran for the Western Islands, which are only from one to two degrees of latitude south of New York, making his first fifty degrees of longitude in nearly an easterly course, and running down his other eight degrees of latitude in his last eight of longitude. The event proved that he judged rightly; for a vessel which left New York three days after us and sailed as well as ours, took a more southerly course, and was four days longer out than we, arriving at Madeira a week later.

But it was in the hour of peril that our captain's sterling qualities were most apparent. I know how prone we all are to consider the dangers we have run as transcending in magnitude those which have fallen to the lot of our neighbors. The gales we have encountered seem more violent and the storms more terrific. Without claiming for this voyage of ours any extraordinary superiority over others in this respect, I may safely say that we had one gale of unusual severity. It came on in the afternoon, about five o'clock, while we were under full sail, but so gradually that the ship was put in condition to meet it without difficulty. The captain commenced reefing his topsails, but no sooner was a sail reefed than it became necessary, from the increasing violence of the wind, to take it in. The spars were thus, in succession, stripped of their canvas, until at eight o'clock (three hours after the gale commenced) the captain found it indispensable to lay the ship to under the storm-staysail. In this condition we continued through the night and until noon the next day. There is certainly nothing so appalling to one unused to such occurrences as a storm at sea. Its terrors are greatly heightened by darkness. The rushing of the wind through the ship's rigging, has a sound which is to be heard nowhere else. I never hear it without thinking of Æolus, as Virgil describes him in the first book of the Æneid, mustering his forces, at the suggestion of the sister of Jove, to carry devastation into the fleet of the Trojans. I generally keep the deck on such occasions; not only because there is a sublimity in them, which is not without its gratification though it be accompanied by a sense of insecurity—but because it is always satisfactory to know the extent of the danger, if there be any. By day you can form a tolerably accurate opinion of your condition. If a wave comes over you, you can measure with your eye its magnitude and its effects. But when all is shrouded in darkness, it is not always easy to determine what the degree of the danger is. If you ship a sea, the fancy is ever busy, and successfully so, in magnifying the difficulty, when the eye can not correct its suggestions. In the cabin your condition is still more disagreeable. You hear the struggling of the ship, the creaking of the cordage, the roaring of the wind, the rushing of the water from one side to the other on deck, as the vessel reels and staggers under the buffetings of the sea—forming, altogether, a complication of sounds and terrors, which, however bold-faced and strong-hearted we may be, makes us long inwardly for a berth on dry land. The praiseworthy but not altogether disinterested idea occurs to us, that we might be in infinitely better condition for the final catastrophe, if we could be allowed further time for preparation. During the whole of the night, and until noon the next day, we lay anxiously awaiting an abatement of the gale. Then the wind became favorable, the storm-staysail was taken in, the foresail set, and in a few moments we were scudding under this single piece of canvas, through a sea more rough than is often witnessed. A more sublime spectacle can not be fancied than that which presented itself: the ocean, lashed by the violence of the gale into foam; the waves rushing on from behind, as if to overwhelm us; and the ship riding over them with admirable buoyancy and ease. It is said that the utmost height of the waves, when the sea is most violently agitated, does not exceed twenty-five feet. They certainly seemed to us much greater. "Father," said little Charley, "the captain has just taken me to see the waves, and they look just like mountains with snow on the tops of them." And so they did, to our sight as well as his. Charley sketched from nature, as she presented herself to him; and when we hear of waves running "mountains high," let us not find fault with the description, whatever the more accurate investigations of science may teach to the contrary.

In my nocturnal visits to the deck, which were equally frequent in fair weather and foul, I was repeatedly struck with the brilliancy of the light emitted by the stars and planets. I know not whether it be a mere fancy, but I have often thought them more bright and sparkling when seen from the sea than from the land. They ought not to be so on any philosophical principle. In contrast with the dark and shadowy earth, they should appear more brilliant than when they look down into the waters beneath, rendering them almost as luminous as themselves. For several nights, in the moon's last quarter, before she had come forth to dispute with the other celestial bodies the empire of the night, we were watching Jupiter and Venus, and admiring their clear and strongly-defined paths of light, extending from the very horizon almost to the ship's side. The reflected light of Venus, though not poured out in so full a flood as that of the moon, seemed scarcely less distinct and brilliant, while that of the larger planet fell upon the sight in a narrow, flickering stream, reminding us significantly of the vast distance which its rays are compelled to traverse in their visit to the earth.

The phosphorescent aspect of the sea, as the waves are broken by the motion of the ship, is another beautiful and impressive feature in these bright nights. The water around the bow and along the vessel's sides becomes bright and luminous; and as the spray comes over the bulwarks, it runs across the deck flashing and sparkling as though it were filled with diamonds. I have often watched these singular appearances, and wondered whether it were possible that such huge masses of water, radiant with light, could become illuminated, as science teaches us, by the presence of innumerable crustaceous animals, which possess, like the firefly in our own country and the glow-worm in Europe, the property of emitting light. Similar effects, in more southern latitudes, are well ascertained to proceed from similar causes; as the brilliant spots with which the sapphirina indicator marks the surface of the Indian Ocean, and the less beautiful but equally well-defined masses of light which the pyrosomæ display in the same seas. Neither of these varieties is, perhaps, either so brilliant or condensed as those I have described, but it seems to be well ascertained that they all have their origin in the same general cause.

A few days after the gale, we came in sight of the Azores, or Western Islands. The peak of Pico first appeared rising from the bosom of the ocean, and resembling, in form and general effect, one of the Egyptian pyramids in the solitude of the desert. We were then directly west of it, and at its northern extremity we could soon after just discern the point of Fayal, apparently in contact with it. The two islands are only about nine miles apart; and we expected, as we went below for the night, that we should be able to pass between them. But, before morning, the wind changed, and compelled us to go to the north of Fayal. The mate, who had the morning watch, called me just before daybreak, as I had requested; and when I came on deck, I found the ship running under the northern side of Fayal, which towered above us, a dark, shapeless mass, almost without outline. We were but two miles off, and we distinctly heard the waves breaking against its rock-bound sides. In a few minutes more the captain came on deck, and directed the ship's course to be changed to the northward, lest she should be becalmed under the lee of the island. Before the day broke, we were four miles distant; but as the island came out before us in the morning light, the ravines, cliffs, and promontories into which its whole surface is broken, became distinctly visible. We saw a church with a low, massive turret, and around it a cluster of houses of the same color, and manifestly of the same material, as the hard, seamy sides of the hills at the base of which this little settlement stood. A large portion of the surface of the island—that part of it, at least, which was within the range of our vision—seemed to be rock, now stretching itself out in wide, sloping plains, or breaking off into abrupt precipices, apparently unsuited to cultivation.

The view of Fayal, as the day broke, was picturesque and beautiful. It was rendered more so by the peak of Pico, a few miles beyond it, elevating the dark and pointed summit, from which it derives its name, high into the heavens, while a profusion of light, fleecy clouds were gathering beneath it. The general form of Pico, as it presented itself to us, is that of a pyramid. It runs down on each side, about half the way from its vertex, in nearly uniform lines, and then stretches itself out into a narrow, extended base. We were informed that it was 10,000 feet high, but I doubted it; and, as I subsequently learned, it is much less. It has been variously estimated, from 6,700 upward, to 10,000. It unquestionably falls below the elevation of perpetual snow, which, in this parallel of latitude, is about 9,500 feet. The best accounts fix it at about 7,700; but it has not, as I can ascertain, been accurately measured. The greater part of the island is highly cultivated, and produces a large quantity of wine of inferior quality, which is sent to Fayal, and thence exported. During one entire day we were in sight of these two islands. At nightfall, St. George came in view; then Gracioso; and the next morning, Terceira appeared in the distance, a dark, indistinct mass. This and St. Michael's are the finest and most productive of the group. Terceira has gained for itself quite a martial reputation, for the firmness and spirit with which it resisted Don Miguel, and repelled his land and naval forces, when the rest of the Azores, as well as Madeira, submitted to him. St. Michael's we left to the south, together with the little island of St. Mary, while Flores and Corvo were at a still greater distance to the north, as we passed Fayal. These islands have always been subject to Portugal, but they are nearly a barren appendage to the Portuguese crown. Terceira alone, I believe, yields a small revenue.

After passing the Western Islands, the wind became favorable and blew fresh, and we felt that we were rapidly approaching the termination of our voyage. It is needless to say how much pleasure this conviction brought with it. But there had been much in the voyage to interest us. In every ship, if one will but look after them, there are sources of entertainment, at least, if not of instruction. They were certainly not wanting in ours. I have always regarded the life of a sailor in a merchant vessel as one of the very hardest a man can lead. Cold, wet, heat, broken rest, exposure of all kinds, are his constant companions. He is sure only of one thing, and that is unceasing occupation. To keep a ship in perfect order is said to be like a woman's work—it is never done. I hardly remember, during the whole voyage, to have seen one of the crew idle. The division of the day and night into watches of four hours, must be one of Jack's greatest annoyances. I am sure it would be with me. He can by possibility have no more than four successive hours of sleep. He never knows, during the voyage at all events, the luxury, on some particularly drowsy occasion, of turning over, after one's regular allowance of sleep, and taking a little extra indulgence. Nay, he is not even sure of enjoying undisturbed the portion allotted to him by the economy of the ship. How often, during the voyage, have I heard all hands called in the middle of the watch, to take in a sail which the violence of the wind would allow the ship to carry no longer! Up he comes from the forecastle, warm and reeking, perhaps, with perspiration, from the close air in which he has been sleeping. As he reaches the deck, a sea comes over the bow and drenches him with just such a cold bath as Priessnitz might prescribe for one of his patients. But Jack does not stand in need of any such reaction of the system, and he will be very likely to express his opinion to that effect by growling out an oath at this unwelcome visitation. However, he goes up into the shrouds, and thence into the top, not the less good-humoredly. The rain is coming down in torrents, and he goes out on the slippery yard, his feet resting, for their only support, on an equally slippery rope, the wind blowing a hurricane; and before the sail is furled, he has not a dry thread on him. In this condition he returns to the forecastle. If he has dry clothes, he puts them on; but if the storm is of long continuance, he is not always so fortunate. In that case, he lies down in his wet ones, and dries them by his own internal heat. I was compassionating the poor fellows on one of these occasions, when the mate remarked that it was nothing in comparison with the wintry storms on the coast, when the rigging was stiff with snow and frost, and when a man could not remain a half-hour aloft without freezing. This was, I must confess, a complication of suffering I had not then thought of. No wonder a common sailor with a gray head is so rare a sight. And yet the life of a sailor is one which he will exchange for no other. He adheres to his ship with German tenacity, as though it were a homestead, which it would be disreputable to part with.

Two better specimens of this professional devotion can not well be fancied than our two mates. They had both been brought up on the salt water.

They had not the slightest inclination to see dry land, and wondered how any one else could have. One of them had been six times in Madeira, and had only been ashore once, and then only to go as far as the custom-house, which stands close to the beach, to transact some necessary business. When I expressed my surprise at this indifference, he coolly remarked, that there was no one in Madeira he knew, and he could see as much of the city as he desired from the ship. The other was second mate of the ship Bristol when she was wrecked on Long Island, about the same time with the Mexico, and was one of the sixteen persons saved out of 109. But he was not the less enamored of the sea; and, so far as danger is concerned, he was perfectly satisfied that the probability of having one's neck broken on land was far greater than that of being drowned in salt water—the only mischance a mariner is exposed to. The two mates had a state-room on deck. There were two berths in it; but only one was in a condition to be used for sleeping: the other was filled with clothes and various articles of their property. There was no need of more than one; they never slept at the same time: one or the other was perpetually on deck. Thus they passed their lives—seeing to the ship, sleeping, in short, doing every thing in turn, but equally contented, equally satisfied that it was wholly useless, if not unseamanlike, to go on shore in a strange country. One of them was from Connecticut, and, as he informed me, he always went to see his friends there once a year, if he was as often in port in New York. His sea life had not extinguished his attachment to his country or his kindred, and his eye lighted up at the slightest allusion to either. Nor had it wrought the least change in him. Though his voyages had been constantly taking him to distant countries in almost every quarter of the globe, he was as genuine a Yankee as when he drew his first breath. He spoke like one; and he saw every thing with Connecticut eyes. One day while talking with him on deck, I said, in answer to one of his questions, that if I went to the Mediterranean I should probably stay a few weeks in some of the cities on the eastern coast of Spain, and among others I named Malaga. "Well," said he, "I *would* stop there, if for nothin' else, *jest* to see the *meetin'-house*."

Shades of Moorish and Castilian chivalry, what a barbarous misnomer! Fancy, on the one hand, one of the noble cathedrals of Spain, the work of centuries gone by—its tower piercing the clouds—its columns, and arches, and pinnacles of stone without—its sculptured marbles, its mosaics, and its incrustations of gold and silver within; and, on the other hand, a thin lath-and-plaster building, covered with clapboards, and painted with bad white lead, with such a multiplicity of windows that one would think the deliberate design was to let in the greatest possible quantity of heat in summer and cold in winter, and you have a fair conception of our mate's confusion of ideas. Give us, above all things, the enterprise, the industry, the ingenuity, the moral and intellectual power of Connecticut, and the love of liberty which her people cherish in common with the great mass of our countrymen; nay, Mr. Mate, give us her meeting-houses, with the freedom of religious opinion which reigns within them, poor specimens as they are generally of the arts; but let us, at least, leave the cathedrals of the old world in possession of their true names!

The attachment of our two mates to their profession was not a universal sentiment among the crew. We had a case quite as striking for its distaste for, as theirs was for devotion to, the life of a sailor. We had noticed, for several days after coming on board, a young man walking about with much such an unsteady and unseamanlike gait as our own, performing a variety of offices which can hardly be considered as coming within the proper sphere of the profession, and which are usually assigned to the raw hand, if there is one on board, such as feeding the pigs and the chickens, and cleaning the cow-pen—that is, the long-boat, for it was there the cow was kept. He was a tall, well-made fellow, with cheeks of the brightest red, his whole frame admirably proportioned and developed, and just arriving at manhood—the very perfection, in short, of health and strength. It was not long before we began to hear him spoken of under the designation of Charley, the raw hand. After the first gale, I observed that his countenance wore an expression nearly akin to that of the weather, and I took occasion to ask him how he liked a sailor's life. He answered, in the most unreserved manner, that it was the most miserable dog's life he could fancy, and that if he could but once set his foot on dry land, he would agree to be a dog if he was ever caught on board ship again. He had been on deck eight hours the previous night, and most of the time ankle deep in water, besides having been aloft to take in sail in a heavy rain. But there were other discomforts in store for him, which were only calculated to increase his disgust for the business he had engaged in. After the storm, we had, as is usual, a calm of a day or two, and it was industriously employed in putting the ship in order. Charley was ordered to bring the tar-pot, by one of the mates. When it came, the mate told him to tar a rope, which he had been serving, to use a sea phrase.

"What shall I take the tar out with?" inquired Charley.

"Why, with your hand, to be sure," replied the mate.

"Must I put my hand in there?" said Charley, looking into the sable mixture of tar and grease with an expression of infinite disgust.

"Why, to be sure you must, you lubber," was the courteous answer; "how do you expect to get the tar out, if you don't?" And in Charley's hand went, though with symptoms of unfeigned repugnance.

As might be supposed, these little incidents had not

raised Charley's reputation among the crew. Another one of a similar character destroyed it entirely. The drenching he had received during the gale, with other exposure, having given him a cold, he stayed below for two or three days, and the first mate, who seemed to be the practising physician of the ship, made daily visits to the medicine-chest on his account, until Charley, thinking he might as well be drenched externally with water as internally with salts, reappeared on deck, but with a pretty general conviction on the part of his messmates that he had been playing old soldier. To use their own phrase, which, like many other figures of speech, borrowed much more significance from the tone in which it was uttered than from the words themselves —"he might have been sicker." A few days after, there was another gale and heavy rain with it, and all hands were called to take in sail. "There," said Charley, who had that moment lain down in his berth for a snooze, "I have just got rid of one cold, and now I have got to get wet again and take another." The idea of a man shipping himself as a seaman before the mast, and not expecting to get wet, was so extremely green that Charley's reputation was, from that moment, lost among his messmates; and when the exclamation just quoted was put forth in the most doleful tone possible, the shouts of laughter with which it was received could be heard from the forecastle for some minutes, notwithstanding the roaring of the storm.

But if Charley, like many greater men than himself,

lacked common sense, he was not deficient either in intellectual capacity or literary acquirement. One day, while on deck with the captain, I observed the first mate with a piece of chalk in his hand, drawing a compass on the broken cover of a claret box, and I asked him, jocularly, if any accident had happened to the ship's compass, as he seemed to be making a new one! He answered in the same tone, that the ship's compass was all right, but that he wanted Charley, the raw hand, to learn the points, and he was drawing them for him to study. He immediately walked forward to set him to work. In a few minutes he returned, and coming up to the captain and myself with an air of the most sovereign contempt, "What," said he, "do you think I found the fellow about? He was down below reading a French novel!" This was the first intimation I had received of Charley being a scholar. On inquiry, I found that he was of a highly respectable family in New Brunswick or Nova Scotia; that he had just graduated at college, and had taken a violent fancy to go to sea; and his father, who certainly proved himself a very sensible man, had, for the purpose of eradicating it in the most effectual manner, sent him to New York, with a letter to a friend, requesting that he might be shipped on a foreign voyage. Never was a disease more radically cured. We saw him a day or two before the Mexican sailed from Madeira on her return to New York, and his distaste for the sea had suffered no abatement. Charley, like many others, had mistaken his vocation. Fortunate would it be for all such, if they could discover their error as soon as he.

On the 11th of November, at two in the afternoon, we came in sight of Madeira. At first it seemed but a dark mass of shadow, veiling the horizon, and hardly distinguishable, by our sight, from the clouds, out of which it was emerging; but the captain's more practised eye readily detected the difference. Before sunset it was in full view, but we were still thirty miles from Funchal, the capital. As it became dark, we could discern the lights on the shore, and at ten we went below with the confident expectation of being safely in port before morning. We were not disappointed. It was about one o'clock when we heard the heavy rumbling sound of the chain cable, as the anchor was cast, and felt the quivering of the ship as the enormous weight of iron was gradually let out at the bow. For nearly four weeks our sleep had not been broken by so welcome a sound. The voyage, with its privations and dangers, its fears and hopes, its depression and excitement, its mingled good and ill, was at an end. The destined haven was reached; and as the buzzing of voices passed from state-room to state-room at the dead of night, proclaiming the joyous intelligence which the anchor gave, as it went to the bottom, I am sure that more than one heart was raised in thankfulness to Heaven that our little corps of invalids, ill as some of them were, had suffered no diminution in number.

CHAPTER II.

FIRST IMPRESSIONS OF MADEIRA.

Aspect of Funchal.—The Landing.—The Harbor and Beach.—Donkeys.—Two Wrecks.—Entrance into the City.—Guard Mounting.—The Praça Constitucional.—Oxen and Cursa.—Market-day and Market-people.—Streets.—Courtesy of the Portuguese.—Wine-bearers from the Vineyards.—Costume of the Inhabitants.—Houses.—Our Lodgings.

The sun never rose more gloriously than on the morning after our ship came to anchor. Almost all of us, invalids included, were up before him; and certainly a more beautiful view can not be conceived than that which disclosed itself as the daylight broke upon Funchal. The city itself, clustering around a slight indentation in the land, hardly deserving the name of a bay, with its spires and turrets, and its ranges of houses piled one above another as it recedes from the water; the Loo rock, some hundred yards from the shore, on the left as we faced the land, rising out of the sea to the height of 80 or 100 feet, with its dark perpendicular sides, and its crest of bristling cannon; the fort within connected with the mainland, ready, with its open-mouthed parapets, to support its advanced guard on the rock, in case of need; the governor's castle hard by, with its antiquated towers, looking out upon the ocean across one of the public walks; the beach, on which the surf is perpetually breaking, covered with boats and boatmen, and overlooked by that curious column of dark stone in its centre, rising like the tall trunk of some enormous pine, which the tempest has stripped of its branches, and seeming to stand there only to tell some tale, like that of Babel, of presumption or folly; the fort in the background, perched high above the city, and which appears, at this distance, as inaccessible as the rock of Gibraltar; the mountains, still farther back, thousands of feet in height, with the morning clouds hanging about their summits, extending their bases down to the very sea, and on all sides, excepting in the direction of the city, pushing out ramparts of mural precipice, as if to defend themselves against the ceaseless fretting of the waves; the deep, dark ravines into which the surface of the island is broken, running down from the very tops of the mountains to the ocean, and rendering more prominent the precipitous banks by which they are flanked; the hill-sides, as far up as the eye can reach, speckled with white country houses, which almost sparkle as they stand out in contrast with the dun soil, clad in vines and foliage; that beautiful thing, near 2000 feet above the city and half way up the mountain, which seems to be a church with two turrets, and which we were afterward told was the celebrated "Nossa Senhora do Monte," or "Our Lady of the Mountain"—

all these picturesque and striking objects crowded into a single picture, constituted, combined, a scene so novel, and, in truth, so rare and beautiful in itself, that it appeared to us like a region of enchantment. As the sun came out in all his brightness, and lighted up the more prominent features of the scene, throwing others into deeper shadow, the picture became still more gorgeous. No pencil can delineate or pen describe it.

While we were yet gazing upon it, we were called back to the dull realities of life. The custom-house boat visited us, and two officers came on board. We were severally presented to them by the captain, to whom they were well known; an account of our baggage was given in, our passports were delivered up, and we each received a written permission to land, with a direction to report ourselves at the government office, which is in the governor's castle, within twenty-four hours. We were not long in availing ourselves of our permission to land. A number of island boats were about the ship, and, after a hasty breakfast, we were all on our way to the shore. To land, however, is a matter of some skill and management. It is always to be done in the surf. No ship's boat attempts it. The island boats are always used, both for landing passengers, and, indeed, for all communications between the shore and the shipping in the harbor. They are shod, on each side of the keel, with a piece of wood running parallel with it, and about one third of its length, so that they appear to have three keels. As they approach the beach, the boatmen get out into the water nearly up to their middle, and when the favorable moment arrives they run the boat up high and dry on the shore. Even then, passengers must land with care, as the surf, when high, is constantly dashing against the stern of the boat, and running up on the beach to the bow, and beyond it. A lady of our party, thinking all was safe when the boat was once upon the beach, jumped out, in her eagerness to touch the land, and found herself standing ankle deep in the water.

We are now fairly on dry land, and before we enter the city, let us look back upon the water and see what conveniences the harbor offers to shipping. Literally none. There is no harbor. It is an open roadstead. Nothing could be worse. There is no shelter for vessels in any direction; and when the wind blows directly in with any degree of violence, they regularly hoist their anchors, or slip their cables, and run out to sea, for fear of being driven on shore. A few weeks after we arrived, it began to blow fresh from the south, and the mercury in the barometer fell slightly. A boat was immediately sent out from the shore to advise that the vessels in the harbor should get under way. Their anchors were weighed, and in a few hours they were all out of sight. It was well that they did not remain in the roadstead, as the wind increased and blew violently during the succeeding night. What an inconvenience is this for a commercial town! Four days elapsed before these vessels were all in port again; and they are often compelled to be for days at anchor, pitching and tossing in the waves, without being able to land the least portion of their cargoes. The mode of unlading is slow and inconvenient. It is done wholly by large boats or lighters. When heavily laden, they can not be taken entirely through the surf, and the boatmen are obliged to strip themselves and carry the cargo ashore through the water. Vessels are, of course, laden in the same manner.

What a busy scene does the beach present! There lies a lighter from one of the ships. It is brought as close to the shore as possible, but not near enough to be unladen on the dry gravel, with which the beach is overlaid. The men are passing to and fro, stark naked, or at best with very insufficient covering below the middle and none above, carrying parcels on their backs, floating ashore casks, which the water will not injure, or dragging in burdens, too heavy to be borne, in smaller boats. Fine-looking fellows they are in general, with broad chests and muscular arms to struggle with their tasks, and strong, pillar-like legs to bear them up under the huge loads they carry.

Here is a boat of finer mould and engaged in a higher department of service; the boatmen are well dressed, each with his ridiculous cap, like an inverted funnel, covering one fourth of his head, serving little purpose of use and still less of ornament, and its stiff-pointed peak running off almost at right angles with his crown. There is an awning over the boat to keep off the rays of the sun, which are falling fiercely around us, and in its stern there are three or four officers with badges of the military upon their shoulders. They have each that other badge, which it is to be regretted is not confined to the military—the mustachio. In the old, honest, antediluvian beard there is respectability and dignity; in the mustachio none. It may make a soldier look more ferocious; but the civilization of modern times, like the chivalry of the middle ages, is, in its teachings, at war with all such exhibitions of ferocity.

Here comes a troop of donkeys, five in a row, marching in single files, and in as orderly a manner, I venture to say, as the soldiers, whom we see idling up there at the gate of the castle, could do it, with their best drill sergeant at their head. What patterns of patience these animals are! Each has on his back two enormous panniers of sackcloth, and both are laden to the brim with heavy black sand from the beach. None but an ass would endure such a load without rebellion; and yet there they go, marching along as though their backs were without burdens. What a barbarous way their drivers have of confining their heads! Each has round his mouth a halter of untanned goat's leather, fastened at the other end to the pad on his shoulders, and drawn so tight that his nose is turned off on one side, at least two points by compass from the axis of his motion. How queer they look as they jog on with their heads awry! Rheumatism and stiff necks to your unfeeling drivers, poor animals, say we with all our hearts.

On the right, as we face the beach, between the Loo rock and the governor's castle, lie two wrecks. The hull of one of them is entire, but her masts and bowsprit are gone, leaving her "a sheer hulk," and looking like some gigantic animal which has turned over on its side and breathed its last. This, they tell us, is the brig Dart, a British packet, which has for years been running as a trader between Old England and Madeira, and has in her day brought hundreds of passengers hither in pursuit of health, and taken them back again in possession of it. She was a favorite, and those whom she has safely carried mourn over her as for one who has done them faithful service. Not far from her lies one of our stranded countrymen; and one, too, not unknown to fame—the Creole. No more shall her decks be stained with human blood, or the intellects of two great nations be tasked to distinguish between mutiny and murder, and a justifiable struggle for freedom. In the poor estate in which we see her, she seems to have been a noble vessel, worthy of a better history and a better end. What a bevy of men she has around and upon her, stripping her of every thing that can by possibility be converted to any profitable use. They have dismantled her, and now they are pulling off her plank and disclosing her timbers to view, like so many vultures upon some huge carcass, tearing off the flesh and leaving the ribs bare and naked. One would think, from the assiduity with which they ply their work, that a corps of enraged abolitionists were in possession, and were wreaking their vengeance on her in retaliation for the things she has done in her day. Her last moments were signalized by a remarkable act of coolness and good judgment. The captain was on shore, and, like all the other vessels in the harbor, she was driven from her anchorage in a storm of unprecedented fury, a fortnight ago. The mate, seeing all hope of saving her at an end, hoisted sail, and drove her high and dry upon a reef of rocks, on which a house stood, and there she remained long enough to enable the crew to run up into the rigging and get in at the windows. By this singular presence of mind every soul was saved.

Unhappily, these are not the only trophies of the storm. The scattered remains of three other vessels lie strewed over the beach. A Sardinian brig came in with such violence, that in five minutes she was in pieces, and in fifteen not a vestige of her could be seen. Of her unfortunate crew every man perished. Of the effects of this terrible tempest on the land, we shall have occasion to speak hereafter. It is time for us now to leave the beach and enter the city.

A finer entrance few cities present. We ascend a flight of six steps of cut stone, about forty-five feet in length, of the same width as the street to which they lead, bounded on each side by a wall with an iron paling above it. The street is divided into three portions, the two sidewalks being separated from the central part by rows of young trees. They serve little purpose of shade yet, for they are small; but in this climate their growth is exceedingly rapid. One good purpose they do serve. They show where the sidewalks end and the central part of the street begins—a matter of no inconsiderable advantage, for both are paved with small stone, and in much the same manner. All the pavements in the city are of a similar character. They are either of round stone, or of flat stone turned up edgewise. At first they seem hard, but the foot soon becomes used to them, and one treads them as easily as the large flat flaggings in our own country. As we advance, a fine broad square opens on our left, with the sea on one side and the governor's castle on the other. It is shaded by trees, and is a delightful walk at all seasons, not only for the noble prospect it affords, but on account of the sea air, which is always pouring into it fresh from the adjoining beach. On the same side of the street is one of the flanks of the governor's castle, in the shape of a heavy, massive turret, then one of its sides running parallel with the street, and on the other side a fine dwelling, which is now occupied as a boarding-house. We pass a species of bastion crowned by a small square turret, and the castle runs off at right angles some hundred yards, then rises into a bastion higher than the first, on a line nearly parallel with the street, forming a broad square or praça. We now reach a second street running across the head of the one through which we have been advancing, still broader than the latter, with sidewalks paved in the same manner, and three rows of oak and sycamore trees, having at one termination an old monastery, now tenanted by soldiers instead of monks, and at the other, the city cathedral, remarkable for its antiquity and want of architectural beauty and nothing else. As we reach the square formed by the junction of these streets, we encounter a crowd of people, and beyond them a body of soldiers, drawn up in military array. It is the city guard, which parades here every morning, and is assigned to its diurnal duties according to the customary formula of the profession. There is a fine band of music, which is just beginning to play a martial air as we come up. It is not possible (as a sprig of aristocracy said on the occurrence of a similar coincidence) that they are going to receive us with military honors! What he said in seriousness, one of our company said in jest. Not only do we plain Americans pass unnoticed in the crowd, but the tall drum-major, who is a fierce-looking fellow with his mildest face on, is turning his eyes this way, while we push forward to get a better view of the show, as though he was going to give us a thrust, to make us stand farther back, with that long, spear-like cane which he carries in his hand, with an enormous gilt head to it, and which he tosses up and flourishes in the most ridiculous manner, by way of salute, as he passes by the officer of the day.

The ceremony is soon over, and we continue our walk through the square. They tell us it is called the Praça Constitucional. What a thrill this word sends through us! In the midst of all this martial pomp and circumstance, this flourishing of swords and glittering of armor, these castellated turrets, the ensigns of a government in which the military constitutes an essential ingredient, it recalls to us our own glorious country, its free institutions, its millions of enlightened people, loving liberty, and sometimes, perhaps, practising it to excess, but cherishing it above all earthly possessions—its cities, and streets, and squares, trodden by freemen—its broad fields and mountains, the abode of constitutional law and of a social order resting upon the basis of agreement, and not of coercion.

Portugal and her dependencies, far removed as they are from the enjoyment of constitutional liberty, as we understand and enjoy it, have, nevertheless, for many years lived under a written constitution. That the people of Funchal appreciate the benefits of a political system with fixed limitations of authority, is sufficiently apparent in the name they have given to the finest part of their city.

We are now out of the Praça Constitucional, and are passing through a narrow street. It is twenty-five feet wide, perhaps—not more; and yet it is fully equal in width to the other streets of the city. It is paved, like them, with small stones—a covering which would not resist for a single day the heavy-wheeled vehicles constantly passing through ours. How is it that these pavements are everywhere so even and unbroken? The cause is soon obvious. We meet no carriages or carts—no vehicles, in short, on wheels. Here comes a sledge, or, as the Portuguese call it, a cursa. It is drawn by two diminutive oxen, and yet it has a pipe of wine, weighing hard upon half a ton. What a primitive vehicle it is! It certainly can not date farther forward in the advance of civilization than the deluge. It is a plank about eight feet long, some sixteen inches wide, and four or five thick, the fore end slightly pointed. On each side, underneath, it has two shoes of wood running from stem to stern; and above, on each end, there is a cross-piece of the width of the principal piece of wood, to prevent the load from slipping either way. The plank is hollowed in the centre from one end to the other, to about the rotundity of a wine-cask, which is its most usual loading, though it carries every thing else that is to be carried. The driver is walking by the side of his cattle, and shouting to them as if it were necessary to compensate for their lack of size and strength by the noise he makes. A small boy accompanies him, carrying in his hand a long mop of rope yarn, or coarse cloth, which he now and then dips in the water he meets with in the streets and throws it down in front of the sledge. The sledge passes over it, and, the bottom being thoroughly moistened, glides over the pavements with greater ease, not only lightening the labor of the cattle, but preventing the danger of fire from friction. Uncouth as this mode of transportation is, it is the only one adapted to the condition of the city. What an ascent the street has before us! it is almost a precipice; and yet a large portion of the city is like it. No wheel carriage could be brought down it in safety. The city is, in this respect, but a type of the island of which it is a part. The whole is but a bed of lava, from the back-bone of the island down to the sea, broken, steep, and in some places inaccessible. As you look at its surface, you can almost fancy you see the burning liquid pouring down the mountains, damming up here, breaking over its barriers there, and leaving the volcanic impress on every thing it touches.

It is Saturday, and Saturday is market-day. This accounts for the throngs of people we meet in the streets, and the loads of provisions, vegetables, fruit, wood, and provender which they are carrying. Here is a man with fowls, carried in the most scandalous manner possible. He has a pole over his shoulder, and on each end the poor animals are tied by their legs, with their heads downward, in just the position to produce an inflammation of the brain in a human subject. The man behind him has a string of pigeons, tied up in the same manner; but he has considerately put them to death, instead of killing them by the protracted process which the man with the fowls is practising. A third man is coming after these two, engaged in one of the most perplexing of all undertakings

—driving a pig to market. In the United States, we often see a man going to market with a drove of pigs, but never with a single one. In this region of full population, where men are more numerous than pigs, a man driving two is probably a thing unseen. This man seems to have his hands full as it is, for he makes very small progress, and is always at cross purposes with his charge. Two or three carriers of wood come along, and pass rapidly by him. Some of them have enormous bundles of light brush-wood on their heads. These are intended for heating ovens, for the very obvious reason that they are fit for nothing else. Others have heavier bundles of short split wood, small and gnarled, no better than the lighter bundles, excepting that they last a little longer. The quality of these loads savors strongly of a dearth of trees in Madeira. But what need has Funchal of any other supply of fuel for household purposes? The thermometer, by day, rarely falls so low as 60°; and wood is only required for cooking and baking. Some of these wood-carriers are women, and their loads seem no lighter than those of the men. There is no country where females are wholly exempt from hard labor: it is the lot of the poor of both sexes everywhere. But in our own country there is this alleviation in the condition of females who work hard: their drudgery is the drudgery of the household; it is all performed within doors; it rarely or never shows itself in the streets or in the fields. To the eye of the mere passer-by the man seems to bear alone the burden of earning "his bread in the sweat of his face."

Though the streets are well paved, they would be infinitely more pleasant for foot-passengers if they had sidewalks. But their width does not admit of it; and as we pass along, we are in danger of being jostled by donkeys, oxen, goats, and other animals, who dispute with us the possession of the best portions of the street. Their drivers are, however, exceedingly respectful and civil, and, if they see us in time, they are ever ready to make their cattle turn out and give place to us. Almost every man we see, no matter what his condition, takes off his hat or cap as he meets a lady. There can be no higher evidence of civilization, in manners at least, than these marks of respect for the fair sex. It is said that since the island has become a place of resort for the Anglo-Saxon race, the practice is falling into disrepute. What an unsocial fancy, to suppose that such an interchange of civilities is only warranted by a formal introduction! And yet such is the frigid rule of the English code of manners. It must be confessed, too, that it is the etiquette of what is called good society in the United States. In crowded cities, the practice is one of convenience; but if you go among the unsophisticated inhabitants of the country, you find the rule of natural politeness prevails, and every one you meet gives you some token of recognition as one of his own species. Here stands a group of Portuguese ladies, nearly a dozen in number.

They have just met, and are kissing each other's cheeks and hands as affectionately as if they had not seen each other for years, though they probably did the same thing yesterday. Three or four Englishmen or Americans (for it is not easy to distinguish the one from the other) are passing by them. The street is so narrow that they almost jostle each other, and yet the gentlemen move on without turning their heads, or, if they do, only enough to give the ladies side-glances. They are closely followed by half a dozen natives, and every one of them touches his hat or raises his cap in the most respectful manner as he passes. How superior is the Portuguese to the Anglo-Saxon rule!

Here is a sight of a still more novel character than any we have seen yet—a body of countrymen from the vineyards. They come in single file, like the donkeys, whose province they seem to have usurped, for they are full as heavily laden. Each one has a goat-skin of wine on his head or shoulders, or around his neck. What a variety of modes they have of carrying their loads! and such loads, too! The skins seem to have been taken off entire. They have no openings excepting at the legs and neck, and these are tied up tightly to keep in the rosy fluid they contain. The man who leads the way is singing at the top of his voice; and the others keep time, as well as they can, with his hoarse intonations. The skins are not quite full; and as the procession moves on, and the liquid within them vibrates with the motion, you feel every moment as if some of these thin coverings would burst, and wine enough to make a hundred hearts glad would be poured out upon the unthankful pavement.

The dress these wine-bearers have on, must be characteristic of the interior of the island. It is nothing more than a cotton shirt and a pair of loose cotton or tow breeches, just long enough to cover the knee, and buttoned tight under it, leaving the leg bare to the bottom of the calf. Below this is a goat-skin boot, coming above the ankle. Some of them have blue cloth jackets, or long, gray, shapeless coats, thrown over the skins of wine, to be put on when they shall have discharged their loads; and these complete their dress.

In the city, the laboring classes are clad in much the same manner, though the pantaloon is always worn instead of the short breeches. The cap, as a covering to the head, if it can be so considered, is common to both sexes. It is a mere skull-cap of dark cloth, covering one third of the hairy part of the head, and running out gradually to a point. It was formerly large enough, beyond doubt, to cover the head properly, but fashion has reduced it to its present useless dimensions. It is, of course, worn here only by what are called the lower orders: the higher classes are dressed like the same classes in Europe.

Some of the females we meet have costumes still more peculiar than the men. One is this moment passing us. She is obviously from the interior of the island. She has on a red-striped petticoat, a large blue cape, trimmed with white braid, reaching to her waist—and as the latter is blown up by the wind, we see that she has no other articles of dress, except a chemise without sleeves. Her legs and arms are entirely bare, and her feet are covered only with a pair of goat-skin shoes. She is without the little cap, but she wears, instead, a clean white handkerchief over her head, and looks all the better for it.

It is remarkable that a large number of the males have fine faces, and some are excellent specimens of manly beauty, while the women we meet in the streets are almost uniformly the reverse. Why should it be so? Where are the mothers and sisters of these handsome men? We almost doubt whether the male and female figure is cast in the same mould, for we see few female faces which would be fine if they were worn by males.

Notwithstanding the crowds of animals passing through the streets, the city seems neat and cleanly. Dirt there must of necessity be; but they tell us it is once a week cleared away, and in general more frequently. Compared with the streets in the city of New York, with its mud in wet, and its clouds of dust in dry weather, the streets of Funchal are certainly remarkably clean.

The houses are generally of three stories. The ground floor has a lower ceiling than the two upper, and it consists, usually, of the hall or passage, and apartments with grated windows, to be used as stores, counting-rooms, or as repositories for household property. Most of the Portuguese transact their business in their own houses. Their wine and their merchandise are below, and their families above. There are exceptions, but this is the general practice. The parlor and dining-room are in the second story of the house, the bedrooms above, and the cooking is usually done in the yard, in a small separate building. The houses are of stone, with very thick walls, and the roofs are covered with fluted tiles. Fires are, of course, with such incombustible dwellings, exceedingly rare.

Many of the houses have a square turret above the roof of the main building, with a single room, and sometimes two, one over the other, with windows on each of their four sides—and making most delightful apartments, either for sleeping or any other purpose. Hardly a house is to be found without its balcony, and most of them have one to each window above the ground floor. Many of the best houses have at least one balcony running across the whole front, either on the second or third floor; and in these the ladies are almost always to be seen in the cool of the day, looking down into the busy streets below them. Indeed, at almost any hour the clattering of a horse's hoofs upon the pavement is sure to bring them out, if they are not there already. Some of the balconies are of tasteful models and ornamented with gilding. Many of the houses, too, may be called fine buildings, though they certainly will not bear the application of strict architectural rules ; but Funchal may, nevertheless, be justly considered a well-built city, if the streets we have passed through are a fair specimen of the others, as the gentleman who is conducting us assures us they are.

But we have now reached the house where we are to be temporarily lodged, and we must reserve for a future occasion what remains to be seen in the streets. We are carried up two stories and ushered into a drawing-room some thirty feet square, with a ceiling at least sixteen feet high, rising from the cornice and narrowing gradually to a square of about fifteen feet. This is lightly ornamented with stucco work, corresponding with the cornice; the walls are of hard finish, painted in fresco, with all sorts of uncouth representations of still life—with fruits, flowers, musical instruments, and now and then a nondescript animal, intermixed. It has two windows on the street, each opening into a balcony which commands a beautiful view of the mountain east of the city, with a mere glimpse of the sea farther on, and the antiquated, ungraceful spire of the city cathedral intervening. A collation is already prepared for us in an adjoining apartment, to which we are conducted; and, with windows wide open, on the twelfth of November, when the friends we have left behind us are probably shivering with cold, and perhaps gazing upon banks of snow, we sit down at a table laden with oranges, figs, bananas, and guavas, plucked this very day from the trees, and look out into gardens where every thing is in bloom, or is rapidly warming, in the rays of the meridian sun, into life, and beauty, and fragrance.

CHAPTER III.

THE CITY OF FUNCHAL AND ITS ENVIRONS.

Objections to the City as a Residence.—Want of Carriages.—Palanquins and Hammocks.—Paved Roads.—Horses and Burroqueros. —Ascent to the Mount Church.—Dragon Trees.—Beautiful Views of the Country.—Aloe or Century-plant.—Camera de Lobos.—Wine-producing District.—A Bridge.—Cape Giram.—A Christening Party.—A Lady in a Hammock—The Portuguese Burying-ground.—A Funeral.—Night in Funchal.—Domestic Habits of the People.—Street Music.—The Machete.—Street Noises.—Milk, and the way to get it.

THE aspect of the city of Funchal, with the surrounding enclosure of mountains and sea, can not, with strict propriety, be called beautiful: it partakes far more strongly of the sublime; but in many of its details it presents features of singular beauty. We have now been three weeks on shore, and have made excursions in various directions from the city. We have, also, seen much of the city itself, and begin to think that we may speak of it as of a familiar acquaintance. We find it, in almost all respects, an agreeable one. We can sincerely say of it, what we are unable to say of many others we have known, that we like it better the more we see of it. The climate is delicious, the inhabitants kind and courteous, and if we do not enjoy all the luxuries which are to be found elsewhere, we have, at least, all the necessaries of life, and as many of its comforts and conveniences as can be reasonably desired. It can hardly fail, we think, to strike others as it does us. Those who leave it with unfavorable impressions, must certainly be disqualified by their moral or physical condition for enjoying fine air and fine scenery. Let it not be supposed that the city is wholly free from objections. It has more than one; what place, indeed, has not? And lest we should be suspected of judging it too favorably, we will proceed to notice them first, and look at the bright side of the picture afterward.

The great objection to Funchal, as a permanent or temporary residence, is the want of wheel carriages. As has been said in a former chapter, the island is a continued succession of hills and valleys, and of such steep acclivities that the use of wheels is wholly impracticable. In Funchal there are, perhaps, two or three small wheel carriages. We never saw them, and they are wholly useless, excepting to drive about a few of the streets near the water, which are sufficiently level to admit of it. The only mode of taking exercise is walking, or riding on horseback, or in a palanquin. Many invalids are too feeble to take much exercise on foot, and for those who have not strength to ride, the only resource is the palanquin, a vehicle which has nothing but necessity to recommend it. It consists of a piece of plank shaped much like the sole of a shoe, with an iron railing running round it, about six inches high, and with a framework at one end to rest the back against. Its length is just sufficient to enable a person to sit up and stretch out the legs to their full extent. It is usually carpeted and comfortably cushioned. It always has a cover of cloth thrown over the pole, by which it is carried, and sometimes it has a covering in the form of an Eastern pavilion, and is finished in a rich and tasteful manner. This may be called the body of the carriage, and it is suspended by iron rods from a pole about twelve feet in length and four inches in diameter, so that when it is in motion, it hangs within a few inches of the pavement. Two men carry it, one end of the pole resting on the shoulder of each, and each having in his hand a staff, with which he steadies himself; and sometimes to relieve one shoulder, he puts his staff over the other, places the end under the pole, and using it as a lever, makes the weight rest upon both shoulders instead of one. It is surprising to observe with what ease and rapidity they travel with this load between them, going up the steepest ascents without slackening their pace, and descending with a sure-footedness which rarely fails them. Sometimes a hammock is suspended from the pole instead of the ordinary seat, and, indeed, this is the usual mode of traveling among the hills. It is not only lighter than the palanquin, but being suspended nearer the pole, it is easily carried over rough ground where the other would be useless. For invalids, both these modes of transportation are a miserable substitute for an easy wheel carriage. The palanquin has one advantage over the latter, however. There is no danger of being thrown out and breaking one's bones—perils which beset most modern vehicles. Certainly a safer conveyance can not well be fancied.

Another very serious objection to Funchal with those who are able to walk and ride on horseback, is the paved roads which lead from it into the interior. For miles, not a rod of unpaved street is to be found, and in many directions you are enclosed within walls so high as to shut out all view of the surrounding country. This is not always the case, however. On the east of the city there is a road open to the sea, and high above it, commanding an unobstructed view on all sides, another nearly similar on the west, and as you go up the mountain, where you are always enclosed in walls, you have frequent glimpses of the sea, the city, and the heights above you. It may be said generally, too, as you get farther and farther from the city, the vision becomes more free from these artificial obstructions. The pavements, however, continue for miles beyond; they are usually of rough stone, not laid in the most even and artist-like manner; and as you ride over them, the clattering of the horses' hoofs is perpetually distracting your attention and diverting it from surrounding objects. We are getting more accustomed to them; but they can never cease to be an annoyance to those who, like us, have been in the habit of looking to the moment when we should pass beyond the city pavements and tread the uncovered bosom of the earth, as the commencement of all that was agreeable in the ride or walk.

As an indemnity for rough roads, you have most excellent horses to carry you over them. The island horses are small, but they are well trained and exceedingly sure-footed. In Funchal there are a few which have been imported from England and America, and they soon become accustomed to the uneven surface of the city and its environs. So far as expense is concerned, one could hardly ask to ride at a cheaper rate. The customary charge at the livery stables is 300 reis per hour—just 30 cents of the money of the United States, or about 15 pence sterling. For this sum, too, a man is sent to accompany you wherever you go; though it is usual to give him 50 or 100 reis (5 or 10 cents) each time he goes out with you. If you take him into the interior, he expects to be furnished with bread and wine. These men are known by the designation of burroqueros (hardly a fair name, by-the-by, for a burroquero is an ass-driver), and they are usually active, athletic, and well-formed young men. They follow you on foot, keeping close to your horse, and when you ride rapidly they seize him by the tail, so that it is impossible to get away from them. The horse knows them, and is much more likely to obey their directions than yours. I have in several instances found my horse going faster than I desired, or refusing to increase his speed at my bidding, and I could always trace it to a quiet communication between him and the burroquero. For ladies, this association of horse and driver is a great convenience. They need no other attendant. He is always ready to render any assistance they may require; and if the horse loses a shoe, he has hammer and nails in his pocket to replace it. It is not easy to fancy a more ludicrous spectacle than a lady riding through a city at full gallop with a man hanging to the tail of her horse; but such scenes are almost every hour before us, and it is surprising to find how soon the eye becomes accustomed to them.

This morning we made our first visit to the Church of Nossa Senhora do Monte—Our Lady of the Mountain. It stands about 1800 feet above the city, directly back of it, and about two miles from the beach. The average ascent, therefore, must be at an angle of not less than fifteen degrees with the horizon. A portion of the acclivity is far more steep; so much so, that the movement of the horse, as he toils up the mountain's side, is exceedingly disagreeable to the rider. During the greater part of the ascent, you are enclosed within high stone walls, rarely low enough to look over, and with about space enough between them to make a street in the city. The same rough pavement, which has been described, lies beneath your feet. It is only when you look up that the eye finds any relief. Then, indeed, all is brilliancy and beauty. The deep-blue sky above; the heliotrope, the rose, and the geranium in full flower, hanging over the walled enclosure, and sending their fragrance down on every breath of air; the orange tree, with its golden fruit and dark green leaves; the wide-spreading banana, the chestnut, the sycamore, the fir, and the solitary dragon tree, with its curious branches, like so many truncated cones extending outward from the top of its long, smooth trunk; these and a thousand other forms of vegetable life, rich, graceful, or fantastic, display themselves at frequent intervals high over your head, and amply compensate for the hard surface over which you are passing, and the rough, inhospitable walls in which you are imprisoned. But, as you advance, your confinement becomes less rigid. The wall now and then is lower, and the view over it is unobstructed. Sometimes the enclosure is, on one side, a precipitous bank of basalt, out of which the prickly pear shoots its ungraceful branches, if branches they may be called, looking like so many bare feet, with nothing wanting but the toes to make the resemblance perfect. Here and there the fig tree stands out from the surrounding bloom—its white trunk and limbs as bare, at this season, as that which the Saviour doomed to perpetual barrenness. This, however, is an exception to the general aspect of the country. Freshness, fragrance, green leaves, and blossoms bursting into life, are the prevailing characteristics of the season. And this is winter in Madeira!

Near the church, which was the object of our visit,

a beautiful view unfolded itself. We reached a part of the road which ran along the bank of a deep ravine, and which required no wall or barrier to protect it, like the grounds about the city. With what delight did the eye, after its imprisonment, rest upon the landscape spread out before us! On one side was the mountain, still rising thousands of feet above us—its ascent not yet more than half gained; on another, mile after mile of hill and valley, covered with houses and terraced vineyards, and with a background of round-topped mountains resembling so many great ant-hills, and with as busy and industrious a set of tenants, if we may judge from the marks of cultivation which they bear from their bases to their very summits; below us lay the city of Funchal, nestling in the little bay around which it circles, with its white houses glistening in the beams of the sun, a fleet of trading vessels in the foreground, and the sea, bounded only by the horizon, spread out beyond them; and on our left, the Palheiro, of which we may speak hereafter, raised its lofty top, crested with a grove of forest trees—the only grove on which the eye rests in the environs of Funchal.

The church of Nossa Senhora do Monte has nothing striking about it but its position. It has two towers and belfries on the same line with its front, and it is reached from a small level space below, where we left our horses, by a flight of broad stone steps. From the terrace below the church, there is a beautiful view of the country between it and the ocean, though the objects are nearly the same which we saw some distance below. The city is, however, concealed by the tops of some large trees on an estate lying directly below the church; but from the belfry it must be distinctly seen. We were in haste, and did not ascend it.

As we descended the mountain we saw, upon a bank high above us, the withered stalk of an enormous aloe. It seemed but recently to have been in blossom, and its branches, running off at right angles from the stem, and then curving up to the perpendicular, were perfect, looking altogether like a huge candlestick set up over the narrow passage which we were threading, as if to light it by night. Three months ago we were examining one of these gigantic plants in the garden of General Van Rensselaer, in Albany, when, least of all things, we expected to be here. It had been sixty years in his family, preserved during the winter by artificial heat. At length its stem began to shoot. In a few weeks it was thirty feet high, and the house built over it was carried up with it as it grew. The general, at the solicitation of the Orphan Asylum, allowed it to be exhibited to spectators for a small sum, for the benefit of that public charity. When we saw it last, it was in blossom: the buds on the lower branches had put forth and perished; those directly above were opening, while those on the upper branches were yet closed. The death it was to die was stealing gradually over it before its blossoms had all burst forth; after its century of sleep, it did not enjoy a single day of perfect life. What a contrast, in one respect, did it present with the one which we have now stopped to look at! It was surrounded by crowds, eager to see what they might not, and probably never would, see again; while this stands alone, and, from the elevation at which it looks down upon us, hardly attracts the notice of the passer by, unless he be, like us, a stranger to the island and its vegetable life. But it will not long be thus neglected. It will be cut down, its stem pounded, and its long fibres carefully drawn out by the natives, to sew the coarse cloth which they use for hats, baskets, and various purposes in their household economy. By what a tardy process has nature elaborated this rude thread!

We are now re-entering the compact part of the city, and are again treading its narrow streets. The ladies are looking down on us from the balconies, and the donkeys are jostling us as we pass. Here sits an old woman on a door stone, to which she has no other title but that of possession. She has a child's head in her lap, and gives indications not to be mistaken that the forest she is scouring abounds with game. Disgusting as the spectacle is, we witness it frequently—in the streets of the city, by the roadside in the country, and even at the windows of houses which wear a decent aspect. Where there is no effort to disguise this shocking want of cleanliness, it is quite clear that it must be a common frailty.

The house we are now passing presents a more agreeable picture—two young ladies in a balcony, with eyes as bright and features as symmetrical as one could desire to see. Their complexion is none of the lightest, but it is enriched by a fine color, which suits well with their glossy black hair and white teeth. These are not the only beautiful women we have seen in Funchal. But they are rarely visible. They walk little and ride less. Their habits are singularly sedentary, and their lives recluse. It is only on Sundays or holidays that they are seen out. It is a great misfortune for strangers that the streets of Funchal are not more frequently enlivened, as they might be, by the presence of her fine women. New York once a day, if the weather is fair, pours out her collected beauty into her principal street, and to the passer by it is the most attractive and gorgeous exhibition which she can make.*

Our next visit was to Camera de Lobos, or, as it is now more generally but not properly called, Cama de Lobos. It is a small village, about five miles, by water, and six by land, west from Funchal. The ride there is exceedingly interesting. It leads you through the finest suburb of the city, by the parish church of

* The lapse of seven years has wrought an astonishing change in Broadway in this respect. Shops, hotels, omnibuses, dust in fine weather and mud in foul, have converted it into a crowded and disagreeable thoroughfare; and the beauty and fashion of the city have, in a great measure, been driven out of it—especially for pedestrian exercises.

San Martino, and near the round-topped hills we saw from Nossa Senhora do Monte. We found them, as we passed, terraced and cultivated to their very summits. The whole country, indeed, may be said to be a succession of terraces and planes. It is only by building up walls and creating artificial levels above them, that the soil can be secured from the effects of the rains, which in winter pour down from the hill-tops, accumulating as they descend, and cutting up the defenceless portions of the surface into gullies and ravines. The quantity of labor expended in creating and securing these artificial levels, is enormous. It would hardly have been sustained by any ordinary object of agriculture. But this portion of the island is devoted principally to the cultivation of the vine. It is within a circle of some twelve miles in diameter around Funchal that the best wines are produced. They have usually commanded high prices, and the proprietors have been enabled to invest largely in the improvement of their lands. As you pass over the high grounds about two miles west of the city, and look back upon it, you have a finer view, if possible, than from the mount church. The church itself, and the mountain against which it rests, the peak fort, and the Brazen Head, the first cape east, are prominent features in the landscape; and the city, when seen in flank, shows better than from the rear. You look up into one of the ravines of the mountain, partially the work of volcanic heat and partially worn out

Funchal from St John's.

of the solid rock by the descending floods, with immense precipices almost overhanging it, and threatening every moment to fill up the chasm below. The entrance is toward you, and you see into it for miles, until the eye is met by the snowy tops of still higher peaks, farther on toward the summit of the island. For four days the snow has lain upon these hills; and though in the valleys, and even on the high grounds we are passing over, all is warmth and verdure, the influence of this wintry visiter is sensibly felt. The sun has been out to-day, almost without a cloud to intercept his beams; but the range of the thermometer has been comparatively low—56° at sunrise, and 64° at 2 o'clock. This is quite a winter's day for Funchal. We ride over the hills without inconvenience, at noon, though the sun is shining on us; but now and then we pass along a whitewashed wall, and his rays are reflected so powerfully, that we unbutton our coats, and contrive by every device to catch the greatest possible quantity of fresh air.

About four miles from the city you meet a work which bears evidence of wealth and mechanical skill. There is a deep ravine, running down from the interior of the island to the sea, with a stream in its centre. It is broad and deep, and as you look into it, it seems to have been the work of violence rather than of the long-continued action of the water. As you ride down one of its sides, over a road remarkably well paved and so graduated as to make it easy for horses, the bed of the ravine lies almost beneath your feet, and hundreds of yards below. The water now occupies but a portion of it, and the residue is covered with gardens and vineyards. You approach the bottom, and you find an immense stone bridge to carry you across. It is about 300 feet in length, and 20 in breadth, and is built up about 50 from the bottom. A single high arch spans the stream, which is now small, but which, after showers, must be large and furious. The whole work is of solid masonry, and of excellent workmanship. And yet this work was erected at an expense of about $7,000. But the stones cost nothing excepting the expense of picking them up, labor is exceedingly cheap, and lime is worth but a few cents a bushel. At a distance of about two miles you reach the village, built upon rock near the sea, and running down almost to a level with it. It may contain from five hundred to a thousand inhabitants. Its situation is beautifully picturesque. It lies at the bottom of a small bay, formed by high projecting land on one side and by broken rocks running out from the main on the other. It is a perfect harbor, but too small for ships. There is a little church, built at the foot of a precipice, where we alighted and gave our horses to the burroqueros, while we walked about and explored the village. At its western extremity we found a gallery cut in the solid rock, some 300 feet above the sea. At frequent intervals there are openings to the light extending from the top to the base of the narrow passage, forming perfect doors, and opening upon the perpendicular side of the cliff in which it is cut. We walked at least 100 feet into it, but meeting water, we returned without passing through it. It was cut, as we are told, to get at a quarry of building-stone on the other side of the cliff.

Two miles above the village is Point Giram, about seven miles from Funchal, an immense precipice rising perpendicularly from the sea to the height of 1800 feet, and forming one of the most sublime objects, when seen from Camera de Lobos, that can be conceived.

On our return to the church, where we had left our horses, we found a christening party before it, waiting for the door to be opened. There were the happy father and mother, both young, and the old grandmother holding the child, their first, from all appearances, sleeping in her arms. Then there were a few friends of the married couple, and a servant with a tray containing a present for the priest, viz., a loaf of white sugar standing up in the centre, with its blue covering stripped off and surmounted with a bouquet of flowers, a bottle of wine on one side of it, another bottle on the other, and what remained of the bottom of the tray covered with fresh eggs, and the interstices between them filled up with wheat to prevent the shells from being prematurely broken. The whole party were dressed in their gayest attire, and looked remarkably neat and comfortable. We talked to them a moment in bad Portuguese, praised the beauty of the child, patted it on the cheek, and saw, by the smiles in which the joyous mother's face was arrayed, that in Madeira, as everywhere else, this is the nearest way to a parent's heart.

On our way home we passed a lady in a hammock. Two men were carrying her, and two more were walking by her side. Her hat lay in her lap, and she was extended at full length; but the cover of the hammock was nearly closed in front, so that we could not see her face. A more lazy or delightful mode of traveling can not be fancied. There is no jolting over stones and through ruts—no bouncing on hard springs, to weary the body and bruise the flesh. Indeed, the motion must be infinitely more pleasant than that of the palanquin. The latter, being fastened to the pole with iron rods, has no elasticity, and every step made by the bearers is felt by the person carried in it. But the hammock is of elastic materials; there is no swinging from side to side; and it has all the luxury of a bed, with the additional advantages of fresh air and gentle exercise. We traveled with as much speed as possible over the hills, but we were several times passed by the hammock bearers. It was only when we gained a level piece of road that we could get ahead of them. At the next ascent or declivity they were sure to go by us, so rapid was their gait. A few days ago, we had a chase of a mile or two up hill on horseback after a hammock, but without being able to overtake it. The rapidity with which the natives pass over the hills, often at an angle of 25° or 30° with the horizon, with heavy loads on their backs and heads, is surprising. No beast of burden can keep pace with them.

We went this afternoon to the Portuguese burying ground, a short distance from the compact part of the city. It is enclosed by a high stone wall on three sides, and on the fourth, which lies upon the street, by a lower wall, surmounted by an iron paling. Through this, a person of ordinary height may look into the interior of the cemetery. The gate in front is of dark cut stone, with a number of carved skulls grinning at you over pairs of crossed thigh-bones, and in spite of this barbarism is striking in its effect; a large cross stands in the centre of the grounds on a heavy pedestal; in the rear there is a small unfinished chapel, designed for the performance of the burial service. The enclosure contains several acres; the grounds are laid out with parallel walks, between which the dead are buried; around the sides there are monuments and large stones, covering the apertures of family vaults; thick hedges or borders of geraniums and flowers of various kinds line the walks; and, with a small annual expenditure, added to the very large one which must have been made to put it in its present condition, it will become a place of great beauty, and, like many of the embellished cemeteries in other quarters of the globe, calculated to disarm the external aspect of death of at least a part of its asperity. As we were about to leave the grounds, we observed a funeral procession approaching, and it was proposed by one of the party that we should return. We did so, and placed ourselves within the gate, at a short distance from a newly made grave, which a man was just finishing. We had scarcely taken our station, when the funeral train passed by us. It was preceded by two priests in their robes; then came the body, on a bier carried on the shoulders of four attendants, and followed by fifteen or twenty well-dressed men in black. Over the bier was thrown a black pall, with a cross of yellow cloth of about the length of the body. As the bearers reached the grave, the bier was set down, the pall taken away, the coffin deposited upon the ground, and the bier and the cover of the coffin removed to a distance of several yards. From these indications, I supposed that we were to witness a mode of sepulture which must naturally be repugnant to the feelings of those who have been unaccustomed to such exhibitions. As it was just at nightfall, the ladies of our party, several of whom were not in good health, retired from the cemetery, and I was left alone with the funeral train.

Let us see in what manner they perform the last offices for their deceased friend. They surround the coffin, one of the priests goes through a short form of burial service, sprinkles the body and the grave with holy water, and he and his associate retire. The attendants take up the coffin and place it upon one side of the grave. One of them removes a pillow from beneath the head of the deceased, and puts a strap under it, drawing out one of the ends on each side. Another strap is put under the feet, and four men raise the body from the coffin. It is stark and stiff, as though it were frozen; and, as it is lifted up, the weight resting upon the straps around the neck and ankles, there is not the slightest relaxation in it. It is held a moment over the grave, to adjust something which is discovered to be out of place, and we are enabled to get a better view of it. It is enveloped in a white shroud of only semi-transparent material, so that we can not see the features or the dress. But it is evidently dressed. The shoes are thrust out at one end, and a dark coat or wrapper is visible through the white envelope. All is now ready, and the body is lowered into the grave; the straps are drawn up, the sexton shovels the earth down upon it, and thus it mingles with its native dust! It is a rigid fulfillment of the Scriptural denunciation, "Dust thou art, and unto dust shalt thou return." There is no attempt to cheat the grave of its due, even for a moment, by enclosing the body in any thing less perishable than itself. But, whatever philosophy or reason may say in favor of this mode of sepulture, there is something in it peculiarly revolting to the feelings of those who are accustomed to the more decent practice which prevails with us. It is, indeed, in a great degree abandoned in Madeira by families in good circumstances. But boards are costly; and, to the poor, the price of a coffin is an expense they can not well meet. Sometimes persons to whom the cost is nothing adhere to the ancient mode of burial. A short time before we witnessed this interment, a rich man requested, in his will, that his body might be committed to its mother earth with no other covering than a winding-sheet; probably from the idea that any thing beyond this is an idle, if not an impious attempt to evade, for a brief space, the common destiny of our species—the union of the body with its parent dust.

It was just nightfall as I entered the compact part of the city, and the inhabitants were everywhere returning to their homes. In the winter months, there is a singular quietness in the streets of Funchal the moment twilight is past. The stores are all shut at sunset; there are no lights in the lower stories of the houses; and, when the moon is not out, you almost grope your way in darkness from street to street. Few persons of any description are abroad, and the city is as silent as it is dark. Now and then a flambeau streams down a street, as some one is lighted to or from home for some purpose of business or pleasure; but in ordinary nights these enlivening scenes are rare. At long intervals of time there is a ball or a concert, almost the only gaieties the city indulges in; and then, for an hour at the beginning of the evening and another at its close, there is a show of life and animation abroad. If the inhabitants are distinguished for any one trait of character more than another, it is for their fondness for domestic life. They pass their evenings at home, with their families, which are ordinarily sufficiently numerous to make them independent of their neighbors for social enjoyment. As a general rule, they may be said to be quiet in their habits and amiable in their character. They are said to be irascible; but we have been in Funchal nearly two months, and have passed through the Christmas holidays, a season of general festivity, without witnessing a quarrel of any sort. The lower classes, so far as we have come in contact with them, seem honest, courteous, and obliging. In trafficking with you, they consider it fair to obtain the greatest possible price for their commodities, without much regard to the value; but it is doubtful whether they carry this point farther than our own countrymen, and they certainly have not a tithe of the shrewdness of the Yankees in driving a bargain. In the respectable Portuguese stores, there is but little variation of the first price asked.

As the inhabitants of Funchal retire to their houses at an early hour in the evening, so, as might be expected, they are out again at an early hour in the morning. I speak more particularly of the working classes. The moment the day breaks, they are abroad, shouting to their cattle or donkeys, and making the streets vocal with their hoarse attempts at melody. There are few musical voices in Madeira. They are almost invariably harsh and discordant. It is said to be a characteristic of the islanders; and, from what we nave seen, there is no reason to doubt it. There is singing enough in the streets, but not a particle of music in it. Nothing can be more grating to the ear. It is remarkable that it should be so. In the cities of the United States, little addicted as we are to the accomplishments, we often hear voices of excellent quality in the streets. The very chimney-sweeps are melodious. But there is no exception here to the hoarse nasal tones in which every attempt at street music is accompanied. Yet the island is not without musical taste. There is a monthly concert given by a corps of professors and amateurs, which is always numerously attended by the Portuguese, the British residents, and many of the visiters to the island; and the performances are highly respectable. They are, however, almost exclusively confined to instrumental music. Now and then a vocal piece is attempted, but there are no voices to sustain it, and it never goes beyond mediocrity. Among the instruments which bear a prominent part in concerts and serenades, is the machete. It is an invention of the island, and one of which the island has no great cause to be proud. In its form it is a dwarf guitar, the body perhaps eight inches long, with four strings of catgut tuned in fifths. Its tones are like those of a violin, when the strings are snapped with the fingers instead of being played on with the bow, excepting that they are higher, and, consequently, more shrill. Its music, by itself, is thin and meagre; but in the streets at night, with a guitar or violincello accompaniment, it is very pretty. There are two or three performers in Funchal who have attained a wonderful proficiency in playing on it. Their execution is astonishing; but I always thought, when listening to them, even when most delighted with their performances, with how much more effect their skill would be expended upon the guitar, which is in all respects a finer instrument. It is not probable that the machete will ever emigrate from Madeira. It is the most common instrument here; but I doubt much whether it would be, if this were not its birthplace. There are several excellent performers on the piano in the city; among others, a private gentleman of the highest musical taste and genius, who not only executes admirably, but has written a number of pieces which would do honor to almost any composer, and on which the inhabitants justly pride themselves. The military band, which is composed principally of natives, is an excellent one. It has recently been formed, and is improving. The Praça Constitucional, where it plays at guard-mounting every morning at ten o'clock, is a place of constant resort for the residents and visiters.

Visiters to the island have often been heard to complain of the noises in the streets, and a book recently published on Madeira makes them a specific ground of complaint; but I much doubt whether they are as noisy as those of London or New York. The greatest clamor is made by the ox-drivers; and this, it must be confessed, is not to be found among the "cries" of

London, or those of our own great commercial metropolis. Persons who are not addicted to early rising, would unquestionably do better to take lodgings a short distance out of the city—though one readily becomes accustomed to noises at night, provided they come regularly. Only that which is unusual disturbs one's sleep. At early day the laboring classes in most cities are about their work ; and certainly nothing can exceed the din of carriages and carts, and the shouting of milkmen, in New York. In Funchal, you hear the voices of the ox-drivers, and the patting of the little feet of the donkeys upon the pavement as they pass under your windows, and now and then one of the latter takes it into his head to bray as he goes along, but this is a nuisance which is rarely inflicted upon you. A little later you hear the tinkling of small bells, and, if you are out of bed, you may see the Funchal milkmen, not coming, as with us, with their carts and huge tin jars filled to the brim with the snow-white fluid, but driving before them a little flock of she-goats tied together two by two. They stop opposite your door, and the man milks before your eyes the quantity you require—a capital plan to get milk without any mixture of water. On the continent, they drive cows about the streets of the cities in the same manner ; and sometimes, it is said, the milkman has a bottle of water under his jacket, which he will contrive to pour into the vessel he is milking in, unless your eye is constantly upon him. Cow's milk is in common use in

Funchal, and not high in price; but it is brought in from the country, and it is extremely difficult to get it pure. The surest way of procuring milk in an unadulterated state, is to patronize the men with the goats. But it is dear. A common-sized tumbler full costs two cents, and when the froth has subsided, and it becomes cool, you find it shrunk to nearly half its original volume.

CHAPTER IV.

CITY OF FUNCHAL.

Our New Lodgings.—The Carreira.—Our Landlord, Baxixa, and his History.—The Comforts of Living in Funchal.—Fish.—Vegetables.—Poultry.—Game.—Butchers' Meat.—Butter.—The Boarding-houses.—Fruit.—Public Amusements.—Clubs, Libraries, and Reading-rooms.—Private Entertainments.—The Civil Governor.—Religious Toleration.—The English Church.—The Sabbath.—The Cathedral.

When we landed, we took lodgings temporarily in a boarding-house kept by a Portuguese, who had lived several years in Quebec, and whose wife was an Englishwoman. Our accommodations were excellent in all respects, our table well supplied, and our cooking unexceptionable. In short, I am not aware that we lacked any comfort within doors, which we could have found at home. There are many other boarding-houses in Funchal which are equally good, and several which have the reputation of being superior. The rooms, however, were not precisely such as we required: and, at the end of a week, we exchanged them for other lodgings.

We now occupy the upper part of a house a few doors from the Carreira, the principal street in Funchal, and so called from having been originally a race-course—not like those of modern times, level and circular, but nearly straight, and as uneven as the surface of the ground can make it. Few streets, however, can be found in the city with less deviation from the horizontal line. Our landlord is an Italian by birth, and a baker and cook by trade; and his house, which is a very excellent one, has just been thoroughly repaired and fitted up for lodgers. The lower floor he occupies himself—the front for a shop and storehouse, our entrance being on one side of them, and the rear for a bakeshop. The latter is magnificent—full forty feet square, with ovens and other conveniences of the finest workmanship and of the best materials. What is of no small consideration, too, it is always kept neat and in good order. The second floor has four rooms—two bedrooms in front, which we occupy, and a bedroom and sitting-room in the rear. The two latter are entirely separated from the others, and are occupied by our landlord and his wife and two little children. The third floor has a parlor, a dining-room, two bedrooms, and a pantry; and these are all ours. Our table is supplied by our landlord, who cooks for us; and we are, in a word, in all respects on the footing of boarders with a private table. For many obvious reasons, this is to be preferred to boarding with a table in common with others not of one's own party; and it is in no respect less comfortable. There are few persons lodged in this manner. In some of the large boarding-houses, parties have private tables; but at most of them the lodgers eat in common. A very considerable portion of the visiters to the island take furnished houses for the season, providing their own linen and servants. This is the most independent mode of living, but it has its inconveniences. Good servants may be procured at comparatively low wages (about four dollars per month for females, and six for males); but, independently of the trouble of house-keeping, it is not easy to escape imposition, without a knowledge of the Portuguese language, which few transient persons possess; and the domestics are almost universally ignorant of English. We have a man-servant, to whom we pay ten dollars per month—the four additional dollars being given on account of his speaking English. But he has scarce any knowledge of it whatever, beyond the names of the ordinary dishes on the tables. Whenever we go farther, and give him a commission to execute out of doors, he is sure to misunderstand us, and to commit some gross blunder; so that I have now taken to speaking bad Portuguese in self-defence.

Our landlord is one of the most well-known personages in Funchal. If there is a great dinner to be cooked, he is sure to have a hand in it. His ices and pastry are indispensable, and they are, in fact, of most excellent quality. He has a large ice-house in the mountain, some two or three miles back of the city, capable of holding a supply of snow, as it is called, for two years ; and when all others are destitute, he has an abundance. A few days ago he observed to us, in great triumph, that if we were to offer twenty dollars for a glass of ice cream, we could not get it, excepting from him. The ice which is laid up in the ice-houses, is frozen rain and hail, or snow partially melted by the sun during the day and congealed again at night. It is only on a few occasions during the winter that it can be procured in a fit state for preserving. The mountains in sight of Funchal, and but three or four miles distant, are frequently covered with snow. For ten days after Christmas they were never entirely bare, but it was too thin to be collected for the ice-houses, which are all near them. When ice is wanted in the city, it is brought down from the mountains by men, often at the peril of their lives. Last winter, the father of our servant, with a load of ice on his head, was borne down by one of the mountain torrents, through which he had to pass, and was killed.

Besides the skill which our host possesses in cookery, he is remarkable for the number of languages he speaks. Italian, French, English, Portuguese, all are alike to him. He speaks them all, including his mother tongue, alike badly. Indeed, he does not attempt to keep up the distinction between them, but passes from one to the other, and jumbles them together in the same sentence, with a fluency which would confound the most skillful interpreter. He has been a man of more consequence, too, though certainly not of greater notoriety, than he is now. He was a merchant at one time, and a successful one; amassed property, spent a good deal of it, embarked more in hazardous enterprises, was cheated out of a part, and he is now pursuing his original vocation with a perseverance and shrewdness which insure him a good living. He has not, however, entirely relinquished his mercantile connections. It was only yesterday that a vessel came consigned to him from the Mediterranean, with 8000 bushels of corn. He has recently purchased, fitted up, and finished the house we live in, and a very excellent and genteel one it is. The rooms are large and airy. A better place for a small party or family, is not to be found in Funchal.

For some days after we took possession, we could hear, at night, the heavy, dull sound of the workmen in the bakeshop, as they were preparing the dough for the oven; and the noisy Portuguese, when they came for bread at daybreak, were sure to rouse us from our slumbers by their vociferous conversation under our windows. But the necessary regimen has been introduced both within doors and without. The workmen make less noise, or we have become accustomed to it. At all events, we hear it no longer. And the good-natured people who come in the morning, having been told that there were strangers in the house, whom they disturbed, stand under our windows in silence, or talking almost in whispers, waiting patiently for the shop door to be opened. The house faces the south, and the sun lies upon our parlor and chamber windows from the time he rises until after two o'clock—a matter of the greatest importance. When there is too much heat, we close our blinds; but when it is cool, we throw them back, and our rooms become bright and glowing with the sunbeams. If we feel cold when we get out of bed, we step into the sunshine and are warm at once. It is precisely like standing before a comfortable fire, and it costs nothing for fuel. No one, who has not tried it, can appreciate the immense superiority of this genial warmth over that on which we have, for eight months annually, been dependent for years—a close stove, heated with wood, and radiating its steaming caloric from thick plates of unwholesome iron, which requires to be constantly watched to guard against too high a temperature.

During the ascendency of the Miguelites in the island, some twelve years ago, our landlord was one of the most important men in it. Madeira, with all the Azores, excepting Terceira, submitted to Don Miguel's forces. Here, there was scarcely any resistance. The fleet appeared off the harbor, and demanded the surrender of the place—a demand which the troops of Don Pedro, who were then in possession, refused. The fleet then sailed for Machico, about fifteen miles east, the forces were landed, marched across the country, and took possession without a contest. The new governor, Monterio, when the city was in the hands of his friends, landed and assumed the reins of government. When he was asked why he did not accompany the troops, he is said to have answered, that he was not sent out to conquer the island, but to govern it after it was conquered; an answer which proves his discretion. Under the new order, Baxixa (for that is the name of our landlord, and the reader should be advised that it is pronounced Bash-shee-shah) became a person of consequence. He was then a baker and a man of property, and he obtained a contract from the government to supply the troops with bread. He acquired the good-will of the governor, soon became intimate with him, and at last a decided favorite at the castle. To tell the truth, his excellency was a very bad fellow in all respects, and it would have been more to the credit of our host if he had enjoyed the confidence of a better man. But his influence was unquestionable. If any one wanted to carry a point with the governor, it was only necessary to enlist Baxixa in his cause. But, like most other favorites, he was beset with difficulties even in his prosperity, and his downfall was sudden and violent. Madeira was politically but a type of Portugal proper. It was divided into two parties. The open and avowed constitutionalists had absconded, or secreted themselves, when Don Miguel obtained the ascendency in Funchal. But with the progress of time, one of the regiments became strongly enlisted in favor of Don Pedro. It was, of course, an object of suspicion and enmity with the governor and his party. It was quartered at the monastery, at one extremity of what is now the Praça Constitucional; and the reverend fathers, its rightful masters, or all that were left of them after the flight of the Pedroites (for the church, as well as the secular branches of the body politic, was divided in political opinion), continued to occupy a part of the edifice. Between these holy men and their military associates a secret enmity sprung up; and on one unlucky day, after the regiment had eaten freely of soup, which was regularly prepared in a large cauldron, they all, with one accord, began to discharge the contents of their stomachs, and with as much uniformity as if it had been done by word of command in the order of their military exercises. Fortunately, no one died. Whether it was intended as any thing more than such a chastisement as it proved, has never been disclosed; but it was satisfactorily traced, some time afterward, to the holy friars, whose order was broken up by Don Pedro when the constitutionalists were in power. The enemies of the governor and Baxixa gave a different turn to it at the time. Whether it was seriously believed or not, they were accused of having conspired to get rid of the regiment by poisoning the bread. The highest excitement existed among the troops. Baxixa was seized and thrown into the city prison. The excitement was only increased by his imprisonment. The ordinary course of justice was altogether too tardy for it. On a feast-day (days of festivity, by-the-by, have, from the era of Pontius Pilate, been the chosen epochs for enacting deeds of blood), they surrounded the prison, broke it open, seized the unhappy Baxixa, and dragged him through the Praça, brandishing their bayonets over his head. They were hurrying him to the Friary, the theatre of the crime of which he was accused, as the most fit place for his execution, when they were met by the colonel, who, if not an unbeliever in Baxixa's guilt, was at least desirous that the forms of justice should be observed in putting him to death. With great difficulty he succeeded in pacifying his followers, and induced them to surrender their prisoner into his hands. They would only do so on the express condition that he should not be remanded to the city prison, which was in possession of the governor and his satellites. He was accordingly taken to the colonel's own house, a few yards from the barracks, and there confined. But in consequence of the disaffection which prevailed in the island, the obnoxious governor was soon afterward removed; and, either because the excitement against Baxixa gradually died away, as all excitements do, or because the mischief ascribed to him was traced to its real authors, he was set at liberty, after having thus narrowly escaped a violent death, as the punishment of a crime of which he was innocent.

The comforts of living in Funchal may fairly challenge a comparison with those of almost any other city of the same magnitude. It has but about 25,000 inhabitants; and it can not be expected to furnish as many luxuries as places ten, twenty, and fifty times as populous; for as masses of men accumulate at a particular point, wealth, and the means of satisfying its demands, increase there also. But all the substantial comforts of life are enjoyed as fully as elsewhere. There is a great variety of fish, of excellent quality. Some, indeed, belong to the class of luxuries. It is but just now that we have been feasting for a fortnight on those delicious little sardines, which we receive, at home, from France, immersed in sweet oil and carefully soldered up in tin boxes. They come about the island once a year in shoals, remain for a few weeks, and then disappear. They are as regular in coming and going as our river shad. When taken fresh from the water, they are very fine. No epicure could ask any thing better. Vegetables are abundant. No better potatoes are to be found, even in the Green Isle itself. Ever since our arrival we have been eating green pease. It is now January, and our table was supplied with them to-day. Then we have the chou-chou, a small vegetable, green without and white within, of an oval shape, with a single seed in the centre. It is, in taste, a medium between the squash and the turnip, if such a medium can be conceived. We have small pumpkins, too, of the size of a citron-melon, cut in two and boiled, with melted butter poured over them when they are brought to the table. If they came in the form of an old-fashioned New England pumpkin pie, we should like them better ; but in their present questionable shape, they are not unpalatable. There is always a plentiful supply of beef in the market, and of very good quality. Chickens are abundant, but poor. Turkeys, on the other hand, are very fine, and so are ducks. Sometimes we have pigeons, both wild and tame, and alike good. Rabbits are abundant, and partridges less so, but always to be had. The mutton is decidedly bad, strong in flavor and lean in condition. The secret of this deficiency is partly explained, when it is understood that no wether mutton is to be obtained. The mountains afford a fine range for flocks ; and on the northern side of the island, within fifteen miles, there is an abundant supply of proper food for them springing spontaneously from the earth. With three or four hundred English here every winter, who certainly are as good judges of mutton as any people in the world, it is surprising that the proper means are not taken by the inhabitants to furnish this first of meats, both for persons in health, as well as invalids, of proper quality.

One of the scarcest articles of diet, and certainly one of the most indispensable, is good butter. It is often brought from England and Germany, and sometimes from the United States ; but the atmosphere is so dry that it can not be kept. The fresh butter from the country is usually unsalted, and tastes strongly of cheese. The inhabitants are learning to understand the English taste, and to cater to it successfully. We have now a supply of butter brought to us every morning fresh from the neighboring mountain parish of St. Roque, salted to the true point and of very excellent flavor. When we add that the best bread, very good tea, sugar, and coffee are to be had, and that the water is excellent, there remains little else to be desired on the score of necessaries or comforts, so far as the table is concerned.

The aspect of the interior of the boarding-houses in Funchal is certainly, to an inhabitant of a cold climate, any thing but cheering. The parlors are now generally carpeted; but the eating-rooms and bedrooms are almost universally bare. The latter have, at the best, strips of green baize or woollen cloth of some kind by the side of the bed, so that, when you rise in the morning, you are not compelled to plant your feet upon the bare floor. There are no fireplaces, or other means of giving you a higher temperature than that of the atmosphere. I have, in one instance, seen a stove-pipe thrust through a tin plate in a parlor window, the glass pane having been removed for the purpose. But fire is rarely, if ever, wanted. Our thermometer has never yet fallen below 64° within doors, nor below 60° without, between sunrise and sunset. In such a climate, an additional garment on cool days is all that is requisite to make one comfortable. I have never yet worn a cloak, even in going out in the evening, though I wear no flannel; but no person in health should be without one. There are few days when a thick coat is uncomfortable; and from the middle of December to the middle of March, woollen clothes are indispensable. To invalids they are so for a much longer period. In short, though a thin coat is often agreeable, persons coming here should bring with them their ordinary winter clothing. Mild as the climate is, every precaution which is necessary at home to preserve the health, is equally so here. Indeed, in all countries a violation of the physical laws brings with it the usual penalty. Exposure to draughts of air, and violent exercise in a hot sun, are to be carefully avoided; and excessive indulgence in eating or drinking is more dangerous, perhaps, here than in climates where the temperature is lower and more bracing.

Though the island abounds in fruits from one end of the year to the other, from November to February they should be eaten in very small quantities. The oranges are not in season till the first of February. Those which come earlier are unripe, and, of course, exceedingly unwholesome. There is no temptation so strong, after a sea voyage, as that of eating fruit, and particularly oranges. Yet it should be resisted. Persons arriving here in November and December usually eat them, and are almost invariably visited with attacks of diarrhœa. It is just as imprudent as it would be for an inhabitant of Madeira to eat green apples in the United States in July or August. Guavas are out of season about the first of January. The banana ripens at all seasons, but it is for most persons a heavy, indigestible fruit. At all events, the greatest caution should be practised in eating it. In winter, the West Indies have unquestionably a great advantage over Madeira in fruits; but it is the reverse at all other seasons of the year. The latter rises, within the narrow compass of three miles, from the level of the ocean to a height of 6200 feet. On the successive planes of elevation which the surface presents, the fruits of widely varying climates may be successfully cultivated. Less attention is paid to them than would be expected. But there is scarcely any fruit known to the temperate or tropical latitudes, which is not to be found here. There are apples, peaches, pears, figs, grapes, pomegranates, pineapples, and a multitude of others, and of good quality. But they are summer or fall fruits, and visiters to the island usually arrive too late, and depart too early for them. To enjoy the island in perfection, and see it in all its beauty, it is necessary to pass the summer and autumn in it. The heat is rarely oppressive in Funchal; and on the northern side, and on the higher elevations, the island is, for its climate, the magnificence of its scenery, and the beauty of its vegetation, unsurpassed. But on this point we may have more to say hereafter.

The public amusements in Funchal are few; and it is well for invalids, perhaps, that it is so. The principal enjoyments are derived from the fine air and scenery, and these are constantly tempting one to healthful exercise. There is an English club and a

Portuguese club, each with its reading-rooms and billiard-table for the use of its members and subscribers. The former has a very good miscellaneous library, consisting, I believe, exclusively of English books, neither very numerous nor very rare, but with a due mixture of scientific works and of the light literature of the day, suited rather to the demands of sojourners than of resident families. Regular, but moderate, annual additions are made to it; and, in time, it will, if the association is continued, become a respectable library. In addition to its books, it has an ample supply of magazines and English newspapers. The Portuguese club has regular files of newspapers and magazines in the national language, but it has no books. Strangers are freely admitted as subscribers, on paying three dollars for a single month, or eight dollars for three months, when introduced by members; and these contributions are the principal source of income. Whenever a name is presented, the person proposed undergoes the ordeal of a ballot on the part of the permanent members of the club; but the rejection of a name is, I believe, a thing unheard of.

Neither dinner nor evening parties are frequent, and they are generally given by the English residents, whose unaffected kindness, courtesy, and hospitality are proverbial. Many of them have amassed fortunes in the island, and have expended their earnings very freely in the embellishment of their houses and gardens, which are generally on the high ground back of the city. Indeed, most of the finest places belong to English merchants. The enterprise, shrewdness, and persevering industry of the Anglo-Saxon race, are, on this side of the Atlantic, as on the other, everywhere visible in accumulations of wealth, and in a liberal and enlightened expenditure. The English are to the old world what the Yankees are to the new—not only busy at home, but perpetually carrying their enterprise abroad, and triumphing, wherever they go, over all competition.

Among the Portuguese part of the population there are individuals of high character, talents, and wealth; nor are they few in number, when we consider the comparatively small population of the island, which does not now exceed 120,000 souls. Entertainments are, I apprehend, much more rare among them than in former years, when the island was in the zenith of its prosperity. Its commerce is now exceedingly depressed; recent calamities have added to the general embarrassment; and few families are so independent as not to participate in it. A monthly ball is given by the Portuguese club in its magnificent rooms, and there all the belles of the city are to be found. Every subscriber can attend, and every stranger may become a subscriber on a proper introduction. It is his own fault, therefore, if any one leaves Funchal without a sight of its assembled beauty.

Among the first men in the city is the civil governor

—not from his station alone, but from his intelligence, wealth, and personal character. He is a native of Madeira, was a practitioner at the bar, and is possessed of all that practical information in relation to the island, and its internal concerns, which a governor should have. With much dignity and courtesy of manner he unites an entire disregard of all ceremony and form in his intercourse with others. He exhibits not the least pride, either of wealth or station; though in the latter respect he has no equal in the island, and in the former very few. One of his dinner-parties, which I attended, was much like that of a private gentleman in New York; and an evening party, which followed, was a very simple, quiet, unaffected gathering, with very excellent music, both instrumental and vocal, from two young Portuguese ladies, who had been taught in England, and quadrilles intermixed. There was nothing, in short, to distinguish it from one of our evening parties at home, excepting the spacious apartment of the old castle, in which it was given, and the antiquated portraits of the Madeira governors, in an adjoining room of equal magnitude, whose eyes seemed, through the open door, to be fixed upon the festive scene near them—a scene which had, probably, been a thousand times enacted during the centuries some of them had hung upon the walls.

Though the established religion is Roman Catholic, a liberal regard is had to the religious opinions of others. "No one," says the constitution of Portugal, "shall be molested on account of his religion, provided he respects that of the state and does not offend against the public morals." The same toleration is not accorded to the external manifestations of religion. A preceding provision of the same constitution is as follows: "The Roman Catholic Apostolic religion shall continue to be the religion of the kingdom. All others are permitted to strangers, with their domestic or private worship, in houses to be set apart for that purpose, but without any exterior form of a church." I believe this privilege has long been enjoyed by the subjects of Great Britain, by virtue of a treaty with Portugal; and it was no more than common justice to accord it to the people of all other countries sojourning in the kingdom. In denying to British subjects the right of worshiping in a building with the form of a church, Catholic Portugal did no more than Protestant England did for centuries in denying the same privilege to all who were not of the national religion. The Episcopal church in Funchal (for it bears that name, though it has no steeple or bell, and looks more like an edifice devoted to scientific or literary uses) is a beautiful structure, and it stands in the midst of a garden laid out and embellished with great taste and neatness. The grounds are full of trees and shrubs, some of them rare, and the approach to them is through a passage of some ten feet in breadth, the walls of which are completely overspread on each side with geranium and heliotrope in full blossom, and ever exhaling fragrance. Indeed, it is quite a fairy little establishment, and it is well calculated to invest the worship of God with bright and beautiful associations, such as appropriately belong to it. The builders, however, seem to have improved upon the constitutional prohibition. It has as little the form of a church within as without, saving the two pulpits, which are perched up on each side of the altar, as it were for symmetry, and the Lord's Prayer, the Creed, and the Ten Commandments, which stand behind in gilt letters. The whole central part of the building is circular in form, from the floor to the ceiling; and in the second story, or gallery, the pews cluster round this circle, looking, in front, precisely like the boxes in a theatre, but without their succession of seats rising one above the other to give spectators a sight of the play. Each pew has a level floor, with chairs for the occupants, and the enclosure in front is so high that it is difficult to look down upon the floor below. Better retreats for drowsy subjects can not be fancied. They might sleep through the whole service, sermon and all, without the least fear of detection. The church in winter is so well filled that not only all the pews are occupied, but chairs are placed in the aisles as close together as possible, each one labeled with the sitter's name, and the use of each brings into the parochial treasury the snug little sum of six dollars. The Rev. Mr. Lowe is a most excellent man, and writes capital sermons; and those who attend to his spiritual instruction as they ought, will be sure to be benefited by it.

The Presbyterians have an organized society also, but they have yet no permanent place of meeting. They have fitted up a room temporarily for their religious exercises, and have it in contemplation to erect a building for the purpose as soon as they can collect the necessary pecuniary means.

The Sabbath is more decently observed in Funchal than on the continent of Europe. The difference may be, perhaps, principally in the fact that there are here no public amusements—a difference of accident rather than of principle. Certain it is that the Roman Catholic churches are well attended, the streets are quiet, and there are no noisy assemblies of the people. Now and then a shop door may be seen open, and a shoemaker within at his work; but these are exceptions to the general rule of respect for the day. Stores and shops are almost invariably closed, and the usual avocations of business suspended. The military are out with unusual splendor, if not always on Sundays, at least on the grand festa days of the Church. But this is the case in most countries where standing armies are an essential ingredient in the political organization. The undress, which is usually worn on working-days, is laid aside, and all the trappings and toggery of the profession are put on. The band plays one or two additional airs in the Praça, and the drum-major, whose countenance, if it be possible, wears an additional shade of sternness and severity, makes an extra flourish with his gold-headed cane as he marches up and down with the trombone and serpent close upon his heels. The usual corps of spectators is greatly reinforced by the addition of many who are about their work at guard-mounting on other days, and whose only opportunity of hearing the music is on Sunday. But the show is all over before it is time to go to church, so that it withdraws no one from his religious exercises. The cathedral is the boundary of the Praça at one extremity, and it is open every day of the week. I have often stepped into it after the military parade was over, and have always found some devout Catholics at their devotions. On ordinary days, however, the corps of priests around the altar, and their assistants, with the young candidates for holy orders whom they are training to the chaunts, are more numerous than the auditors.

The interior of the cathedral has nothing remarkable in its architecture. It is spacious, and has the usual provision of side altars, gilt figures, and paintings, but none which hold out, on a superficial examination, any strong inducement to a closer inspection. There is a communion chapel on one side, which is usually shut off from the body of the church by curtains. On Christmas eve they were drawn aside, as they are on all great occasions, and they disclosed one of the richest apartments that can be fancied. The whole chapel is a mass of gold and gilding, with a much greater display of wealth than of taste or skill in workmanship. The floor of the church is a layer of doors, about six feet in length and three in breadth, and beneath each of these there is a vault. It was formerly the principal burial-place, and it contains the bones of more than 20,000 persons—nearly as many as now inhabit the city of Funchal. On Christmas eve the whole body of the church was filled with the city population: the gentry occupied rows of seats near the altar; the humbler classes were crowded together farther back—the men standing, and the women sitting cross-legged (a strong indication of their Moorish origin) upon the floor, or rather upon the doors of the vaults beneath; the priests stood in close array about the altar, in their sacerdotal robes; and the organ was pouring forth a strain of triumphant melody, its tones half drowned by the hoarse voices of a corps of male choristers, but hardly powerful enough altogether to fill the immense space between the living mass below and the vaulted roof above. It was an imposing spectacle, and not the less so for the reflection that, full as the cathedral was of living worshipers, it numbered not the tithe of the successive generations which had in their turn been assembled there to usher in the day of the nativity, and were now slumbering in the silent vaults below.

CHAPTER V.

CITY OF FUNCHAL.

Water.—Fountains.—The Great Flood of 1803.—The Flood and Storm of 1842.—Depression of the Commerce of Madeira.—The Monopolies of Tobacco and Soap.—Impost on Foreign Grains, and Export Duty on Wines.—Measures of Relief.—Exports of Wine from 1828 to 1842.

No city is better supplied with water than Funchal, or with water of better quality. It comes down from the mountains, through the ravines which intersect them, as clear as crystal, leaping over the rocks and sparkling in the sunbeams, wherever the sun shines upon it. It is so soft that the washerwomen use little, and most of them no soap, so that they are in some degree independent of that shameful tax upon cleanliness, the soap monopoly, of which we shall have something to say hereafter. The inhabitants of Funchal have not failed to avail themselves of the facilities which the formation of the island affords, for bringing within their reach this first necessary of life. They have intercepted the descending streams, and, conveying them under ground in clay pipes, have distributed them through the city, bringing them to the surface again in fountains at convenient distances from each other. These fountains are generally found in some square, or open space, forming slight recesses, and presenting an exterior of stone, the flat surfaces turned to the street, with large brass cocks inserted in them. In a square near the cathedral, the fountain consists of a marble column about twenty feet in height, on a pedestal, with four open-mouthed heads, with expressions so repulsive as almost to disgust you with the sparkling streams they are spouting into a receiving basin. Near the river is another column of dark stone, plain and massive; and by the governor's castle there is a wall from which fine jets of water issue. To these fountains the inhabitants resort for water for domestic uses, sometimes with large jars on their heads, but more frequently with little wooden casks, precisely like a hogshead in shape, but somewhat more slender in proportion, and holding about ten gallons. After all, this is but an inconvenient mode of procuring water. How easy would it be to introduce it into every house, and what a saving of expense and trouble! This is done in some cases, but by far the greater number of the best houses in the city, and of course the inferior, rely on the fountains and the water carriers.

In one respect, the city has used its supply of water to the best advantage. It is conducted in sewers through every street, and the houses are drained into them, so that all filth and impurities are swept into the sea by the constantly running currents. This, of itself, would be sufficient to ensure the city the healthfulness for which it is distinguished.

Fortunate as the city is in this respect, its water is its greatest enemy. It has been twice deluged within the last forty years, and with the most disastrous consequences. The first of these great floods was in October, 1803. The rain began to fall in torrents at noon, and at eight o'clock in the evening the devastation commenced. Houses were swept from their foundations, broken into fragments, and carried into the sea. The floods came down from the mountains with such force as to bring large stones with them, thus adding greatly to their destructive powers. No structure could resist such a battery. One house was swept entire into the sea, and remained some time above the surface, with the lights burning in the upper story. The darkness of the night added to the confusion, and to the loss of life. In many instances individuals rushed into the very destruction from which they were endeavoring, in their terror, to escape. About four hundred persons perished. The narrow streets were blocked up by earth, the ruins of houses, the carcasses of cattle, and the bodies of men, women, and children. As the streets were afterward cleared of their obstructions, the bodies were collected and burned upon a general funeral pile. For some time despondence, apathy, and despair pervaded the city. The ignorant and superstitious considered it as the precursor of the destruction of the world, and abandoned themselves to their terrors instead of laboring to diminish the general calamity. But the floods at length subsided, to be renewed at the end of forty years with equal force, though, fortunately, not with the same disastrous effects.

On the 26th of last October the storm, of which we have spoken in a previous chapter, burst upon Funchal. For two successive days the rain had fallen heavily, and on the third a furious gale from the sea met the descending floods from the mountains, and in the collision the whole lower part of the city was buried in water, and every vessel in the harbor was stranded upon the beach. The torrents, which had for two days been pouring down from the mountains, brought with them enormous masses of earth and stones, sweeping away the cultivated soil from the terraces by which it was supported, and blocking up the artificial rivers constructed to facilitate the passage of the water to the ocean. Proprietors could no longer distinguish the boundaries of their domains. Walls, terraces, rich beds of earth, vines and their trellis-work, all were carried away; and where gardens and vineyards flourished, the volcanic rocks beneath them were laid bare-and every thing wore one common aspect of desolation. The channels, which were prepared and fortified at an enormous expense to guard against the recurrence of the disaster of 1803, proved wholly inadequate to the security of the city.

Funchal may be said to be built upon two ridges of land, formed by three ravines, which afford a passage for the rains from the mountains to the sea. All these ravines pass through the compact part of the city. To prevent them from washing away their banks and undermining the houses near them, immense walls of solid masonry have been constructed, so that they are completely enclosed, from the points at which they enter the city, to the places where they are discharged into the ocean. One of these enclosed channels is about 1,400 yards in length, from 30 to 60 feet in depth, and about 150 feet wide, and it is spanned by several arched bridges of excellent workmanship. The cost of this work alone was near half a million of dollars. The others are not so great in extent, and were less costly. So large was the quantity of descending water that they were all filled nearly to the brim; and such was its force in these narrow channels, that immense masses of rock were rolled down their sloping bottoms, until they were so clogged at their lower extremities that the water flowed over their banks on each side and inundated the whole of the lower part of the city. In some of the streets the water was twenty feet in depth, and when the flood subsided, the apartments on the ground floors of the houses were filled to the height of two or three feet with mud and earth. If the disaster had occurred at night, the loss of life would probably have been as great as in 1803. As it was, streets were blocked up with the ruins of gardens and vineyards; public walks were overwhelmed, their ornamental work destroyed, and their shrubs and plants beaten down or torn up by the roots; bridges were demolished, houses undermined, and property to the amount of at least a million of dollars lost. As if all this destruction were not sufficient to appease the anger of the elements on the land, a new enemy attacked the city from the sea. A violent hurricane came in from the south at the very moment when it was under water. The ships in the harbor were driven from their anchorage. Fortunately they were only five in number. As the gale blew directly in upon the land, they could not go out to sea. To save the vessels was impossible. All that could be effected was to save the crews. For this purpose their only resource was to hoist sail and run up as far as possible on the beach. In two instances it was entirely, and in a third partially successful. In two it failed, and ships and crews were buried in a common destruction. When we entered the city, traces of the ravages of the flood, as well as the gale, were seen on all sides. They are yet by no means obliterated. But much has been done to remove them. Streets are cleared out and repaved; the channels of the artificial rivers are partly opened again by the removal of the stone, gravel, and earth brought down from the higher elevations; the wrecks of the stranded ships have been broken up and carried away; and the city begins to wear a renovated aspect. But years will elapse before the effects of this disaster will be repaired. Falling upon the island, as it has, at a season of great commercial depression, it is far more severely felt than it would be under ordinary circumstances of prosperity.

The decline of the commerce of the island of Madeira is to be traced, in some degree, to the pecuniary embarrassments which exist in other countries, though it is also, to a great extent, to be attributed to causes of domestic origin. Its entire product for exportation consists of its wines, an article of luxury. When the countries in which they are consumed are prosperous, its annual supply is absorbed. But when commercial depression and embarrassment call for economy and retrenchment on the part of the consumers of its wines, the usual demand is diminished, and a surplus accumulates. This is the case at the present time. Such a season of inactivity in business has never before been known. Little wine is exported. Large quantities remain on hand; and the islanders, who rely on sales for the support of their families, are reduced to great embarrassment for want of money. As a temporary resource, many are selling off ornaments and jewelry which they can dispense with. Almost every day some such articles are offered to us—laces, ear-rings, breastpins, and gold chains—the former at very low prices, and the latter for the value of the gold contained in them. But for the annual influx of invalids, who come here to pass the winter months, and who expend, at the lowest calculation, $150,000 in Funchal, the suffering would be still greater. This foreign tribute is, in fact, to a large portion of the amount, a consumption of the products of the island, or the employment of its labor. It puts in requisition the services of a great number of persons in the city, and brings from the interior the articles of subsistence which are necessary for the support of the foreign visiters.

The Madeira wines were first brought into notice in the western hemisphere by the city of Charleston, in South Carolina. From that city the island received large supplies of rice, which constituted a considerable portion of the subsistence of its inhabitants. A more natural or beneficial traffic to the islanders there could not well be. They were profiting largely by it. They found a ready and advantageous vent for their staple, and they received in return a cheap and nutritious article of food. In an evil hour, Portugal, under the influence of the protective system—a system which too often turns the industry it seeks to regulate and benefit into unnatural and unprofitable channels—imposed a heavy duty on rice imported from any but its own dominions. The object was to protect the rice of Brazil. The object was accomplished: the rice of Brazil obtained a monopoly of the Madeira market. The trade with Charleston was destroyed; for the impost on rice amounted to a prohibition. But Brazil does not want the wines of Madeira; and the people of the island, at least those who can afford it, eat bad rice at prices comparatively high, without being able to pay for it directly with their own products. What a comment on the folly of governments in attempting, for the benefit of particular districts of country or classes of people, to give a direction to human industry and force it out of the channels in which it naturally circulates!

The people of Madeira have other causes of complaint of the same sort against their government. They are taxed on two articles—one a necessary, and the other a luxury—for the united benefit of the government and a few monopolists. The importation of soap and tobacco is in the hands of a contractor, who, for the exclusive privilege of supplying the kingdom, pays the government over a million of dollars a year. The contract is usually sold once in three years to the highest bidder; though it has for several years been in the hands of an individual, to reimburse loans made of him by Don Pedro. These articles, excepting in the hands of the contractor, are, of course, contraband. Nor is this all. To make the monopoly complete, no person in the island is permitted to make soap in his own house, or raise tobacco on his own land. There is an old woman now imprisoned in Funchal for making her own soap in violation of the monopoly. A more arbitrary exertion of power can not be fancied. The tea-tax, and other kindred impositions, which gave birth to the American revolution, were, as mere grievances, nothing in comparison. So far as tobacco is concerned, the consumers may not be considered entitled to any special sympathy; though the principle of controlling an individual as to the particular articles he may raise on his own soil, is equally offensive in the sight of all political justice. But the soap monopoly is an unmixed evil, oppressive in principle and iniquitous in practice. It is a tax on cleanliness; a bounty on squalidness and filth, on fleas, and other vermin of a more loathsome character; and it can hardly fail to produce a fruitful crop of all. The poorest soap (such soap as no one would use in the United States—coarse, dirty, and of horrible odor) is sold by the monopolists at twenty-two cents the pound. They are not allowed to sell it at a higher rate! But on all fancy soaps they may charge what they please. With the poor privilege of using their own ashes and soap-grease according to their own pleasure for domestic purposes, there is no doubt that the health as well as the neatness of the islanders would be greatly improved. To deny it to them is, in a small way, one of the worst evidences of bad government. It is singular that, under a representative system containing so many excellent practical provisions, and so many declarations of high political principle, as that of Portugal, an abuse like this should be allowed to exist.

There is one honest feature in this soap and tobacco contract: it does not disguise its true character. In every store where these articles are vended in Funchal, a board is hung out with the following words inscribed on it—"RAMO DE ESTANCO"—which are equivalent, in English, to "A BRANCH OF THE MONOPOLY." How many of the monopolies in our own country (for we are not without them) would be able to endure the popular ordeals through which they pass, if they were compelled to advertise themselves in this way under their true names, instead of assuming, as they do, appellations significant of public benefit, to which they are in no manner subservient!

It is by no means probable that these Portuguese monopolies will be endured much longer—at least the monopoly of soap. It is the subject of discussion and complaint; and if Portugal has a tithe of the liberal spirit which her constitution contains, arbitrary as some of its features are, a speedy remedy will be applied to what is really, in practice, a domestic, and in principle a public evil.

The local, as well as the national government, has contributed its share to the existing impositions on the necessaries of life. There is a tax on imported grains, though Madeira can not raise, in breadstuffs, more than one third of its consumption. This is an impost with a view to revenue. The only objection to it is, that it falls upon an article of first necessity, and, in consequence of the high price of bread, the laboring classes are forced to subsist principally on potatoes, chestnuts, and the very coarsest grains.

Under the pressure of embarrassments abroad and

burdens at home, the commercial business of the island has fallen off to a deplorable extent. It has been gradually declining for several years; but its recent diminution has been rapid beyond all former example. The receipts at the custom-house in Funchal for the fiscal year ending in 1840, were reduced to $129,492; and for the year ending in 1842 they were only $111,420; exhibiting in two years a falling off of about one seventh of the whole amount—a large loss upon an already reduced rate of income. Formerly, Portugal derived a large revenue from Madeira. The island now does not yield enough to pay its own expenses. Measures framed with a view to the restoration of its commercial prosperity have recently been proposed and submitted to the government for its consideration. Among the first of these is a proposition to negotiate with Great Britain a treaty of commerce, stipulating a reciprocal reduction to the amount of ten or fifteen per cent. of the duties paid on the productions of the two countries in their respective custom-houses. Another is, the abolition of half the export duty on the wines of the island—another imposition on its industry, which we have not before alluded to. This duty is $4 80 a pipe, and in very prosperous years amounts to a tax of $70,000.

It will be perceived, by the following extract from the report of a committee appointed by the queen, to suggest measures for the relief of Madeira from the consequences of the disasters of October, 1842, that the decline of its commerce is attributed to the application, generally, of the custom-house regulations of the kingdom to the island. The committee consisted of the civil governor and some of the most judicious and enlightened citizens of Funchal, among whom was Daniel D'Ornellas e Vasconcellos, a peer of the realm, and a gentleman of learning and distinguished talent.

"This minute and careful examination has resulted in rendering the committee more thoroughly convinced that, of all the scourges and misfortunes which have weighed and now weigh with new force upon this unhappy island, no one has assailed it in so vital a point, no one has plunged it so deeply into the abyss of misery, as the fatal application of the national tariff of custom-house duties to the island! And how could it be otherwise, when the exorbitant rates of duty fixed by the tariff, putting an end to the introduction of foreign merchandise, prevent us from exchanging our only article of production, wine, from which we derive the necessaries and comforts of life, and which is, unfortunately, an article of great luxury? It was not reasonable to suppose that foreigners would send vessels to Madeira in ballast, to purchase, with cash, wines which they might advantageously dispense with by substituting for them the infinite diversity of others which are produced by Spain, Italy, France, the Rhine, and the islands of the Mediterranean; it was not reasonable to expect, by forcibly and violently compelling us, in this way, to draw the merchandise we require from Lisbon, which does not purchase in money for its own consumption a single gallon of our wine, that we could continue to have money to support so ruinous a commerce."

The extent to which the commerce of Funchal has fallen off might be better understood, if its shipping-list for the last year could be compared with those of former years. This, unfortunately, is impossible, for want of authentic registers. The number of vessels which entered the port in 1842, was 366; of which 72 were Portuguese, 188 English, 29 American, 15 French, Danish 5, Sardinian 33, Spanish 7, Greek 6, and 11 from various countries. From 1807 to 1815, the number of vessels entering the port is said to have been from 400 to 500 yearly. A better criterion, perhaps, of the commercial prosperity of the island, may be found in its exports of wine, its only product for foreign consumption. The amount entered for exportation at the custom-house in Funchal, for a series of years, is as follows:

1828	9623 pipes.	1836	7913 pipes.
1829	8104 "	1837	8123 "
1830	5499 "	1838	9828 "
1831	5533 "	1839	9043 "
1832	7163 "	1840	7975 "
1833	8683 "	1841	7157 "
1834	9228 "	1842	6270 "
1835	7730 "		

It will be seen that the export for 1842 was the

least during the eleven years of which it terminates the series, and nearly half of this amount is said to have been sent abroad on speculation to find purchasers, and not on actual sales and orders. In earlier and more prosperous years the annual export sometimes rose to 15,000 pipes.

Whether all the measures of relief sought for by Madeira will be granted, is questionable; those, especially, which would diminish the revenue of the kingdom. Portugal is, as a nation, in as embarrassed a condition, in respect to her finances, as her province of Madeira. She has a debt of about $100,000,000—a debt she is wholly unable to pay. Indeed, her income is not sufficient to meet the annual installments of interest. She pays only part of the interest now; and, of course, the debt is constantly accumulating, while her ability to discharge it is becoming less. She, however, promises to pay, and is, in this respect, much like some of our Western states, which do not pay their debts, but deny, theoretically, the dishonest doctrine of repudiation.

CHAPTER VI.

CITY OF FUNCHAL.

Death of one of our Party.—Common Error of Pulmonary Invalids.—Funeral Trains in Madeira.—The Protestant Cemetery.—Invidious Distinction between British Subjects and Foreigners.—February in Madeira.—Beauty of the Nights.—Visit to the Palheiro.—Artificial Planes and Embankments.—Beauty of the Road to the Palheiro, its Groves, and Parks.—Destruction of the Forests.—Ball of the Portuguese Club.—Chicken Broth.

We have to-day paid the last tribute of respect to one of our fellow-passengers in the Mexican—a young gentleman of fine talents and most amiable character. He embarked with little prospect of ever again seeing his native land, and against the earnest remonstrances of his friends. But the love of life—the hope, faint as it might be, of gaining a few additional months, perhaps years, through the influences of a genial climate—prevailed over all other considerations. His disease had advanced so far that nothing could retard its progress. The voyage, instead of giving him new strength, as it might at an earlier period, seemed to enfeeble him. It is a common error of pulmonary invalids to leave home when home is the only fit place for them. It should be impressed on them and their friends that nothing is to be hoped from a change of climate, unless it is made in the first stages of the disease. To go from home when it is far advanced, and has become firmly seated, is, in a vast majority of cases, but courting a foreign grave. Every possible mitigation, of which a deathbed abroad and at a distance from one's kindred is susceptible, our countryman enjoyed—comfortable lodgings, excellent attendance, the best medical advice, and a crowd of surrounding friends ministering assiduously to his wants. But how poorly do all these alleviating circumstances compensate for the absence of those who are endeared to us by the ties of blood, of friendship, of associations which have grown strong with the lapse of years ! In the struggle of the spirit against the strong arm of the destroyer, for the possession of its frail tenement of flesh, how is it encouraged and sustained when the failing ear continues, to the last, to hear familiar voices, and the cold grasp is returned by kindred hands ! If in this hour of trial the beauties of surrounding nature have a soothing influence, in no other part of the globe is it more likely to be felt than here. When the last hour of a distinguished philosopher was approaching, he begged that his bed might be moved to his window, that he might look out once more upon the groves and fields he loved. The death of our countryman was in the midst of scenes which, for natural beauty, could not well be surpassed. The window at his bedside opened upon a grove of orange trees, laden with their golden fruit. Beyond them rose a mountain, thousands of feet in height, clad with vineyards, terraced, and spotted with cottages, as far up as the eye could reach, and crowned with a dark crest of firs; while below the broad ocean was seen rolling in its ceaseless waves against the huge basaltic cliffs, which stand there as a perpetual barrier against its encroachments. But this scene, beautiful and majestic as it was, had not for him the charm of familiarity. It was a foreign land. These were not the groves in which he had strolled, the mountains he had climbed, or the sea-beaten rocks on which he had stood in his boyhood and his youth. If there is any power in natural scenery to render the last moments more tranquil, is it not in that which presents well-known aspects, and which is associated with recollections of pleasures enjoyed, of difficulties conquered, or of favorite objects achieved? When the dying philosopher desired to be carried to his window, to see the trees he had planted, the woods in which he had rambled, and the garden he had tilled, it was from the same feeling with which we take leave of old and familiar friends, who have been the partners of our pleasures, our sorrows, and our toils. In the last struggle of humanity against its destiny, it is to the familiar objects of life that the heart clings. Majestic and beautiful as nature may be, is not its influence lost upon the sinking spirit, unless it is endeared by the powerful charm of association? There is reason and truth in the wish expressed by the ancients on the departure of friends: "May you return and die among your kindred!"

There is something impressive in the funeral trains in Madeira; far more so than in the long processions of carriages (often empty) which in some countries attend the body to its burial-place. Here it is carried on the shoulders of four men. A heavy black pall is thrown over the coffin, having, with the Roman Catholics, a cross of white cloth upon it, and with the Protestants, a wide flounce of white satin. The bearers are dressed in long black coats, coming down to their ankles; and as they move on with their heads and bodies buried beneath the sable pall, the effect is singularly solemn and striking. The cemetery for strangers is in an elevated part of the city, enclosed with a high wall, and filled with trees and shrubbery. Every thing connected with it is neat and tasteful; every thing, in short, gratifies the eye and the fancy; there is nothing bare or neglected, like too many burial-places in other quarters of the globe. It is under the direction of the Episcopal church, together with another adjacent cemetery for residents.

It is painful to qualify this praise by alluding to other circumstances, connected with the interment of strangers in Madeira, of an offensive character. The cemetery was prepared, and is kept in order, at considerable expense, and it is but just that those who use it should pay a reasonable compensation. The charge for a mere permission to bury a British subject in it, is $40. It seems a large price; but it may be necessary; and there would be no cause to find fault with it, if it were uniform, but it is not so. For the privilege of burying an American citizen, or any person other than a British subject in it, the sum of $80 is exacted. The distinction is invidious and illiberal—neither in harmony with the spirit of the times, nor with the character of those who are responsible for it. The British residents, by whom the church is principally supported, are distinguished for their hospitality and courteous attentions to strangers. There is probably not one of them who would not feel his character impeached, if he could be supposed capable, personally, of such illiberality. But how true is it, that associations and bodies of men, where there is a divided responsibility, are ready to assume and act collectively upon principles so narrow and repulsive that each would individually consider his honor concerned in renouncing them in practice! The death of a friend in a foreign land is always peculiarly afflicting. How much more so is it to his kindred, when those among whom he breathed his last, instead of putting him on the common footing of a brother, follow him to the grave with an invidious exaction, and make a heartless speculation out of his dead body! It is difficult to suppose that this distinction will not ere long be abolished. When it is once fairly brought under the consideration of its authors, there is little hazard in saying, that they will lay aside the corporate feeling, and dispose of the subject in accordance with their true character as gentlemen and men.

There is another exaction, which is of the same character. By the cemetery regulations no stone is allowed to be placed over a grave, and the charge for affixing a tablet to the wall, is $40 for a British subject, and $80 for all other persons. In most cases, a mass of plaster, of the shape of a coffin, and of the color of dark stone, is placed upon the grave, with the name of the deceased painted on it. But these are, of course, exceedingly fragile: the action of heat and moisture, with the accidents to which they are subject, soon destroy them, and every memorial of the spot where a particular individual is buried, is obliterated and lost. To avoid this alternative, those who can afford it pay the charge for the privilege of placing a tablet upon the wall. As the island becomes more frequented by invalids, and particularly by persons from other countries than Great Britain, the continuance of these exactions must lead to the establishment of another strangers' cemetery, on a more liberal foundation, and, at all events, on the principle of entire equality for people of all nations.

It is now the first of February, and the country wears much the same aspect as it did when we landed, on the 12th of November. Every thing is fresh and verdant, excepting a few trees, which have shed their leaves, and are standing up, with a kind of monumental air, amid the prevailing bloom and fragrance. And yet they wear an aspect of life. They are not dry and sere, like the sapless trunks which are seen here and there, and which have put forth their leaves for the last time ; but they look vigorous and firm, as if they were recruiting their strength to come out again with redoubled beauty and luxuriance. Among the bare trees, the fig occupies a conspicuous place. No other seems so entirely divested of foliage. It is a peculiarity of the island—the southern part of it, at least—that the deciduous trees are rarely found bare in mid-winter. Their old leaves cling to them almost until they put on their new dress in spring. But the vines—one of the principal elements of rural beauty in Madeira—are dry and leafless. Some of them are, however, at this early period, beginning to put forth new leaves ; and still they are far in rear of some of the fruit trees. Many of the latter have already shed their blossoms, and the peaches are as large as walnuts. I have just been taking a solitary ride through the surrounding country, mile after mile, with these refreshing objects, with flowers in endless profusion, and fields of verdure around me, climbing precipices, crossing ravines, and winding around the declivities of mountains with the broad sun-lit ocean stretching itself out and bounding the horizon at the farthest compass of the eye. More than once during my ride did the remembrance of the good friends we have left behind come over me, and always with regret that they could not be snatched away from that hard-coal fire over which they are shivering, or picked out of that snow-bank into which they have probably just been upset, and brought here to share with us a winter of flowers, and verdure, and genial warmth.

Among the other charms of Madeira, is the beauty of the nights. They are usually clear and brilliant, even when the days have been overcast. The vapors, which the sun had not power to chase away while he was above the horizon, seem, as he descends below it, to vanish of their own accord; and, almost before the brief twilight is past, the stars begin to come out, and the moon, if she is in this part of the heavens, lights up the encircling hills with an effect as beautiful, if not as brilliant, as that which is produced by the glare of mid-day. I was very much struck, a few days ago, with the aspect of the heavens at sunset, from the public walk between the governor's castle and the beach. As the sun went down in the Atlantic, and while the whole west was red and glowing with his beams, the moon was rising over the mountains, and seemed already to have taken full possession of the opposite east; so sudden is the transition from day to night! As I turned from one to the other, I could scarcely believe that I was not under the influence of an optical illusion. One might almost fancy the moonbeams pouring down the mountains like an armed host, and driving the retreating daylight into its last stronghold in the west. The sun's shadows seemed scarcely to have disappeared, before the moon threw new ones from the same objects in an opposite direction. The general effect of this brief contest for the mastery between the day and the night, was singularly beautiful. It is difficult to describe it. But it reminded me forcibly of the light which prevails during an annular eclipse of the sun—somewhat warmer in its tone, as the painters say, but in intensity a medium between the brilliancy of the day and the pale lustre of the moon on a clear night.

This morning we made an excursion to the Palheiro, an estate belonging to the heirs of the late count of Carvalhal. It occupies the summit of a mountain, 2,000 feet above the city, and about three miles to the northeast of it. The first part of the ascent is uninteresting enough. It leads you through narrow passages, with high walls on each side, shutting out the view, and rendering the air, as the sun shines upon them, hot and oppressive. But as you advance, the scene changes. The road, which is remarkably well paved and less steep than most of those around the city, runs out upon the brink of a ravine, down which you may look hundreds of feet into its stony bed, with its perpendicular face of columnar basalt on the opposite side, and with artificial walls rising one after another, from top to bottom, like a huge staircase, and supporting narrow patches of earth wherever the least deviation from the vertical line allows a level of the most contracted dimensions to be formed. It is surprising to see with what an expenditure of money and toil the sides of these ravines are made tributary to the wants of man. To create an artificial level of twenty or thirty feet in width, a wall as many feet in height is built up, and every inch of the little surface of soil it sustains is reduced to the most elaborate state of cultivation. Where the whole face of the country is broken and furrowed, as this is, by mountains and ravines, it is only by such contrivances that it can be made to furnish the absolute necessaries of life for even a portion of its inhabitants. With all this labor and expense, at least one third of the sustenance of the island is drawn from other portions of the globe.

At an elevation of perhaps 1,500 feet above the city you cross the ravine by a narrow bridge, and at a short distance beyond you enter an avenue of chestnut trees. The road is so narrow that the branches of the trees on the opposite sides are interlaced. They are now leafless. At such an elevation, and standing exposed to the wind in long, narrow files on the mountain's side, deciduous trees must necessarily be so. But in summer, when they are in leaf, the road must be in perfect shade, and the freshness must be delightful after leaving the hot streets of the city. For nearly a mile you may ride without the least molestation from the beams of the sun. The beautiful groves and parks of the Palheiro must be still more grateful to visiters from Funchal in hot weather. The greater part of the grounds is covered with large trees, not unworthy of countries which boast of their forests. They stand in close array, nearly excluding the rays of the sun even now, when they are but partially covered with foliage. The situation is exceedingly beautiful. Occupying the summit of a mountain, which stands out toward the sea, in advance of the higher elevations pressing most closely upon the city, it commands an extensive view of the ocean, the Desertas (three uninhabited islands about twenty miles to the east), Funchal and its harbor, and a long line of coast farther west. How diminutive is every feature which the art of man has added to the scene! The houses in Funchal seem like cabins, and the seven or eight vessels in the roadstead like the toys which our children were sailing last summer in a little stream in the interior of New York, three thousand miles hence toward the setting sun. It is only when you turn to the mountains behind, or to the ocean in front, that the objects before you become vast and majestic, the emblems of consummate wisdom and unlimited power.

The general aspect of the Palheiro is suited to its position. It is on a scale of no inconsiderable magnitude; the trees are large, the shade dense, and the improvements, in general, simple, without any mixture of the finical. There is a fine garden, several fishponds, and a multitude of beautiful avenues and walks. The house does not correspond in magnitude with the grounds. The late owner was a bachelor, and it was built with a view to his own accommodation. Still, it is large enough for a family of some size. It is enveloped in shade, and has a retired and quiet air. Near it stands a chapel, which contains the remains of the late count. After expending several hundred thousand dollars in embellishing this beautiful place, he rests in the scene of his labors, and his absence is from year to year more distinctly visible, in accumulating evidences of dilapidation and neglect.

The beauty of the Palheiro may have been heightened in our sight by the contrast it presents with the whole aspect of the country by which it is surrounded. Its characteristic feature is its parks, while for miles around Funchal there is hardly to be found a grove of even moderate size. Yet the island was covered with magnificent forests when it was discovered. It derives its name from the abundance of its woods. In the progress of improvement they have been sacrificed to the purposes of cultivation, at least on that portion of the island which is devoted to the vine. The great demand for wine in times past, has caused almost every acre of ground on the southern and southwestern parts of the island to be stripped of its native covering, and has substituted for the walnut, the vinhatico, the dragon tree, and the til, the webs of trellis-work on which the vine is supported, and which, as you look down upon them from the surrounding hills, appear like white cross-lines penciled out upon the red soil. In winter they are everywhere seen overspreading the surface of the ground; but in spring, summer, and autumn, they are buried beneath luxuriant foliage, and the whole country wears a totally different aspect. In particular situations the vine is already in leaf, and we can easily fancy how much the beauty of the scenery will be improved, as we pass from winter into the bloom of spring and the fuller luxuriance of summer. In all new countries covered with forests, the settlers are apt to consider trees as their great enemy. They wage an implacable warfare against them, until the whole face of the land becomes naked, the streams dried up, the summers made hotter, and the winters colder, by opening the earth to the sun and winds. The succeeding generation labors as industriously to produce shade as its predecessors did to destroy it. Madeira is old enough to court more generally the luxury of cultivated shade trees. They are now confined to a few estates like the Palheiro. On the northern part of the island, indeed, they are not wanting; the mountains are in forest, instead of being, like those around Funchal, stripped of their covering; and in the cultivated portions, the vines, instead of being supported by trellis-work of cane, are trained upon trees, forming the most graceful exhibitions of vegetable life that can be fancied. There is no comparison between the two sections of the island in rural beauty.

In the evening, we attended one of the monthly balls given by the Portuguese Club, an association of which we have already spoken. We found a large number of the Portuguese and English residents and a few of the visiters to the island. The ball-room is a fine one, with a very lofty ceiling, and an orchestra elevated eight or ten feet above the floor. There was nothing in the entertainment generally to distinguish it from balls in our own country. There was the usual succession of quadrilles and waltzes in the ball-room, with lemonade, sangaree, and ices between; and in other apartments near by, the amateurs of whist and ecarte were seen seated at card-tables, with more lookers-on than performers, watching the progress of the games. The building is on a magnificent scale. It is, indeed, both in external appearance and internal arrangement, one of the very finest in the city. The entertaining rooms are spacious and handsomely finished; and there are smaller apartments without number, well suited for the accommodation of a numerous and wealthy family. And for the use of this immense and costly establishment the club pays $300 a year. The dancing commenced at half-past nine, and was continued without intermission until two o'clock in the morning, when we returned to our lodgings. It probably did not end until two hours later. Every thing was well arranged, and the party was a very agreeable one—sufficiently numerous, and yet not so much so as to be crowded. Among the ladies, who numbered about sixty, there were, perhaps, half a dozen who might be called beautiful, and two who would have been so considered in any part of the world. If this assemblage is a fair specimen of the ladies of Funchal, beauty is certainly not a general characteristic. They are, however, genteel and graceful. We saw but one coarse woman among the dancers, and she was a visiter to the island for the winter. She could hardly have come to Madeira for the improvement of her health, for there was no one on the floor whose performances were so vigorous and athletic.

One part of the entertainment deserves a distinct notice—more especially as it was the only one which was strictly national. At half-past one o'clock the company were served with chicken broth, handed round in cups and saucers; and most excellent broth it was —so strong that a whole brood of chickens must have been immolated in preparing it. It has been often sneered at by visiters. But why should it be? It is in every sense as appropriate as the roast ducks, stewed oysters, and ham sandwiches with which guests are regaled, with us, at the termination of an evening's entertainment. For the purpose of repairing the animal strength wasted by exercise, there can hardly be a more appropriate prescription than a strong infusion of chickens' flesh; and after a cup of broth, one's slumbers are certainly much less likely to be disturbed than after tasking the digestive organs with the assimilation, as the doctors have it, of a mass of solid food. We vote with the Funchalese, for the chicken broth.

CHAPTER VII.

CITY OF FUNCHAL.

Mendicity.—Wood-Carriers.—Burroqueros.—Extreme Destitution of the Poor.—An Assassination.—Demoralizing Tendency of Civil War.—Criminal Statistics of the Island.

FUNCHAL has its share of mendicity, and yet I doubt much whether there are more beggars to be met with than in Albany. There is, undoubtedly, a larger number of persons in extreme indigence, and obtaining, with great difficulty, a sufficient quantity of food for their subsistence. But though you see them in the streets, they do not beset you in crowds, as they do in some of the cities of Europe. They come singly, as with us, and if you turn away from them, they usually pass on without giving you any annoyance. They rarely come to your house; and in this respect Funchal is, in a great degree, exempt from one of the principal vexations with us—the ringing of street-door bells by applicants for alms. In the street you often meet with wretched objects; sometimes in the shape of a man without hands or feet, a Calvin Edson, or a boy with half a pair of breeches, and a corner of a blanket wrapped about his shoulders. But in every city there are to be found a few of these old stagers, who meet you at every turn. Taking such a corps here into the account, I consider Funchal, for its population, far from possessing more than its proportion of mendicants, whether it be compared with the cities of the old world or the new. Nor is their condition one of extreme suffering. They want no fire, and very little clothing, and a crust of bread satisfies their hunger. The great end of life, not only with them, but with a considerable portion of those who labor, is to get enough to eat; and this remark is true of the country as well as the city population. As you go into the interior, however, you reach higher elevations, with a northern temperature in the winter months. Snow, frost, and cold winds prevail, and fires and warm clothing become necessary. Almost every winter, some of the peasants are overtaken by storms in the mountain-passes, and perish with cold. On the northern part of the island, where fires are most necessary in winter, there is an abundance of wood, and fuel can always be obtained by the most needy.

The wood-carriers, who supply much of the fuel consumed in Funchal, lead hard lives; and yet they are, perhaps, not more severely tasked to procure the means of subsistence than some other classes of the population. They live among the mountains, where they gather their wood. At daybreak they are at their work. The wood is prepared, cut in small sticks, and made up in bundles, each bundle containing, perhaps, fifty sticks. They carry these bundles upon their heads three, five, and even seven or eight miles to the city, and sell them, when they can find purchasers, at from fourteen to eighteen cents each. With these small gains they buy a little corn and codfish, and reach their dwellings again at night, to take a few hours' sleep, and recommence the same routine of labor the next day. Women are often engaged in this laborious service, and yet they come down from the mountains, with their immense burdens, as gayly and with as little apparent inconvenience as their more hardy fellow-laborers of the other sex. The very nature of the country of necessity converts a large portion of the inhabitants into beasts of burden. From their infancy they are trained to carry enormous loads upon their heads. In the streets of Funchal, you often meet boys of fourteen or fifteen years of age, from the interior, staggering under burdens, which seem large enough to bear down any ordinary man. The greater part of this transportation would be performed by cattle and carts, if the roads would admit of it. As it is, the inhabitants are literally carriers of wood and drawers of water.

The habits of life of the burroqueros are, perhaps, more characteristic than those of any other class. They and the horses are as inseparable as the jackall and the lion; yet their connection with the horses and the stables is very equivocal. They are not hired by the owners of the livery-stables, they receive no wages, and yet they eat and sleep with the horses, as though they were of the same family. In winter, when the weather is what they call cold in Funchal, or, in other words, when the thermometer ranges from 62° to 70° in the day, and from 52° to 62° at night, they make up their beds of straw or weeds in the stables, and lie down with the horses. In summer, when the temperature is higher, they sleep in the streets, at the stable-doors. In this way they pass their lives. The subsistence they gain is, for a portion of the year, of the most uncertain and precarious nature possible. When they go out with horses, they receive one third of the earnings—that is, if a horse is out an hour, the charge is thirty cents, and of this the burroquero receives ten. He also asks, and generally receives, each time he goes out, of the person who hires the horse, a few cents more, under the name of drink-money, but which he is quite as likely to spend for bread as for wine. During the winter, when the island is frequented by strangers, they are almost every day sure of earning something; but at other times their gleanings are small, and at long intervals of time. They are generally active, athletic, fine-looking fellows, in all respects worthy of better employment, and more of it.

I was never more strongly impressed with the extreme difficulty with which the poor procure their daily subsistence, than on a recent occasion. I was walking up one of the ravines which constitute the beds of the rivers intersecting the city. Three months ago it was filled with a raging torrent. It was now almost dry.

A small stream only was running along the base of the cliff which forms one of its sides. I had walked about a mile over the loose stones and gravel which covered the bottom, when I perceived two women washing at a short distance before me; and, as I came up, I had observed one of them descending the precipice by a narrow footpath, which led to a small cottage perched high upon the rocks above. Near them were two boys, who, as soon as they discovered me, came running toward me, asking alms. Not being disposed to advance farther up the ravine, and being equally disinclined to retrace my steps, I asked them if I could reach one of the roads leading to the city by the footpath up the cliff. They answered in the affirmative, and I then told them if they would guide me to it, I would compensate them. One of them instantly led the way, while the other turned back toward the women and shouted in Portuguese with all his strength —" Mother, we are going to earn some bread." The ascent of the cliff was steep and laborious, but we soon gained the main road, and, agreeably to my promise, I gave them each a small piece of silver. Their countenances immediately brightened, and away they ran down the precipice, calling out, as they went, " Bread, mother, bread!" What stronger evidence could there be of the difficulty of procuring this first necessary of life than the joy with which these two boys hastened to put into the hands of their mothers the means thus accidentally obtained of procuring their next scanty meal? The bread, and not the money, was the reigning thought.

The tranquillity of Funchal has just been disturbed by a deed of violence; and it has produced the more excitement from the extreme infrequency of such occurrences. The British war-steamer Megæra has been several days in port, from England, on her way to the Gulf of Mexico, with Mr. Doyle, who is going to Texas as the minister of Great Britain to that republic. Two days after his arrival his servant was missing, and on inquiry it was ascertained that he had left the house of the British consul in the evening to go on board the steamer, which was lying close to the beach. It was immediately suspected that he had been murdered, and the police was set in motion to discover the assassins. After two days they were detected. They have been examined, and have made a full confession of their guilt. They are, happily for the character of the city, not regular boatmen, but hangers-on about the beach and custom-house, laboring and begging by turns for their subsistence. Seeing a stranger in quest of a boat, they took possession of one and offered their services to take him on board. The darkness of the night favored their design. They rowed him out to sea, knocked him down with one of the seats of the boat, rifled his pockets, and threw him overboard alive. The whole amount of the plunder which they gained by this act of atrocity, was a silver watch and two or three dollars in money. They will be tried at the regular term of the court in about two months, and will probably be executed in Funchal.

Capital punishment, when inflicted at all, usually takes place in Lisbon, even when the offences are committed in Madeira. It is said there is only one hangman in Portugal, and he performs his office in the most revolting manner. When the convict is swung off, he jumps on his shoulders and breaks his neck. No wonder the Portuguese have the utmost horror of hanging! The judicial proceedings in criminal cases are subject to revision by the supreme court, and the body of the convicted person is taken to the capital. Death is rarely inflicted where there are extenuating circumstances, or where the conviction rests upon circumstantial evidence. The sentence is commuted, in such cases, to transportation to Africa; which is, in truth, exchanging a violent death for a slow one; for, of 300 persons transported, not more than 50 are alive at the end of twelve months. The crime of murder has, until of late, been exceedingly rare in Madeira. Murder for the purpose of plundering may be said to have been heretofore unknown. When life is taken, it is in the heat of passion, or in the spirit of revenge. Family quarrels and jealousies lie at the foundation of almost every deed of blood committed here. Since the civil wars, which, from 1826, distracted the kingdom for several years, crimes of this description are said to have become more frequent. It would be strange if it had been otherwise. The example of fraternal discord and hatred presented to the people of Portugal in the contest of the two rival branches of the House of Braganza for the throne, could not fail in some degree to demoralize the nation. In wars with foreign countries, deplorable as they are in almost all respects, there are moral fruits which atone, in some degree, for many accompanying evils. There is the strong sense of national honor, the parent of high achievement; the sentiment of patriotic devotion to the country, which shrinks from no labor or sacrifice in the public cause; and the feeling of mutual dependence which pervades the different classes of the community in the hour of adversity and peril. Far as these are overbalanced by the domestic bereavement and the public evil which war brings in its train, they may serve, for the moment, to purify the thoughts of something of their selfishness, by turning them out of the more sordid channels in which they are but too apt to run. But civil war has no such ameliorations. It is pure, unmixed demoralization; it cements no national or domestic tie; it tramples down all the principles of morality and affection; and it renders selfishness more odious, by wedding it to hatred and cruelty. Its crowning evil is the inheritance of bad passions which it transmits to posterity. The after generation, which reaps the bitter harvest of intestine war,* is scarcely

* A part of this paragraph was differently written in the original manuscript. It is now made to correspond with what the author said on another occasion.

less to be commiserated than that by whose hands the poisonous seed is sown.

The criminal statistics of the island are highly favorable to its moral condition. The whole number of committals for crimes in 1842, in the district, which includes not only the island but also Porto Santo, was eighty-three. Not more than one third of the prosecutions resulted, or would result, in convictions. Of the whole number of persons accused, five were charged with crimes of the greatest atrocity—four with assassination, and one with infanticide. The great mass of the residue were committed for theft or rioting. In respect to all classes of crime excepting assassination, Madeira will bear a favorable comparison with almost any other country. For the reasons already assigned, murder has become a crime of frequent occurrence—the well ascertained cases ranging from one to three in a year. This is certainly a very large number for a population of one hundred thousand souls. It exceeds vastly the proportion existing either in the United States, England, or France. Its very recent introduction into the island, and especially its regular occurrence as a characteristic feature of the criminal statistics of Madeira, exemplify in a striking manner the contagion of evil passions.

The former moral purity of the islanders can now only be restored by a higher intellectual culture. The inhabitants are generally simple-hearted and kind, but exceedingly ignorant. The constitution of the kingdom guaranties to all its citizens gratuitous primary instruction; but, in whatever manner the government has redeemed this pledge in Portugal proper, it has certainly done little for Madeira. By a proper system of education for its poorer classes, the complexion of its criminal statistics may yet be cleared of the blemishes by which it is disfigured.

CHAPTER VIII.

CLIMATE OF FUNCHAL.

Climate.—Snow on the Mountains.—Extremes of Temperature.—Duration of the Cold.—A Tornado and a Gale.—Arrival of the Great Western.—Meteorological Tables.—Dr. Heineken's Observations.—Sir James Clark.—Rain.

He who supposes that it is always brightness and sunshine in Madeira, will, if he passes a winter there, be convinced of his error. Our summer visions have just received a severe check. On the 8th of February, the snow began to fall upon the mountains some five or six miles back of Funchal, and four or five thousand feet above it. In the city it rained copiously through the night; and during the whole day on the 9th it was showery and cold, with occasional gleams of sunshine. On the night of the 9th, the snow fell in still greater quantities; and at six o'clock on the morning of the 10th, the thermometer stood at 48°. For four hours it only varied two degrees. About nine it rained violently, and the mercury rose to 50°. At ten it had ceased raining, and the mercury fell again to 48°. So low a temperature in Funchal, between sunrise and sunset, is not to be found on record; nor has there been so great a fall of snow, at so short a distance from the city, for half a century. All day it was to be seen on the summit of the mountain back of the Mount Church. Its elevation could not have been more than 2200 feet above the level of the sea, and it might have been reached at a distance of about two miles and a half from the city. While the mountains are covered with snow, the currents of cold air usually pour down into the warmer regions near the ocean, cooling the atmosphere rapidly, and causing frequent rains. During the whole day on the 10th these effects were displayed in a striking manner. There were several violent showers, preceded by cold blasts from the mountains, and uniformly accompanied with a rise of the mercury in the thermometer as the vapors were condensed into rain, and gave out their caloric to the atmosphere. The night of the 9th was rainy and cold. At six o'clock on the morning of the 10th, when the thermometer was at 48°, I immersed it in a jar of water, which had been standing all night on a balcony, and the mercury fell to 45°. The jar had a narrow throat, so that scarcely any portion of the surface of the water was exposed to the air, and at a temperature so low, and so near that of the surrounding atmosphere, the influence of evaporation upon the thermometer could have been but very slight. In the open air, an hour or two before daybreak, the thermometer would, without doubt, have indicated as low a temperature as that of the water when I tried it.

The whole of the 10th was exceedingly uncomfortable.

The 11th was still more so, though the thermometer did not fall as low. There are few fireplaces in Funchal, and, in general, no convenient means of creating artificial heat in bedrooms and parlors; though in perhaps half a dozen houses there is to be seen a stove-pipe of sheet-iron or tin, thrust through the window into the street. After all, such a provision against the weather is very rarely necessary. The thermometer within doors is almost always above 60°. Ours has ranged from 64° to 69°, and on cold days an additional garment is all that is required to keep the surface of the body at a comfortable temperature. Up to the middle of February we have had not more than two or three such days. We have had a stove at our command all winter, but have not thought it necessary to put it up in our apartments. Invalids who come here in a very feeble state might do well to bring one, no matter how small it is. If it holds a handful of charcoal, it is all that is necessary. A small tin pipe can be fitted to it, and a pane of the same metal substituted for one of glass in the window, so that the smoke and gas can be carried off into the street. During half a dozen days such a provision would conduce to one's comfort, though persons in tolerable flesh and strength may do very well without it; and with invalids there need be no want of comfort, if they regulate their clothing by the temperature. Out of the city a fire is indispensable. It is only within the compact and sheltered part of it that the sun shines upon the houses and pavements during the day, and exerts a lasting influence upon the temperature.

The duration of cold weather is always very brief in Funchal. Although on the 11th of February the thermometer at two o'clock stood at 54°, and at no time in the day rose more than four degrees above it, on the 12th, at the same hour, it was at 67°, and on the 13th at 69°, and the air was again as warm and balmy as in spring. Still the snow maintained its position on the mountains, although it was gradually disappearing. The range of hills nearest to the city, which, two days before, raised up their white crowns against the dark northern sky, were again bare, and reappeared in their usual dress of volcanic red and brown. The hills more remote are still covered with snow, and as long as the wind continues to blow from them down upon the city, we shall have alternate rain and sunshine through the day, or catching weather, as the farmers expressively say, when they are disturbed in hay-making by frequent showers. But as the snow becomes more remote, the temperature grows milder, and the showers warm, so that in an hour after a rain, if the sun comes out, you may walk the streets on a dry pavement.

The promise of the 12th and 13th was, after all, deceptive. On the 16th, before the snow had disappeared, the weather again became cold. The thermometer fell to 65° at mid-day, and in the night there was a furious tornado in the harbor, with a fresh fall of snow on the mountains. In the afternoon the aspect of the heavens was lowering, and the last vessel at anchor in the roadstead put to sea for safety. The wind had been fresh for a week, and the other vessels had left the harbor some days before. Under shelter of the Loo Rock, and between it and the shore, lay a brigantine at anchor. She had recently arrived from Demerara, and having unladen, had taken that station for the purpose of making some repairs. She was almost without ballast, and could not go out to sea; but as the night approached the weather became unpropitious, and the crew were advised to land. Fortunately they did so. When the squall struck her, she capsized in an instant, and she is now lying on her side, filled with water, and still held by her anchor; her hull invisible, but with her masts and yards partially above the surface. She was not the only sufferer. The telegraph house on the Loo Rock—an object to which more eyes are turned than to any other in Funchal—was torn from the battlements, and pitched into the sea. We were in a central and sheltered part of the city, and were entirely out of reach of the wind, but we heard the minute-guns fired from the Loo Rock, heralding the fate of the brigantine. Though the violence of the gale had subsided before morning, it still blew steady and fresh, and the next day at noon the sea beat upon the beach with unprecedented fury. The surf was at least thirty feet higher than the ordinary level of the sea. It broke over the wall built up in front of the Governor's Castle, and filled the public walk with stones and sand. It came over the steps and through the street, which we described on landing, at least 100 feet from the usual high water mark in calm weather. It was amusing to observe the people as they came down to see it. Those who had been some time there were profiting by their experience, and stood at a respectful distance from the beach, while the new-comers pressed forward, until a sudden splash sent them back with wet feet or dripping jackets. Among others, a soldier, with a dignified and martial gait, advanced, at the moment the waves had receded, to the steps, when the surf unexpectedly broke upon him; and not only was his coat thoroughly drenched, but he found himself, to his astonishment, up to his ankles in salt water. He was too much of a soldier to run, or to turn his back upon the enemy, and he therefore retreated, with his face to the sea, looking daggers all the time, as if he had sustained a personal insult, and apparently distressed because he could not find some responsible person whom he might call to account for it. His ill-humor was obviously not at all diminished by the shouts of laughter with which he was greeted by the bystanders, many of whom were consoling themselves in this way for similar misfortunes, which they had just before sustained in their own persons.

On Sunday, the 19th of February, the steamer Great Western arrived, on her way from Liverpool to New York. The wind was blowing a gale, and it was with difficulty that the visiting-boat boarded her. On the following day the wind had somewhat abated, and a few passengers she had brought for the island were landed. But on the same afternoon she proceeded on her voyage without being able to take in a supply of coal, as she intended. Of the passengers on board destined to New York, some twenty or thirty came on shore, and wandered for an hour or two about the city, obviously surprised to find such vile weather in an island which enjoys so high a reputation for clear skies and mildness of temperature. How much our lasting impressions are influenced by accidental circumstances! Every one of these casual visiters is undoubtedly satisfied, from personal observation, that the winter climate of Madeira is very bad, and each will inoculate a circle of friends and acquaintances with the same unfriendly opinion. Yet, in three days after their departure, the skies were again bright, and for three weeks there was almost uninterrupted sunshine.

It must be confessed, however, that for fifteen successive days the weather was exceedingly disagreeable; not only colder than usual, but rainy and blustering. Fifteen such days have never before been known in Funchal. But, with this exception, the winter has not been unusually severe or inclement. The following meteorological tables will show the range of the thermometer during the day, and the general character of the season. Though founded upon observations made, in a central part of the city, with some care, they do not profess to be perfectly accurate, nor ought they to be taken as an unerring guide. Still, as a whole, they vary but slightly from the results of other observations taken during a much longer period of time, and under circumstances more favorable to accuracy. My thermometer hung in the open air, effectually sheltered from the direct rays of the sun, and as far as possible from their reflection. It was observed only at particular hours of the day, and, therefore, does not show the maximum and minimum temperature during the twenty-four hours. The mean for the month of January, however, corresponds very nearly with the mean obtained by Dr. Heineken for January, 1826, from a series of careful and systematic observations.

1842.	Degrees Fahrenheit.				
Dec.	7 A.M.	2 P.M.	7 P.M.	Wind.	Weather.
1	64	70	65	W.	Clear.
2	[illegible]	69	64	W.	Clear.
3	58	67	57	W.	Rainy. Snow visible on the mountains.
4	57	67	58	W.	Showery.
5	58	73	64	N.E.	Clear.
6	54	69	59	N.E.	Clear. This morning at seven I immersed the therm. in water which had been standing out doors in a jar all night, and it fell to 52°.
7	58	68	60	N.E.	Clear.
8	59	71	62	S.	Clear.
9	57	70	60	S.E.	Clear.
10	61	68	66	S.W.	Showery.
11	66	71	67	N.W.	Showery.
12	67	70	66	W.	Clear.
13	66	69	64	W.	Showery.
14	65	70	69	S.W.	Cloudy.

7

1842. Dec.	Degrees Fahrenheit. 7 A.M.	2 P.M.	7 P.M.	Wind.	Weather.
15	61	67	64	S.	Cloudy, with rain.
16	61	72	60	S.	Clear.
17	56	71	63	S.E.	Clear.
18	56	70	61	E.	Clear.
19	56	70	64	E.	Clear.
20	58	72	64	E.	Clear.
21	57	68	65	E.	Clear.
22	59	69	66	E.	Clear.
23	60	70	63	S.	Clear.
24	57	68	60	N.E.	Cloudy, with slight showers.
25	57	62	59	N.W.	Rainy. Snow on the hills.
26	56	70	62	N.W.	Showery.
27	57	67	60	N.E.	Clear.
28	56	64	57	N.E.	Clear.
29	54	66	59	N.E.	Clear.
30	58	64	60	N.E.	Cloudy.
31	58	65	56	N.E.	Cloudy.
Jan. 1843.					
1	53	68	58	E.	Clear.
2	54	68	60	E.	Clear.
3	55	71	61	E.	Clear.
4	55	67	58	S.E.	Cloudy, with slight showers.
5	60	66	60	S.E.	Cloudy.
6	59	67	60	E.	Clear.
7	59	69	60	S.E.	Clear.
8	54	69	61	S.E.	Clear.
9	60	64	56	S.	Clear.
10	55	64	55	E.	Clear.
11	53	69	59	N.	Clear. This morning immersed therm. in water—50°.
12	53	70	58	N.E.	Clear. Ditto. ditto.
13	55	69	60	S.E.	Clear
14	54	69	61	S.E.	Clear.
15	52	69	58	N.E.	Clear.
16	51	67	58	S.E.	Clear. Overcast part of the day.
17	55	67	59	S.E.	Clear. Ditto.
18	57	66	60	S.W.	Overcast.
19	56	66	61	S.W.	Overcast.
20	59	67	59	W.	Overcast. Light shower.
21	56	69	60	W.	Overcast.

	Degrees Fahrenheit.				
Jan. 1843.	7 A.M.	2 P.M.	7 P.M.	Wind.	Weather
22	58	69	60	W.	Overcast.
23	57	70	59	W.	Clear.
24	58	69	62	W.	Overcast.
25	59	71	64	W.	Overcast. Slight shower.
26	57	70	62	W.	Overcast.
27	57	71	60	E.	Clear.
28	55	70	61	E.	Clear.
29	54	66	62	E.	Clear.
30	54	64	58	E.	Overcast.
31	57	66	59	E.	Overcast.
Feb. 1843.					
1	54	67	58	E.	Overcast.
2	54	68	58	E.	Clear.
3	54	67	60	N.E.	Clear.
4	57	69	58	N.E.	Clear.
5	56	68	57	N.E.	Clear.
6	53	67	61	W.	Clear.
7	54	66	58	W.	Overcast.
8	58	66	58	N.W.	Rainy.
9	54	62	54	N.W.	Rainy. Snow on mountains.
10	48	60	52	N.W.	Rainy.
11	50	54	54	N.W.	Rainy.
12	54	67	58	N.W.	Showery.
13	57	69	63	S.W.	Showery.
14	60	69	63	S.W.	Showery.
15	60	67	60	W.	Showery.
16	61	65	62	W.	Showery.
17	60	65	56	W.	Rainy. More snow on mountains.
18	52	61	54	N.W.	Showery.
19	52	67	61	N.W.	Rainy.
20	62	66	58	N.W.	Rainy.
21	57	65	58	N.W.	Rainy.
22	60	66	60	N.W.	Rainy.
23	54	68	62	N.N.W.	Clear.
24	61	70	60	N.W.	Clear.
25	60	70	60	S.E.	Clear.
26	54	68	61	N.W.	Clear.
27	60	68	60	N.W.	Clear.
28	61	71	65	N.W.	Clear.

An analysis of the table for January, 1843, gives the following results:

	Deg.	
Mean temperature at 7 A.M.	55 9	
" " 2 P.M.	67 9	
" " 7 P.M.	59 6	
Mean temperature for the month	60 3	
Highest temperature at 7 A.M.	60	on the 5th and 9th.
Lowest " "	51	" 16th.
Highest " 2 P.M.	71	" 3d, 25th, 27th.
Lowest " "	64	" 9th, 10th, 30th.
Highest " 7 P.M.	64	" 25th.
Lowest " "	55	" 10th.

By Dr. Heineken's tables for January, 1826, it appears that the mean was 59°.9—four tenths less than the mean for January, 1843. His mean was, however, deduced from the maximum and minimum temperature for the twenty-four hours, obtained by a self-registering thermometer. The maximum during the month was 69°, 2° less than the maximum in January, 1843; and the minimum 51°, which was also the lowest temperature in January, 1843, at the hours of observation.

It will be seen that on the 12th and 15th of January there was a variation of 17° during the day, the thermometer having risen from 53° to 70° in one case, and from 52° to 69° in the other. This is the greatest diurnal variation noticed during the winter, and it is greater than I had anticipated from a general knowledge of the climate. Yet it does not exceed the variation noticed by Dr. Heineken. On the 8th of January, 1826, it was precisely 17°; on the 4th of the same month, 16°; and on several other days, 15°. From all the observations which have been made in past years, the greatest diurnal variation may be set down at 17°, and this is, of course, of very rare occurrence. The mean annual range does not exceed 14°, and the mean diurnal range about 10°. The results of the meteorological observations made at Funchal have been so well summed up by Sir James Clark, in his valuable work on climates, and compared with observations at other places of common resort for invalids, that I can not forbear to insert them:

"The mean annual temperature of Funchal is 64°, being only about 5° warmer than the Italian and Provençal provinces. This very moderate mean temperature, relatively to its low latitude, arises, however, from the summer at Madeira being proportionally cool; for while the winter is 20° warmer than at London, the summer is only 7° warmer; and whilst the winter is 12° warmer than in Italy and Provence, the summer is nearly 5° cooler. The mean annual range of temperature is only 14°, being less than half the range of Rome, Pisa, Naples, and Nice. The heat is also distributed through the year with surprising equality, so that the mean difference of the temperature of successive months is only 2°.41: this at Rome is 4°.39, at Nice 4°.74, at Pisa 5°.75, and at Naples 5°.08. Whilst there is much equality in the distribution of temperature through the year, there is no less so in the progression of temperature for the day; the mean range of the twenty-four hours being 10° by the register thermometer, whilst at Rome it is 10°, at Naples 13°, at Nice 9°, by the common thermometer, which gives only the extremes observed during the day. The steadiness of temperature from day to day also exceeds that of all other climates. In this respect it is not half so variable as Rome, Nice, or Pisa, and it is only about one third as variable as Naples. The degree of variableness from day to day at Madeira is 1°.11; at Rome it is 2°.80, at Nice 2°.33, and at London 4°.00."

Our residence in Madeira commenced on the 12th of November, and terminated on the 17th of March; and my own observations fully confirmed the favorable impressions I had long before received in respect to the general character of the climate. The autumnal rains, which usually begin in September and end early in November, were over; and from our arrival until the 8th of February, when the fifteen days of rain commenced (nearly three months), there were but fourteen days on which any rain fell, and of these, only three could be called rainy days. During the whole month of January, there were three days on which there were slight showers. During the other twenty-eight days not a drop of rain fell. Nor was this a solitary instance. During the month of February, 1826, according to Dr. Heineken, there was not a single shower. In the months of March, April, and May, showers usually occur. From June to September there is no rain. But it is as a winter climate that Madeira is sought by invalids, and certainly no district of country can be found which, for dryness and moderate warmth combined, presents so many advantages. There is scarcely a day on which an invalid need be kept within doors during the whole twenty-four hours on account of rain; the sun is rarely too warm for exercise in the open air; and with an overcoat the cold is never uncomfortable. It would be difficult to find a climate, within the reach of European or American invalids, of which as much can be said. There may be particular instances in which valetudinarians require a higher temperature, and in these the West India Islands, where the thermometer regularly rises to 75° and 80° during the twenty-four hours, may be preferable; but such cases are not of frequent occurrence. It is rare that an invalid is not most likely to be benefitted by a temperature which, like that of Funchal, never reaches in winter the point of summer heat.

CHAPTER IX.

GOVERNMENT OF PORTUGAL.

Government of Madeira as an Integral Part of the Kingdom of Portugal.—Portugal Proper, and the Azores and Madeira Islands divided into Administrative and Military Districts.—Constitution of Portugal, and its chief Provisions.—Right of Self-expatriation.—Legislative Power.—Absolute Veto.—Checks on the Sovereign.—Power of the Cortes in interpreting its own Laws.—Independence of the Judiciary.—Trial by Jury.—Amendments of the Constitution.—Inviolability of Civil and Political Rights.—Chamber of Deputies elected indirectly.—Qualifications of Voters and of Deputies.—Constitution of 1821.—Constitution of 1838.—Regulations for Elections.—Early Government of Portugal.—Alfonso Henriques.—Assembly at Lamego.—Historical Sketch of the Government of Portugal from the Twelfth Century.

THE island of Madeira is a dependency of the kingdom of Portugal. It has its governor and other provincial officers appointed by the crown; but it has an equal voice with other portions of the kingdom in the election of the chamber of deputies, the lower branch of the Cortes or national legislature. It has also its local representative authorities chosen by popular suffrage. It had formerly a colonial government, but it has, within a few years, been put upon the footing of a province; and in this respect, though it has some local peculiarities in its administration, and in its municipal organization, it is treated as an integral part of the kingdom. Portugal proper consists of six provinces, one of which is composed of the former kingdom of Algarves. But these political divisions have ceased to be of any practical importance. A new organization has been introduced. The kingdom and the Azores and Madeira islands are divided into twenty-one administrative and ten military districts. The former contains seventeen administrative and eight military districts; the Azores one military and three administrative districts; and Madeira, which is the ninth military district, is also an administrative district by itself. The name it bears is the District of Funchal.

Before we proceed to a sketch of the domestic or municipal organization of the government of Madeira, let us glance at some of the leading provisions of the constitution of the kingdom of Portugal, which was granted by Don Pedro in 1826, and which has recently been re-established by the present queen, Donna Maria II. The government of Portugal is declared to be an hereditary representative monarchy, and the reigning dynasty is continued in the House of Braganza. The groundwork of the constitution is the following declaration of political principle, of itself sufficient evidence of the spirit of freedom which pervades the people of Portugal, whatever practical non-conformity may be found in the political organization of the kingdom: "The kingdom of Portugal is the political association of all Portuguese citizens. They constitute a free and independent nation." This fundamental declaration is supported by an enumeration of rights, which gives Portugal a high rank in the scale of representative government, when compared with the established political organizations of Europe. In designating the particular circumstances which constitute the condition of citizenship, the right of self-expatriation—a right which has given rise to a good deal of discussion, and which is theoretically denied by one of the most powerful nations of the age—is distinctly recognized. In free countries no difference of opinion ought to exist on this point. If the right of the citizens, as a body, to abolish their form of government, when it ceases to promote the general happiness and welfare, and to establish a new one in its stead, is founded in reason, the right of a single individual peaceably to withdraw himself from one political association and unite himself to another, if his comfort or prosperity seem to him to require it, is equally defensible on every principle of rational liberty. The cases of expatriation provided for are, first, when a citizen of Portugal becomes naturalized in a foreign country ; and, second, when he accepts, without the permission of the king, an office, pension, or title from a foreign government.

The legislative power resides in the Cortes, with the sanction of the king. In other words, the Cortes legislates, and the king has an absolute veto upon their acts. This is virtually depositing the whole legislative authority in the sovereign, who is hereditary, and who is no otherwise the representative of the people than through the assent given by them, in the various revolutions and changes which have taken place within the last forty-five years in the government of Portugal, to the ascendancy of the House of Braganza. It is the same control which the king of Great Britain has over acts of parliament; and it may here as there be annulled in practice by the force of public opinion. The right possessed by two thirds of the members of both branches of the legislature in the United States to pass a law, from which the chief magistrate had withheld his assent, is a vast step in the progress of the representative principle. Such a provision, however, in the constitution of Portugal would not be equally efficacious as with us. The Cortes consists of the chamber of peers and the chamber of deputies. The latter only is chosen by the people. The chamber of peers is in no sense their representative. It is composed of members for life and hereditary, named by the king, and without any fixed number. It would, of course, always be in the power of the sovereign, by the creation of new peers, to defeat a vote of two thirds, if, under the constitution, a law could be carried by such a vote without his assent.

But the unconditional veto of the king does not rest solely upon the provision above cited. It is more distinctly conferred by an article concerning the proposal, discussion, sanction, and promulgation of the laws.

When a bill is presented to him, if he declines to give his consent to it, he sends the following message to the chamber which has last deliberated on it: "The king wishes to consider the bill until he can have time to decide on it;" to which the chamber is required by the constitution to answer, that "it is much pleased with the interest his majesty takes in the public welfare." And all this dalliance is designed to cover up the exercise of the most important prerogative that can possibly be vested in the crown. For the next section of the constitution declares, without any equivocation of terms: "This refusal shall be absolute." What a comment on the poverty of the absolute monarchy principle in the present age! In asserting one of its essential attributes, the unqualified veto on constitutional legislation, it resorts to indirection. It refuses, under the pretext of taking time to consider. When it is observed that the constitution of Don Pedro superseded one of a much more popular character, the equivocation with which the consent of the sovereign is withheld from laws he disapproves will be more readily understood.

On the other hand, the Cortes has some checks upon the sovereign. It determines every year the amount of the public expenditure, and reapportions direct taxes. With the exception of such as are applicable to the administration of justice and the payment of the public debt, all direct taxes are to be annually laid, but they are to be continued until their abolition is published, or until others are substituted for them. Public loans can only be made on the authority of the Cortes. It fixes every year the number of the land and naval forces, or, when it fails to do so, the existing establishments remain unaltered: the king can neither diminish nor increase them. These are so many limitations of the powers of the sovereign in respect to some of the most delicate and important functions of government. Either house, by withholding supplies of money, may bring the sovereign to terms in any matter of controversy between them. Though the king has the power of declaring war and making peace, the whole fiscal power is in the Cortes; and he would, therefore, not be likely to involve the kingdom in hostilities, excepting under such circumstances as to command the approbation of his subjects. He has the power also of making treaties; but where they provide, in time of peace, for the cession or exchange of the territories or possessions of the kingdom, they require the ratification of the Cortes. In like manner, though he may grant titles, military orders, and distinctions, he can not annex to such grants any pecuniary benefit without the sanction of the Cortes, unless they are already provided for by law.

Among the powers secured to the Cortes is that of interpreting its own laws. If it were only intended that the legislative body may, when it passes a law, declare its meaning, the power would be innocent in its exercise. But if the legislature may give a subsequent interpretation, it is obviously open to great abuse; and certainly the power is conferred in unqualified terms. The interpretation of laws is essentially an attribute of judgment: it belongs to the judicial, and not the legislative department. To adjudge the application of a law is to interpret its meaning, so far as the particular facts to which it is applied are concerned. If the interpretation of a law by the judiciary does not conform to the intention of the legislature in enacting it, the latter may obviate the difficulty by an amendment. The publication of the new enactment is a notice to all concerned, and it is equivalent to a contemporaneous declaration of the intention of a law. But if the judiciary, by its judgment in a particular case, were to decide that a law did not reach a certain class of persons, and the legislative body, by virtue of its power of interpretation, were subsequently to decide that it did reach them, this would be virtually legislating *ex post facto*, and would come within the very definition of tyranny. It would be doing in effect what the constitution of Portugal as well as that of the United States forbids: it would give the law a retro-active effect.

The independence of the judiciary in Portugal is secured by the perpetuity of their office. The judges can only be deprived of their places by judicial sentence, and for abuse of trust. In this respect the organization of the judiciary conforms to that of the United States. The principle of making the judicial tenure perpetual does not prevail, however, in the domestic establishments of all the states. In some the judges are appointed for a term of years, and public opinion has been gaining ground in favor of a limited tenure, from the idea that judicial officers, like those charged with the performance of executive duties, unless periodically subjected to such a test, lose an important stimulant to a devoted execution of their trust. The hope of reappointment is supposed to add to the moral incentive of honor and love of reputation the more homely stimulus of personal interest. The independence of judges is an essential attribute of free government. Whether a judiciary can be rendered perfectly independent and beyond the reach of all temptation without placing them, in respect to the tenure of their office, above party vicissitudes, is a question to be settled by practice. In an enlightened and virtuous condition of society they undoubtedly may be so. Where corruption and venality prevail, a periodical reappointment of the judges might render them the instruments or the victims of dishonest combinations.

The trial by jury is guaranteed by the Portuguese constitution both in civil and criminal cases. With this fundamental provision in their social system, no people can be other than freemen.

The constitution may be amended in the following manner: 1st. The proposed amendment must be introduced to the chamber of deputies by the vote of two thirds of the members; 2nd. It must be read three times after intervals of six days, and after the third reading, it may be discussed; 3rd. It must be sanctioned and promulgated by the king, and the electors of deputies for the next legislature are directed to give them special authority to pass upon it; 4th. It must be sanctioned by the next legislature, and is then to be solemnly promulgated as a part of the constitution.

The inviolability of the civil and political rights of the citizens of Portugal, which have for their basis freedom, personal security, and property, is guaranteed by thirty-four separate declarations, in the nature of a bill of rights. Among them are the following: Every individual may communicate his thoughts by words, and may publish them in print, independently of all censorship, but may be held to answer for any abuse of the right. Any person may depart from the kingdom if he chooses, and may carry with him his property, subject to the police regulations, and provided the rights of third persons are not prejudiced. Every person has in his own house an inviolable asylum; it can not be entered at night without his consent, or in case of any outcry for help made within it, or to defend it from fire or inundation; and by day an entrance can only be made in the cases and in the manner which shall be prescribed by law. Every citizen is capable of exercising public offices, civil, political, or military, with no other difference but that which is founded upon talent and virtue. Whipping, torture, branding with hot iron, and all other cruel punishments are abolished. No punishment can extend beyond the person of the guilty; in no case can his property be confiscated, or his infamy be transmitted to his relatives of whatever degree. The right of property is guaranteed in all its plenitude. If the public good, legally shown, requires the use and occupation of the property of a citizen, he is to be previously indemnified to its full value. The privacy of letters is inviolable; the administration of the post-office will be held rigorously responsible for any infraction of this article.

With such declarations as these in their fundamental charter, the public liberty of a people can not be otherwise than secure. The practical operation of the system may not always rigidly conform to them, but they are a part of the political creed of the people; they become interwoven with the prevailing habits of thought; and any gross or long continued violation of them can hardly fail to produce resistance and bring the moral and physical force of the community to their support. Such at least would be the result in a community even moderately imbued with the love of liberty. The most recent change in the government of Portugal has been accompanied with increased restrictions in the application of the representative principle and with the reorganization of the aristocratic branch, the chamber of peers, in full vigor. Yet it is not to be credited that any great abuse of the established system, or any flagrant infraction of the constitutional rights of the people, would be patiently endured. Freedom of opinion and of speech is in perpetual progress, and this is but one of the developments of the spirit of liberty.

Though the chamber of deputies is a representative body, it is not directly so. The members are chosen by a body of electors, much as the president of the United States is elected, the great mass of the people voting in their primary assemblies for the electors, and the latter choosing the deputies. Each district chooses its separate corps of electors, and the deputies for the district are chosen by its electors independently of the action or participation of other portions of the kingdom. This is carrying out but imperfectly the doctrine of popular representation. Where the people vote directly for the representative, there is every reasonable ground of assurance that in his official acts he will conform to the popular opinion on questions of public policy as well as on those which more immediately concern his constituents. The indirect representative has not the same strong tie to bind him to fidelity. He is chosen by a different body. He can not look back to the direct vote of the people in his favor—the strong evidence of their confidence in him and of their claim to a faithful execution of his representative trust. He can not, in the one case, without the grossest ingratitude and infidelity, lean to the side of privilege and power in opposition to the interests of the people. He may, in the other case, be equally in error in disregarding the popular will; but he does not render himself so clearly obnoxious to public censure. One of the very objects in interposing a body of electors between him and his constituents is to render him more independent of them, and in this respect it is a palpable departure from the true principle of representation. In practice it has proved, what it was designed to be, an additional support to the irresponsible branches of the government. It is said that electoral bodies favorable to the minister are more easily carried in the primary assemblies than deputies would be, if voted for directly by the people. The former are chosen to perform a specific act—the latter to legislate for years on subjects deeply affecting the public interests. The same enthusiasm at the polls is not felt in both cases. The people might lose the electors through indifference, when they might be successfully rallied by a popular candidate for the legislature. With us this is not the case in the choice of electors of president. There is as much effort and spirit as there would be if the president were elected directly by the people. But the people of Portugal have neither our party machinery, nor are they so thoroughly informed on public questions. For this very reason an indirect election of representatives in the popular branch of the legislature is a greater grievance. It is the more so, too, for the reason that the electoral bodies may be influenced, more readily than the deputies, to go counter to the wishes of their constituents, and disappoint the public expectation, with which they were chosen. Some instances of this description have already occurred. Individuals have been chosen deputies, who never could have been elected by a popular vote.

The principal qualification of voters in the parochial or primary assemblies is founded upon property. No one can vote unless he has an annual net income of one hundred dollars from real estate, from property invested in industry or commerce, or from some office or employment; nor can any one vote under the age of twenty-five years, unless he is married, holds a military commission, is a bachelor of arts, or a clergyman in holy orders. Servants are also excluded, and sons residing with their parents, unless they hold public offices. No one can be an elector of a deputy unless he has an annual income of two hundred dollars, and no one can be a deputy unless he has an annual income of four hundred dollars. These provisions are far more liberal than those of France, though they are much less so than those of Great Britain. That which requires a deputy to have an income of four hundred dollars is certainly altogether inconsistent with the spirit of one of the fundamental declarations of the constitution, that every citizen may be admitted to public employments, whether civil, political, or military, with no other distinction than that which is founded upon talent and virtue. If a citizen without income is worthy of a high civil or military office, why should he be excluded from a seat in the national legislature? Public employments are generally conferred by the crown; and to suppose that they would ever be given to persons without income, would be expecting from the sovereign a degree of liberality exceeding that of the constitution.

The constitution established in the reign of Don Juan the Sixth, the predecessor of Don Pedro, in 1821, was far more popular in its provisions than the one now in force. The nobility of the kingdom were wholly disregarded in the political organization. The legislature consisted of a single body, a chamber of deputies chosen directly by the people without the intervention of an intermediate body of electors, in this respect conforming to the system existing in Spain. Any person could vote who had been domiciliated or resided a year in the district where the election was held. There was no property qualification whatever, and to encourage education, the only durable basis of political liberty, it was provided that any person reaching the age of twenty-five years should not vote unless he could read and write, provided he was under seventeen years of age at the time the constitution was published. There was no specific qualification for deputies other than for voters, excepting that no person should be eligible who had not a sufficient income to support him. It was also provided that no bankrupt should be eligible, unless he could show that he was so in good faith. What a comment on the fraudulent bankruptcies of the present day, and on the public opinion which countenances and upholds the fraudulent bankrupt in the face of all moral principle! No treaty of alliance, offensive or defensive, nor even a commercial treaty, could be executed without the approbation of the Cortes. The absolute veto on acts of legislation vested in the king by the existing constitution, was in that of 1821 a mere right of objection. If the king disapproved a law, he sent it back to the Cortes with his objections. If after fully considering them the Cortes were of opinion notwithstanding that it should become a law, he was required to give it his sanction. If he refused to sign it, the Cortes were authorized to publish it in his name. All laws fixing the military and naval forces, regulating the imposts, taxes, and public expenditures, authorizing money to be borrowed, and providing for many other important objects, were wholly independent of the royal sanction. It must be confessed, that where the legislative power is vested in a single body, it is questionable whether the chief magistrate ought to be deprived of the absolute veto on acts of legislation. There is danger to be apprehended from the legislative branch of the government as well as the executive; and certainly the organization of a legislature consisting of one house, with power by a majority of votes to pass a law without the sanction of any co-ordinate branch, comes nearly up to the idea of a legislative dictatorship. From this glance at a few of the leading provisions of the constitution of 1821, it will be seen that it was of a highly popular character; that the attributes of the crown were exceedingly restricted, and the participation of the people in the government, through representatives chosen directly by themselves, was enlarged in a corresponding degree.

A third constitution was proclaimed in 1838, under the authority of the present queen, in its provisions a medium between those of 1821 and 1826. The national legislature, or Cortes, consisted of two houses, both elective—the first the chamber of senators, and the other the chamber of deputies, the former having half as many members as the latter. The senators were elected for six years, and the deputies for three. By the constitution of 1821, the Cortes were elected once in two years, and by the present constitution (that of 1826) the chamber of deputies is elected once in four. By the constitution of 1838, senators and deputies were chosen directly by the people, and by the same class of voters. No person could vote unless he had an annual income of eighty dollars, and no one could be elected a deputy unless he had a like income of four hundred dollars. No proprietor could be elected a senator unless he had an income of two thousand dollars, and no merchant or mechanic unless his annual gains could be valued at four thousand dollars; but certain privileged classes, the principal of which were the clergy and military, were eligible without any qualification of property. The unconditional veto on acts of legislation was again vested in the crown in the power of sanctioning laws. The provisions of this constitution were perhaps generally considered better suited to the condition, social and intellectual, of the people of Portugal than that of 1821; yet it lived only four years after its promulgation. It gave place to the more restricted charter of 1826, which has been briefly noticed.

The regulations for elections, adopted in furtherance of the existing constitutional provisions, are well devised, not only to secure the rights of the voters, but to protect the ballot-boxes against illegal voting. With a property qualification there must, of course, be a registry of voters. The election lists for the election of deputies are made out once in four years, that being the period for which the chamber is elected. The lists are three in number: 1st. Of those who are entitled to vote in the parochial assemblies; 2d. Of those, who are eligible to the office of provincial electors or electors of deputies; and 3d. Of those, who may be elected deputies. The lists, which are prepared throughout the kingdom by the municipal chamber in each concelho, and in Lisbon and Oporto by commissioners, are completed on the 20th of April; an authentic copy is affixed to the door of each parish church, and the original lists are subject to the inspection of any person who wishes to examine them. From the 20th to the 25th of April, any person who has not been registered may present his claim to the municipal chambers or commissioners of registry, and any one, during the same time, may object to the enrolment or complain of the omission to enrol a third person. By the 28th of April the commissioners are to decide all such cases, and on the 30th all alterations in the lists are to be published. From the decisions of the commissioners an appeal lies to the municipal chamber of the concelho or municipal district, to be made in writing by the 3d of May.

The primary assemblies, as they are denominated, are formed of convenient districts. No district can contain less than 1000 fogos—literally fires, but in the practical understanding of the term, families—unless the concelho or municipal district contains a less number. Each assembly of 1000 families chooses one elector; each assembly of 2000 and less than 3000 families, two electors, and so on progressively. The island of Madeira contains nine concelhos, with 24,633 families. The neighboring island of Porto Santo, with 413 families, belongs to the same administrative district, and together they choose twenty-two electors, who elect four deputies.

The whole number of administrative districts in Portugal proper and the adjacent islands is 21, the number of concelhos or municipal districts 413, and the number of families 918,122. Their aggregate population by the latest enumeration was 3,601,000 souls.

At the elections the priest of the parish is required

to be present to give information as to the identity of the voters. At every poll the table, with an urn for the reception of votes, is to be so placed that all may have free access to it, and all the doings in respect to the election may be open to public inspection. No one can appear at the polls with arms under the penalty of expulsion. These, and a variety of other provisions in relation to the duties of the persons holding the poll, and the rights of voters, are calculated to secure a free and at the same time a pure exercise of the elective franchise.

The electoral colleges, when constituted, proceed to the election of the deputies, choosing one deputy for every number of families not less than 6500 nor more than 7000. They continue in existence during the period of four years, and in case of a vacancy, the electoral college of the district in which it occurs is assembled, by order of the government, to fill it.

The people of Portugal boast of having enjoyed from the earliest period of their history, as an independent community, with the exception of a short interval, the benefits of a constitutional government; and they refer to the era of Alfonso Henriques, their first king, for the origin of their personal freedom as citizens and of their sovereignty as a nation. They cite the proceedings of an assembly at Lamego, consisting of the representatives of the nobility and clergy, and of the great body of the people, proclaiming him king, settling the succession, and establishing a few general principles of criminal and civil jurisprudence. The declarations of Alfonso on the one hand, and some of the distinguished persons who officiated in investing him with the sovereignty on the other, are quoted to show that the government was in its inception strictly constitutional, and that the kings of Portugal derived their authority essentially from the pleasure of the nation, represented by the different orders of the state. A different view of the subject is taken by some writers. In the history of the civil law of Portugal, the following passage occurs: "Quare Alphonsus et Regiam magestatem præ se tulit, et loca a Mauris capta dominio suo adjecit optimo sanguinis, legitimæ successionis, et belli, seu occupationis jure, non Populi suffragiis, Pontificisve liberalitate." This treatise was published in the reign of Maria I., when the government was absolute. The subject is one of importance as connected with the constitutional history of Europe, and a very brief reference to the rise and progress of the Portuguese kingdom may not be out of place.

Portugal until the beginning of the twelfth century was a dependency of Spain. In 1109, it was given as a dowry to Donna Teresa, wife of Don Henriques, the Count of Portugal, by her father Alonso, the 6th king of Castile. Don Alfonso Henriques, surnamed the conqueror, was their eldest son, and at a very early age became distinguished for his valor and military address. In 1139 he fought the great battle of Orique, in which the Moors were completely routed. This was a precursor of a series of brilliant triumphs over them and of their final expulsion from Portugal. The history of the whole of this period is tarnished by absurd fables invented by the priesthood for the purpose of animating the followers of the Cross in their contests with the Infidels. The baptism of Alfonso Henriques was said to have been accompanied by a miraculous expulsion of a devil from one of the bystanders. His feet were said to have been united from the heels to the toes from his birth. Through the intercession of a devout relative, the Virgin Mary promised that if the intercessors would clear out an old church erected to her honor, and then almost buried in rubbish, and place the prince every day upon the altar, for a series of years, he should be made whole. At the end of five years the promise was fulfilled. In like manner, before the battle of Orique, the Saviour is said to have appeared to him, and promised that the Moors should be expelled from Portugal, that it should be an independent kingdom, and that he should be made king. These inventions, as incredible as they are impious, are gravely cited by the Portuguese historians down to a very recent period, to prove that the royal authority in Portugal is a direct emanation of divine favor. Within the last fifty years enlightened opinions have made rapid progress, and it may be safely said, that no Portuguese writer of reputation, whether layman or divine, would at the present day introduce these fables into a sober history of his country without characterizing them as the false inventions of a superstitious age. Alfonso Henriques was himself the authority for one, and the most striking of these miraculous interpositions of divine power—the appearance of the Saviour to him before the battle of Orique ; and he was rewarded for his subserviency to the priesthood by a formal acknowledgment of his authority as king of Portugal by Pope Alexander III., in 1179, whose bull, signed by himself and twenty cardinals, is still preserved among the archives of the kingdom; and it is written in a tone of superiority which might be expected from a pontiff whose stirrups had been held a few years before by two of the most powerful sovereigns of Europe, when he dismounted from his horse.

The mixture of so much fable with the history of so late a period as the 12th century, is by no means calculated to support the facts with which it is associated. There is no authentic record of the proceedings of the Cortes of Lamego, as it is called, and the very existence of such a body for the organization of a political system, is called in question. But there is a document said to have been issued by the authority of Alfonso Henriques, reciting the principal acts and declarations of the assembly. Much that is said of it is unquestionably apocryphal. But that there was such an assembly about the middle of the 12th century, and that the authority of Alfonso Henriques as the first king of Portugal was recognized by it, can hardly be doubted; nor is it denied that at a very early period the fundamental laws of the kingdom were framed by a legislative body in concurrence with the sovereign. About two centuries afterward (in 1385), the celebrated Cortes of Coimbra was assembled, at the commencement of the reign of John the First. The direct line of the Alfonsos ended with his predecessor. He was chosen from a collateral branch, and before he was proclaimed king, he bound himself to observe certain conditions prescribed by the Cortes in limitation of his power. Among other obligations was that of consulting the Cortes on all subjects of national importance, and of neither making peace nor war without their consent. From this period the Cortes were frequently assembled to deliberate on matters of public concern, and to frame laws; and among the conditions which are considered fundamental in the organization of the sovereign power, is one, which in every constitutional system is of vital importance—that the supreme executive magistrate shall lay no pecuniary impositions on the people without their consent, expressed through their representatives. Even during the usurpation of the Philips of Spain, from 1580 to the restoration in 1640, the Cortes were convoked for the purpose of giving the form of a constitutional sanction to their authority. With the restoration, and the elevation of Juan the Fourth, of the house of Braganza, to the throne, the limitations of the royal authority were distinctly proclaimed by the Cortes. All tributes previously exacted were abolished, and the whole subject committed to the Cortes, as well as the number of troops necessary for the defence of the kingdom, and the mode in which they were to be supported and paid. In this reign also the Cortes established the principle that the clergy should not be exempted from the pecuniary contributions required by the state, but, like all other classes, should be subject to taxation—a principle far in advance of most other countries of Europe at that day.

The long and disastrous reign of John the Fifth, from 1715 to 1750, was a reign of superstition, hypocrisy, extravagance, and usurpation. The Cortes were not once called together during these thirty-five years, and a death-blow may be said to have been given to constitutional liberty in Portugal. From this period the government was absolute until the revolution of 1820, which led to the promulgation of the charter signed by John the Sixth, to which we have already referred. During a portion of this period the affairs of the kingdom were ably and justly administered; but the sovereign power was wholly free, in practice, from all constitutional restraint.

The revolution of 1820 was a great popular movement. It was the fruit of a long continued departure from the ancient usages of the kingdom in the administration of its affairs, of its position in relation to Brazil, and of a complication of abuses and evils, which at last became too great for endurance. In the reorganization of the government, though there may have been defects, the popular principle was carried perhaps beyond the public expectation. During the protracted discussions which took place in the Cortes, by which the constitution was framed, a strong opposition grew up, and in the year 1823, it resulted in a counter revolution, while the new system was yet hardly tried. The death of John the Sixth, in 1825, led to the establishment of the constitution or charter of Don Pedro, the same year. The political changes which have taken place since that time, have been the work of parties or factions, aided by the military force—movements in which the feelings of the great mass of the people of Portugal have been but partially enlisted. This remark ought to be taken with some limitation when applied to the constitution of 1838. In the movement by which it was introduced the middling classes in Lisbon and Oporto had a large share. This is known as the revolution of September, and the Septembrists have still an organized party. Of the several constitutions which have been proposed and temporarily adopted, the most restricted provides for as full an acknowledgment of the representative principle as could perhaps be claimed on the strength of ancient usages and institutions, with the exception of the indirect election of the only popular branch of the government in the constitution now in force. This is a very serious defect, and one which can hardly endure for any length of time. In all political reorganizations through the interposition of the people, the right to make the remodeled government conform to new emergencies is implied. The right is independent of all authority of ancient usages or forms. In the present advanced state of opinion, it would be singular if the people of Portugal should not ere long assert their claim to be directly represented in the legislative branch. One would think that it only required a few strongly marked abuses to bring forth such a demand, under circumstances calculated to insure a compliance with it.

The sovereigns of Portugal have in most cases been the passive instruments of the parties by which the recent revolutions in the government have been brought about, in some instances assenting with reluctance to the alterations introduced into the pre-existing systems. This has not always been the case. The present queen can hardly have looked with disfavor upon the late change, which restores to her the control of one branch of the legislature, by re-establishing the chamber of peers, and by giving her the power to add to the number of members, with no other limitation than her own will. She is very naturally suspected of having connived at it, notwithstanding her assent to the constitution of 1838. If she was the passive victim of this revolution, she was more happy than crowned heads usually are on similar occasions.

8*

CHAPTER X.

LOCAL GOVERNMENT OF MADEIRA.

The Civil Governor.—Municipal Chambers.—The Council of the Concelho.—The General Junta.—The Council of the District.—The Parochial Junta and Regedor.—The Administrator of the Concelho.—Powers of the Civil Governor in the Islands.—Judicial Establishment and Divisions of the Kingdom.—The Relaçao, or the Superior Court.—Inferior Judges.

LET us now look at the local government of Madeira. As has been already said, the island is treated as an integral part of the kingdom, and its provincial government is in all essential particulars the same as that of an administrative district in Portugal proper. The highest administrative officer is the civil governor. He is appointed by the crown, is charged with the general supervision and management of the civil affairs of the district, and takes care that the laws are duly executed. His official powers and duties are minutely defined by law. They are principally executive. He is president of the council of the district—a body of which we shall speak hereafter. In respect to many objects with the accomplishment of which he is charged, he consults with the council, and in respect to others, in which its concurrence is required, he votes on the questions to be decided, and has no more power over them than one of its members.

In each concelho, of which there are nine in Madeira, there is a municipal chamber, composed of five members, or vereadores, in concelhos which have not more than three thousand families, and of seven members in those which have a greater population. The chamber is elected by the voters of the concelho, and the vereador who has the greatest number of votes is the president. In concelhos with a number of families not exceeding two thousand, any voter may be elected a vereador; but in those which contain a larger number of families, the property qualification is higher. In the first case, those may be elected vereadores who pay a tax of ten dollars per annum on incomes from personal property, pensions, benefices, etc., five dollars from occupied real estate, or one dollar on real estate unoccupied, or who have an annual income of one hundred dollars. In the second case the taxes and incomes required are trebled where the concelho contains more than two and less than six thousand families, and quadrupled where the concelho contains over six thousand. The chambers are chosen once in two years, and the registry of voters, the elections, the ballotings, and returns are all regulated in the most careful manner. The powers of the chambers are much like those possessed by our city corporations. The most important is that of borrowing money and giving security for the repayment of the loan, and this can not be exercised without a special act of the Cortes, or national legislature.

The council of the concelho, or, as it may properly be called, the municipal council, is a body very peculiar in its organization, but limited in its functions. Its members are equal in number to those of the municipal chamber. It consists of the voters of the concelho who pay the major part of the taxes, and they are selected as follows:

A list of the voters who are tax-payers is made out, the names being written down in the order of their respective contributions, the greatest contributors first, and the highest on the list are taken for members of the council, until the number equals that of the municipal chamber.

The council has authority to determine, in conjunction with the chamber, whether loans shall be contracted or taxes laid, and to fix, with the concurrence of the chamber, the expenses of the municipality for the ensuing fiscal year. The policy of organizing this body, and giving it a voice in respect to the matters referred to, is obviously founded upon the very rational consideration, that those who pay the largest taxes shall participate in imposing them, and in applying them to the objects of public interest for which they are laid.

There is still a higher deliberative body, whose powers are coextensive with the administrative district. It is denominated the general junta, and is composed of thirteen procuradores, who are elected by the municipal chambers and the municipal councils jointly, for the term of two years. Those only are eligible to the station of procurador, who may be elected to the chamber of deputies. The civil governor opens the sessions of the junta, which are annual, takes his seat on the right of the president, and must be heard when he desires it. On the first day of the session he renders an account of the state of the district, with the documents and information necessary for the deliberations of the junta. When his own doings are under consideration, he may make explanations, but he can not be present when a vote is taken upon them. Extraordinary sessions may be called by the king, and in such cases the procuradores are entitled to travelling expenses and a daily compensation not exceeding $1 60. The principal attributes of the junta are to distribute the assessment of taxes among the concelhos of the district, to decide upon claims for a reduction of their respective quotas, to prepare the annual estimates of expenses and receipts, vote the taxes necessary for the expenditures of the district, to contract loans when authorized by a special act of the Cortes, and to choose a treasurer-general for the district from among the citizens residing at the capital town. The doings of the juntas are annually reported to the secretary of state for the affairs of the kingdom, or the home secretary, as he would be called in England, and are annually published as an appendix in the Diario do Governo, or government paper.

To render the systems of local government in the provinces, or districts, still more complex, there is another deliberative body, to which allusion has already been made—the council of the district. It consists of the civil governor, who is president, and four members, or vogaes, selected by the king on the nomination of the general junta, from a triplicate list prepared by the latter. There are also four substitutes chosen in the same manner, and from the same list, who act in case of the absence or disability of the vogaes. Any one who may be elected a procurador is eligible as a vogal, or member of the district council, and the two stations are compatible. The council, like the juntas and the cameras, is chosen for two years. It has a regular session once a week, and its extraordinary sessions are as frequent as the public service requires. Its powers and functions are of the highest importance. It has a general supervision over the acts of the municipal cameras within the district, and may reverse their decisions and deliberations in cases specified by law. It decides upon all complaints and claims against the ordinances, regulations, and deliberations of the chambers ; on appeals in relation to the registry of voters ; on complaints in respect to the decisions of the electoral boards, or inspectors of elections, or the validity of elections generally within the district ; on applications from individuals for the remission, in whole or in part, of their quotas in the assessment of direct taxes ; on the decisions of the municipal chambers ; on appeals from individuals who deem themselves aggrieved by any act of the parochial junta, a deliberative body of more limited jurisdiction than any of which we have spoken; and over a variety of other subjects the district council has an appellate power. In fact, the great mass of powers vested in the subordinate deliberative bodies results, to the district council, either by virtue of this appellate jurisdiction, or by virtue of its power of revising the acts of the cameras, the most important of the municipal authorities, without complaint. Every member of the council, including the governor, who presides over it, is appointed by the crown. Thus, by means of its agents, the sovereign enters into and controls the minutest details of the local administrations—a system altogether at variance with every just conception of popular government. In our own country, if questions arise between individuals and the local administrations, they are disposed of like controversies between two individuals, by the judicial tribunals; and suits may be brought in Portugal against the local authorities by individuals. But the important judicial function of disposing of claims, complaints, or questions arising under the deliberations and acts of the municipal authorities, as well as that of interpreting contracts, is vested in the district council, a body, as has been seen, appointed by the crown, and for the short period of two years. The council becomes to this extent a judicial tribunal, but without the essential attribute of independence of the executive. It is true, the district council is composed of individuals nominated by the junta. From twelve names the sovereign selects four. But the junta itself is but remotely responsible to the people. There is some security in the mode of nomination. But it is not quite clear that a body thus constituted will always be possessed of the proper qualifications for the important functions it has to fulfill.

In each parish, of which there are forty-two in Madeira, there is a parochial junta and a regedor. The junta is composed of the parish priest and two members, or vogaes, if the parish has not more than five hundred families, and of four if it has a larger population. The members are elected by the voters residing in the parish, for the term of two years, and any voter is eligible. The regedor, who is appointed by the civil governor on the nomination of the administrator of the concelho, is entitled to a seat in the junta, and sits on the left of the president. The parochial juntas form no part of the organization of the public administration, and their powers are limited to the care of the church edifice, the management of the property of the parish, and the performance of certain acts in the capacity of commissioners of public charity. In Madeira, in fact, the church edifices are in the custody of the priests, who receive their pay from the government, so that the attributes of the parish junta are exceedingly limited. With the approbation of the civil governor, they may borrow money, execute mortgages for its repayment, make contracts for work necessary for the parish, and provide for other objects of parochial benefit. The regedor executes the legal determinations of the junta, communicates to the administrator of the concelho any proceedings of the junta which he may consider exceeding its authority, or contrary to law or public convenience, opens wills in the manner prescribed by law, and performs such administrative acts as may be delegated to him expressly by the administrator of the concelho. He is also charged with the duty of keeping the peace, and for this purpose he has under his control a body of police constables.

The administrator of the concelho, who is an important administrative officer, is, like the civil governor, appointed by the crown. This is an innovation. Until very recently he was elected by the people. He is charged with the general supervision of the affairs of the concelho, and in respect to mere executive functions, he is to the concelho much what the governor is to the district.

In the islands of Madeira and the Azores, the civil governors have the power of dissolving the administrative bodies, subject to the confirmation of the sovereign. In Portugal proper this authority is not given to the governors of districts. It is in consequence of the difficulty of prompt communication between the insular districts and the government that it is conferred on the governors of the latter. The dissolution of a camera or junta, when confirmed by the crown, is always followed by a new election, thus virtually referring the questions at issue between the executive and deliberative bodies to the people for their decision.

Though the great body of the people have a voice in the election of many of the administrative officers in their respective districts, the ultimate control over most of their local concerns, those which affect their property as well as their personal security, is exercised by persons almost entirely independent of them in respect to the mode of appointment and the tenure of office. This feature in the system of local government existing here will be found essentially defective when tried by any correct principle of popular freedom. In Madeira, it must be confessed that this organic defect is effectually cured in practice, so far as the highest officer is concerned. The civil governor, who is wholly independent of the people of his district, is not, what provincial governors often are, ignorant of the condition of the territory and the people under his jurisdiction, or alien to their interests. On the contrary, the government has had the wisdom to appoint him from among the citizens of Madeira; his property, which is large, is on the island; he is intelligent and discreet; he is bound to the people of his district by the ties of long association and of personal and pecuniary interest. He could not be better disposed to consult their true welfare in all the important concerns of government, if he had been chosen by themselves. In all matters of his administration, not directly involving essential interests, it is, of course, to be expected that he will consult the wishes of the ministry from whose hands he received, and at whose pleasure he holds, his authority.

The organization of the judicial establishment of Portugal is regulated by a decree issued in 1841, and is generally known by the name of the new judicial reform. The kingdom is divided, for judicial purposes, into districts, comarcas, julgados, and parishes. Each district has a relaçao, or superior court; each comarca, excepting Lisbon and Oporto, a judge of law, and one or more jury circuits; each julgado an ordinary judge and one or more judges of the peace; and each parish an elective judge. There is also a supreme court of justice at Lisbon, the jurisdiction of which is coextensive with the limits of the kingdom; and in each comarca a tribunal of correctional police, composed of the judge of law and commissioners elected annually by the municipal chambers and councils jointly. The island of Madeira has two comarcas, nine julgados, and forty-four parishes. The exclusive jurisdiction of the superior court extends to suits to the amount of $600. It is a court of appeal from inferior tribunals, and is charged with many important judicial functions. The exclusive jurisdiction of the judges of law in civil causes is limited in respect to suits concerning lands to the amount of twenty dollars; in suits for movable property to thirty dollars; and in criminal cases to fines of ten dollars, and imprisonment for a month. The exclusive jurisdiction of the ordinary judges is limited in civil causes to suits concerning lands to the amount of four dollars; to suits for personal property to six dollars; and to fines of two dollars, and imprisonment for three days. Within these limits their decisions are final, and without appeal. It is their duty also to prepare criminal and civil causes, which are to be tried by the judges of law. The judges of the peace are a tribunal for the amicable adjustment of differences, and no suit can be brought into court for litigation until the case has been submitted to a judge of the peace, unless by command of the latter, or by mutual agreement of the parties. The exclusive jurisdiction of the elective judges is limited to suits for movable property, or money, to the amount of $2 50 in Lisbon and Oporto, and half that sum in other parts of the kingdom. The ordinary judges, the judges of the peace, and the elective judges, are chosen by the people for the term of two years. The judges of the higher tribunals are appointed by the crown, and can only be deprived of their office by judicial sentence, though they may be suspended by the crown, under certain legal restrictions, for official errors, or for crimes; and they may be sent into retirement with pensions, for just cause, clearly shown.

There is one feature in the judicial system of Portugal which might be advantageously introduced into our own. Each tribunal, within certain defined limits, pronounces final decisions—decisions from which there is no appeal to a higher tribunal. These limits are for the inferior officers of justice exceedingly low. The judges of law, who may be considered as of the same grade as our circuit judges, have an absolute jurisdiction in suits concerning real estate, to the amount of twenty dollars, and in suits for personal property to the amount of thirty dollars. From their decisions in such suits there is no appeal, either on the ground of inequity or erroneous applications of the law. The rule is founded upon the reasonable consideration, that in suits involving small amounts an erroneous decision is likely to work less inconvenience, even to the party prejudiced by it, than a tedious and costly resort to a higher tribunal for the correction of the error. The supreme court is a tribunal of review for alleged errors in the proceedings of the inferior tribunals, in suits for amounts not within the limits referred to. The superior courts, of which there are two, one for the kingdom and the other for Madeira and the Azores, have an absolute jurisdiction to the amount of $600. In suits not involving sums exceeding that amount, there is no right of resort to the supreme court, even to correct errors of law. The system proceeds, in this respect, upon the principle that there shall be a speedy end to litigation. At the same time, justice may be said to be brought to every man's door, so far as the organization of the system is concerned. For the external provinces, or districts, there is, it is true, some inconvenience in resorting for the correction of errors to a tribunal in the heart of the kingdom—but this is an inconvenience in the nature of things incapable of remedy.

CHAPTER XI.

MADEIRA.

Geographical position of Madeira.—Porto Santo and the Desertas.—The Leste.—Geological Character of the Island.—The Forja.—Geological connection of Madeira with the Azores and Canaries.—Legend of Robert Machin and Anna D'Arfet.

THE island of Madeira is assigned by geographers to the African portion of the globe, and justly so, as it is about one hundred miles nearer the coast of Africa than that of Europe, and several degrees of latitude south of the European continent and the islands appertaining to it. This geographical arrangement has given rise to a very great absurdity; it has subjected Madeira in some countries, and I believe in the United States, to the same quarantine regulations, in respect to commercial intercourse, as the African continent itself, though it is uniformly healthy, and especially free from infectious diseases. The city of Funchal, which lies near the southern termination of the island, and on its southwestern face, is in N. latitude 32° 38,′ and in W. longitude 16° 54′ from Greenwich. The 36th parallel of latitude runs through the Straits of Gibraltar, leaving Madeira about three degrees south of the dividing line between Africa and Europe. The island of Teneriffe lies south by west at a distance of about two hundred and fifty miles, and the African coast on the east is about three hundred and fifty miles distant.

There are four other islands belonging to the Madeira group: Porto Santo, about forty-five miles to the east, and the Desertas, about eighteen miles to the south-east. The former has about eighteen hundred inhabitants. The latter are three in number; they are uninhabited, and are in all respects worthy of the name they bear. A few hares range over them, and the sea-fowl hover around their rocky and almost inaccessible sides. Ordinarily, they exhibit no other signs of life. On one of them barilla is produced; but the men who go there to prepare it are obliged to take with them the very water they drink.

Porto Santo has a strong interest in its association with the name of Columbus. He married there, and was a frequent visiter to the island, as well as to Madeira, before the discovery of America. In one of the streets of Funchal, the house in which he resided is pointed out. There are two in the same street which have the reputation of having sheltered him in his visits to the city, and it is not unlikely that both may be justly entitled to the distinction.

The vicinity of the African continent is at times the cause of some singular effects in the meteorological condition of Madeira. Though Funchal and the surrounding district is so mild in winter, it is exempt in summer

House of Columbus.

from the great heat of tropical climates. The thermometer rarely rises above 80° in perfect shade. Occasionally, however, the east wind, or leste, as it is called, blows directly from the African coast, and then the temperature is sometimes near 90°. The upper strata of the atmosphere are said to be the most highly charged with caloric, even in the higher portions of the island, and in Funchal the inhabitants seek the basements of their dwellings as the most free from the effects of the wind, which are very remarkable. Though it traverses three hundred and fifty miles of ocean, it brings no moisture with it. It seems to come charged with some of the peculiar properties of the great desert over which it passes. It is singularly dry. Furniture shrinks and cracks, as it does with us when exposed to the heat of anthracite coal; and the eyes, nostrils, and mouth have the sensation of rapid evaporation. When it continues for several days, it brings with it insects, and sometimes, it is said, birds, which are known only as inhabitants of the African continent. The leste is, however, not a frequent visiter. We had it twice during the winter, and though we were conscious, in a very slight degree, of its enervating influence, it did not sensibly increase the heat.

For the geological student Madeira possesses a fund of interest. Its whole structure is volcanic. A mere glance at the island, as you approach it so nearly as to be able to discern the outline of its cliffs and ravines, is sufficient to disclose its true character. Bowditch, in his "Excursions in Madeira and Porto Santo," and James Macaulay, in an admirable article on Madeira, in the Edinburgh New Philosophical Journal of 1840, have pointed out some of the most interesting features in the geological structure of the island. One of the most characteristic localities is in close proximity to the city, near the Pontinha, a battery on an isthmus of rock, connected with the land above by a bridge, for the use of the garrison. A cliff from 50 to 100 feet in height, and about three quarters of a mile in length, extends from the city to the rock, which forms the Pontinha, exhibiting on its face some remarkable effects of volcanic action in a succession of beds, which commence with columnar basalt above, and after running through a succession of tufa, scoriæ, cinders, and fragments of pumice, in horizontal bands, terminate in a bed of tufa, nearly buried in masses of basalt, which have fallen from the upper part of the cliff. Passing on to the westward, equally distinct effects of volcanic action are visible. At short distances from the shore, and immediately upon it in some places, huge vertical masses of columnar basalt stand out from the banks of earth, which they support. In immediate contact with the shore the rock is often cavernous, indicating that the currents of lava must have run over beds of sand, which have been gradually worn away by the action of the sea, or that these liquid currents, coming in contact with water before they reached the ocean, were raised up by the gases and vapor, which were the product of this contact, and sustained until they had cooled in the forms in which they now appear. About three miles west of Funchal one of these formations takes a very striking form. It is a cavernous rock, with a vaulted roof, strongly resembling an inverted funnel, with a narrow opening at the top. The base is, perhaps, fifty feet in diameter, with a low opening towards the sea. The waves are constantly pouring into it, always with a loud roar, and when the sea is powerfully agitated, the water comes in with so much violence that it forces itself out through the opening above, rising to the height of forty or fifty feet in a column of spray and foam. The Portuguese give it the expressive appellation of La Forja. Seen and heard from below, it might very well have passed, in an age of superstition, for the abode of some sea-monster, perpetually bellowing in his den, and when attacked by the ocean, venting his rage upon it by hurling its waters into the sky above him.

From the similarity of some of these volcanic products it is supposed that an intimate geological connection exists between Madeira, the Azores, and the Canary group. The only essential differences are supposed to arise from the remoteness of the periods at which the volcanic action existed in each. Madeira has obviously enjoyed a long period of repose. In Teneriffe and some of the Azores, on the other hand, there have been very recent volcanic eruptions. The products of these eruptions bear no resemblance to those in Madeira, though between the older formations in all these islands there is a strong similarity. In Madeira the abruptness of the hills, the immensity of the cliffs (that at Cape Giram being 1800 feet in height and perpendicular), and the depth of the ravines (the Coural being 1300 feet from the bottom to the summit of the hills which surround it), indicate that the volcanic action, which produced such remarkable geological features, must have been on the most gigantic scale. Recent observations have effectually overthrown the theory that Madeira and some of the neighboring groups of islands are the remains of a submerged continent. Every manifestation shows that they must have been elevated at periods, more or less remote, from the sea. In the great Oceanic district, of which the Azores are one of the centres, the same volcanic agencies still exist. A few years ago, a submarine volcano was discovered in the neighborhood of this group, and disappeared before its exact position could be ascertained. Throughout this interesting region there is a vast field for inquiry and investigation which has yet been but very imperfectly explored.

Notwithstanding the inequalities of surface which Madeira exhibits, it has two great plains. Poul da Serra, the first, lies in the western part of the island. It is, according to Bowditch, 5159 feet above the level of the sea. It is a plateau, nine miles in length, and three in breadth. From its great elevation it is sometimes covered in winter with snow and ice. This extensive plain is a perfect desert, though its vegetation shows that with proper cultivation it would furnish a large portion of the breadstuffs which the island now imports. The rapid elevation of the land, from the sea to the interior, furnishes, in the compass of a very few miles, every variety of temperature, and a capacity for the production of nearly every species of vegetable and fruit which is found in continental districts, extending over ten or fifteen degrees of latitude. It needs only a proper application of agricultural skill to make the island wholly independent of foreign countries for all the necessaries, and most of the conveniences, of life.

The second plateau, or table-land, is San Antonio da Serra (or St. Antonio of the Desert). It lies on the eastern side of the island, about 2000 feet above the level of the ocean, and is several miles in extent. The eastern and northern portions of Madeira are said to exceed the southern and western in rural beauty, though they fall below the latter in the grandeur and sublimity of their scenery. In the former there is greater variety in the native vegetation, and art has been more successful in embellishing it. The vines are trained upon trees, as in portions of Italy, instead of trellis-work, and they give to the vineyards a character of gracefulness in which those around Funchal are sadly deficient; though even in the latter, with a vast screen of leaves and clusters of fruit covering entire acres, there is a richness which belongs to very few forms of cultivation.

The Coural das Freiras (the fold of the nuns) is another of the distinguishing features of the geological formation of the island. It is an immense chasm, more than thirteen hundred feet in depth, with Pico Ruivo, the highest peak of the island, looking down into it. A stream runs through this valley, and a few houses have been built upon it. Nothing can be more striking than the aspect of this little cluster of dwellings, seen from the height. The ride from Funchal to the Coural is one of the most interesting the island affords. It leads through a country rich in rural beauty, and abounding in scenes of grandeur rarely to be found. Nor is it wholly void of danger. In some places the only passage is a narrow footpath, cut in the side of a steep precipice, and winding round it at a sharp angle with the horizon. It requires strong nerves to thread these precarious passages with perfect composure, with a gulf five or six hundred feet deep beneath your feet, and overhanging rocks as many feet above your head. The Alps may be traversed with less danger than some of these hills. The day we visited the Coural, a heavy mist came over us as we were crossing one of them, and at the very moment when we were winding round its side, with a chasm from six to eight hundred feet below us, and by the narrowest conceivable footpath. The mist was so dense that we could not see more than five or six yards from us. Above, below, wherever we turned, all was enveloped in this shadowy veil. We seemed to be standing upon a mere strip of earth, with nothing tangible beyond it. It was far more exciting to the imagination than a clear view of the gulf would have been, and infinitely more fruitful in ill-defined apprehensions of danger.

We can not close these hasty notes on Madeira without a brief reference to a legend connected with its discovery. It is said that a young Englishman by the name of Robert Machin, in the reign of Edward the Third, fell in love with Anne D'Arfet, the daughter of a nobleman, through whose influence the lover was imprisoned under a false accusation by virtue of a royal warrant. Having found means to escape, he eloped with the object of his affection and embarked for France in a small vessel, which was driven from its course by a violent storm, and after twelve days, exhausted by fatigue and nearly famished, they reached the island of Madeira. They landed about twenty miles east of Funchal, in 1344, at a place now called Machico, and in a few hours afterwards their vessel was driven from her moorings by another storm and they were left upon the island, then uninhabited, but abounding in the most magnificent forests and scenery of exquisite beauty. Worn out by fatigue and disheartened by the desolate condition in which she was placed, Anne D'Arfet died in three days after the landing, and Robert Machin followed her in five days more. They were buried in one grave, and the place of their sepulture is the site of the village church of Machico. Their followers committed themselves to the ocean in a small boat, were captured by Moors, and carried into captivity. Their story at length reached the ears of one of the sovereigns of Portugal, and an expedition was fitted out under John Gonsalves Zarga, who discovered Porto Santo in 1418, and Madeira in 1419.

This is the legend, and its truth in Madeira, at least, is not doubted. Indeed, there are many in other countries, not half so well authenticated, which are received as true. The histories of Madeira contain an elegy in Latin hexameters on Anne D'Arfet, said to have been written by Machin, and an inscription in the same tongue marks his sepulchre. The whole story is in harmony with the character of the island. The sweetness of its climate, the beauty of its scenery, and the gracefulness of its vegetable life seem to require that its discovery should be laid in some such tale of tender and romantic interest.

CHAPTER XII.

VOYAGE TO CADIZ.

Departure from Funchal.—The Voyage and the Captain.—Arrival at Cadiz —The Harbor—.Boatmen.—Landing at Cadiz.

On the 17th of March we bade adieu to Madeira, and with the most sincere regret. The winter had not passed away without bringing with it some inconveniences and trials; but these were far overbalanced by the mildness of the atmosphere in which we lived, and the beauties of the scenery by which we were surrounded.

It was about four in the afternoon when we left the beach to embark in the little brig which was to convey us to the European continent. In an hour more we were sailing slowly out of the roadstead. The sun shone with unusual splendor, and as he sunk down in the west, casting heavy shadows across the ravines back of the city, and bathing the tops of the mountains in golden light, the scene was scarcely less beautiful in our eyes, familiar as it had become, than when it first broke upon our sight. During the night we passed the Desertas near enough to make out their harsh, ragged outlines in the moonlight. At dawn the next day they were far in the distance, faintly relieved by the shadowy form of Madeira in the back-ground. In a few hours more they had all disappeared, and nothing remained to bound the sight but an unbroken horizon of sky and waves.

The passage from Madeira to Cadiz, the port to which we were destined, averages six or seven days. The vessel in which we had embarked was a small one, not measuring more than 170 tons, but she was strong, skilfully commanded, and had a crew of fine young men. She was from the city of Boston, and bore its name. She had for eight years baffled the fogs and northeasters which preside over the New England coast, and there was a guaranty in this that she would do her duty in case of need. Her cabin was small, but having discharged her cargo at Funchal, and being in ballast, a roomy apartment was fitted up in her hold, and a neat and delightful one it was, of clean, freshly planed, but unpainted boards, far outdoing the principal cabin in convenience and comfort. It had got the the name of the steerage while the carpenter was fitting it up, but it soon sunk this cognomen in the more appropriate one of the gentlemen's cabin. The passengers were seventeen in number, including ladies, gentlemen, children, and servants, and, with the crew added, we mustered twenty-six souls. The wind was fair, the skies serene, and the moon was in her third quarter, giving us fine bright nights. Time never hangs heavily at sea under such circumstances. Even sea-sickness loses half its horrors, when you know that you are speeding on to your destination, and that your sufferings will soon be at an end. For two days and nights the wind blew steadily, but was constantly though almost imperceptibly increasing. From five and six knots an hour our log began to report seven and eight, and at last nine and ten; the sky became overcast, the rain came down at intervals in torrents, without any abatement of the wind, and a dense fog set in on the morning of the fourth day, just at dawn, when we were indulging the hope of seeing land. Our situation was now extremely unpleasant. The wind blew violently—so much so that the courses were taken in, and the vessel was running under close-reefed topsails—and we were on a lee-shore in a thick fog. The captain had never been at Cadiz, but he had been up all night studying an excellent chart, which he had found at Funchal, and had made himself as familiar with the coast and harbor as though he had navigated them all his life. At nine in the morning he told a few of us that he should be opposite the light-house in an hour, if his reckoning was right, and he must then choose between the alternatives of standing in or of attempting to beat out to sea. The latter would have been full of peril, for if the wind had continued to increase, as in fact it did, we should in all probability have gone ashore before night. The captain at half-past nine took his station in the foretop, and in half an hour more stood boldly in for the land. To those of us who understood the matter, the next half hour was a period of extreme anxiety. But it was hardly over before the captain's clear voice was heard amid the roaring of the storm, giving his orders to the helmsman with as much confidence as if he had been on his own native coast. He had descried the light-house at a distance of about half a mile, the first object we had seen, excepting a few vessels which crossed our path, since we lost sight of the Desertas. He was now at home. He had so thoroughly mastered his chart, that he knew the bearings of all the shoals and breakers, which lie at the mouth of the harbor, from the light-house, and he remained in the foretop until we had passed them all, directing the motions of the vessel with perfect calmness and confidence. It was certainly no small triumph of nautical skill on the part of our Yankee captain. He had sailed nearly six hundred miles, and had hit the light-house at the mouth of the harbor to which he was destined within fifteen minutes after his reckoning was up. It must be confessed, too, that there was some good luck in it. But his subsequent management of the vessel, steering her through breakers and reefs of rocks without the aid of a pilot, was all skill and good judgment.

The harbor of Cadiz is one of the finest in the world; it is defended on the south by a narrow tongue of land, at the extremity of which is the city, with its enclosure of battlements and walls, and its white houses rising above them. From the point at which it is connected with the main body of the island of St. Leon, about six miles distant, the shore curves to the northwest, gradually narrowing as it reaches the meridian of the city, and forming a broad, capacious bay, with an entrance some three miles in width. On the opposite side, about five and a half miles distant, lies the port of Saint Mary, and farther to the west, beyond the mouth of the harbor, the smaller town of Rota; on the north-east a range of hills, a few hundred feet high, forms a pretty back-ground, with a long wavy outline, rising at one point to a precipitous mountain, and near the summit of one of them there is the little town of Medina, the Sidonia of the ancients, with its white houses glistening in the sunbeams, and presenting altogether a pretty view, but a very tame one when compared with Funchal, or with most of the maritime towns on our own bolder coast, in the eastern Atlantic states. The light-house lies at the western extremity of Cadiz, about half a mile from the walls, and connected with the city partly by a reef of rocks, and partly by a bridge resting upon stone piers, though at low water you may pass over the whole intervening space on dry land. Between the light-house and the harbor and nearly half a mile out from the shore, there is a succession of reefs and breakers, with channels both without and within them, though the inner one is, I believe, rarely used by vessels of any magnitude, excepting when compelled by stress of weather.

Sheltered as vessels are, when at anchor in the harbor, they are not altogether secure from the violent gales with which it is sometimes visited. One of our own frigates was a few years ago driven from her moorings, and went ashore on the sandy beach near Saint Mary's, though her commander succeeded in getting her off without injury. A French ship of the line was soon afterward stranded near the same spot, and lay there six months. A corps of engineers was sent down from Toulon, and by some very scientific means they succeeded in raising her sufficiently to float her off. A large brig is now lying on the shoals near the inner harbor, stripped of every thing but her two lower masts. She was driven ashore in the gale of October, which desolated the island of Madeira, and filled the city of Funchal with ruins. Notwithstanding these occasional disasters, there is no harbor lying so directly upon the ocean which affords a greater degree of security to ships.

When we had fairly entered the port, and were approaching the anchoring-ground, the lazy pilot came on board, just in time to see the vessel stripped of the little canvass she was carrying, and to secure his fee of nine dollars. We were soon at anchor, with a Spanish frigate outside of us, and two French man-of-war brigs, two Neapolitan war-steamers, a dozen or more square-rigged vessels, and a multitude of feluccas and fishing-boats, of the most picturesque rig, filling up the whole space between us and the shore. Some two miles east there is an inner harbor, still more secure, and it was filled with vessels which had been laid up for the winter. The wind continued to blow a gale, and though it came across the city, the vessel rocked nearly as much as she did at sea. Some of the gentlemen landed at the expense of a wet jacket, but the greater part of the passengers were compelled to remain on board until the next day. Being anxious to provide lodgings for our party as soon as possible, three of us took a boat, which had come alongside after dinner, and went on shore. Before starting, we made an agreement with the boatmen to land us for two dollars, and to bring us on board again for an equal sum. After scouring the city and looking at the principal lodging-houses, we returned to the dock. Our boatmen were waiting, but refused to take us on board, unless we would pay them five dollars. Their pretext was that the city gates would close before they could get back, and that they would be compelled to stay outside till morning. We reminded them of our agreement, but a man who has made up his mind to be dishonest, is not likely to be made otherwise by assisting his memory. They had no sort of recollection on the subject. On the contrary, they were quite sure that their agreement was only to land us. Here we were, on the dock, in a strange city, the wind blowing a gale, and all the other boats anchored at a distance from the shore. There was a crowd of boatmen about us, and from what we had heard of them, it was not unnatural that we should fancy ourselves the objects of at least no very friendly intentions. What should we do? make a merit of necessity and submit to the imposition, or get into the city before the gates were closed, and find a lodging-place for the night? We determined on the latter, not as the most convenient alternative, but on the principle of making no compromise with rogues. We accordingly turned back toward the walls, the boatmen who had brought us on shore and a large number of others following us. But in modern times controversies are settled by negotiation. The boatmen were not behind the age in this respect. We had not gone far before we were met with overtures for a reconciliation. They proposed to take us on board for four dollars, then for three, and at last for two and a half. We might have made a merit of our necessity and accepted the last offer, but before we had time to consider it, another boatman came forward, expressing great indignation that strangers should be so imposed on by his countrymen, and said he would take us on board for a dollar. This interference produced an abundance of violent gesticulation on the part of the boatmen who had brought us on shore, and was near leading to blows; but the proposition was altogether too favorable to be declined, and the boatman having borrowed a small boat to bring in a larger one from its moorings, we were soon embarked, and in due time on board. But when we came to pay off our generous friend, who had so conscientiously interposed, we found we had only exchanged a plurality of rogues for a single one. He demanded three dollars, and insisted that he had not offered to take us for less. We at last got rid of him by giving him two, though he went off grumbling as though he had been wronged. This first specimen of the Spanish character went far to convince us that the author of "A Year in Spain" had reason for saying that "the lower classes on the coast of Andalusia are the most quarrelsome, cheating, and vindictive rascals in the world." But I am happy to say, that during the six weeks we passed in Andalusia, this was almost the only instance in which we found cause to complain of any thing like dishonesty, extortion, or want of kindness on the part of any portion of the inhabitants, although we were constantly in contact with them.

The next day, at ten o'clock, although the gale had but very slightly abated, we embarked for the shore in a large sail boat, having previously enveloped the ladies and children in blankets, and covered them with canvass. After lying twenty-four hours in port, a few hundred rods from the shore, we were scarcely less rejoiced to touch the land than we should have been after a long voyage, though less than four days and a half had elapsed since we were weighing anchor at Funchal.

CHAPTER XIII.

CITY OF CADIZ.

The Walls.—The Seville Gate.—Smuggling.—The Pier and the Bay.—The City Gates.—Custom-House Examination.—The Market.—Houses.—Doña Antonia, our Landlady and her House.—The Cathedral.—The Chapel of the Capuchins.—Murillo.—The Walk around the City Walls.—History of Cadiz.—The Drawing Academy.—The Cemetery.—The Neighboring Country and the Banditti.

The city of Cadiz is completely surrounded by walls. On three sides they are washed by the sea, and on the land side there is a regular series of bastions and ravelines, terminated by a glacis, which is separated from the inner works by a ditch. Across this ditch there are several bridges, affording a passage to the numerous pedestrians, animals, and vehicles which enter and leave the city by day. At night they are drawn up, and all intercourse with the country is cut off until daybreak, when the city gates are again thrown open. The points of communication with the water are two—one for the foreign commerce of the city, and the other for the ingress and egress of the inhabitants or strangers, and for the articles of consumption required for daily use. The first is a dock built out into the water between two projecting angles of the wall, and opening into the city through the Seville gate. Though exceedingly limited in extent, it was the centre of the vast intercourse of Spain with the countries of Europe, and with the western hemisphere, during the commercial prosperity of the city. On this narrow platform were received the countless millions of gold and silver dug from the mines of Mexico and Peru, and the supplies of merchandize, the products of European industry, which were sent back in return for all this treasure. It is now literally deserted. Cadiz receives nothing from abroad, excepting what she consumes, and the high tariff of Spain has given a death-blow to all legitimate commerce. A large portion of the articles which enter the city are either contraband or charged with enormous duties; yet there is an abundant supply of both classes to be found in the shops. The importation of cotton fabrics from other countries is prohibited; yet English muslins and French calicoes are as freely vended as though no such prohibition were in force. Other articles of merchandize, the introduction of which is charged with duties prohibitory in effect, are as freely sold, though the duties are never paid. They are, of course, introduced by smuggling, the necessary fruit of every system which has for its object to annihilate, or clog with unjust and injurious restrictions the commercial intercourse of mankind. The smugglers have as little respect for the direct as for the indirect prohibition; and the consequences are, that the consumers pay dear for the commodities they require, the government is defrauded of its revenue, the open contempt in which the law is held tends to engender a spirit of hostility to all law, and the community is demoralized through the large numbers who gain their livelihood by an illicit traffic. It is said that smuggling is carried on through the connivance and by the aid of the public authorities, and that it has become a source of revenue to individuals high in power, whose influence is employed to perpetuate the commercial system out of which it has grown. Some months ago an individual connected with the court was urged to lend his efforts to a reduction of the rates of duty fixed by the present exorbitant tariff, and one of the arguments addressed to him was, that it would put an end to smuggling. His answer was, If you put an end to smuggling, what will become of the sixty thousand families who live by it? It may readily be seen how large a portion of the commercial transactions of the kingdom depends on it. This species of commerce makes very little show. It neither requires the aid of public docks, nor carries on its operations in the face of day; and as Cadiz has scarcely any other, there is as great a want of commercial activity externally as can well be imagined.

The dock connected with the Seville gate now runs round another projecting angle of the wall, fills up a space between two bastions farther on, and terminates in a pier projecting into the water, at the extremity of which is Fort St. Philip, a small battery, with about a dozen guns mounted *en barbette*. The pier and battery are but slightly elevated above high-water mark, while the main wall of the city rises some thirty feet above them.

The other point of communication between the city and the sea is a pier about forty yards in width, and extending about one hundred yards into the water, with flights of stone steps at intervals along its sides, for landing passengers and supplies from the city. At the extremity of the pier is the health-office, and near by the holy martyrs Servando and German, two of the patron saints of the city, are perched up on high stone columns, erected by Philip the Fifth, a hundred and forty years ago. As the pier approaches the wall, it runs off at an angle, forming a dock parallel with it, and having on its inner side a low range of ship-chandlers' shops, and two or three public stores, where articles requiring to be weighed are carried and sometimes temporarily deposited. Near the centre of the dock stand the two city gates, side by side, with their arched passages, their double columns and high pediments, and St. Francis Xavier, another patron of the city, on a marble column, all facing the bay. Through one of these gates the human flood pours into the town, while another stream flows out of the other. If you attempt to go against either of these currents, the sentinel turns you back with his bayonet and points you to the other gate. At each of these thoroughfares there is a corps of custom-house officers, to see that nothing enters or goes out but in conformity to law. In small matters their duty may be well performed. How it is discharged in weightier commercial transactions has been already seen.

Let us stop a moment before we enter the city, and look back upon the pier and the bay. What a busy scene it is! Hundreds of boats, with their masts and yards projecting in all directions, lie at anchor. Some are getting under way, and are spreading their huge lateen sails to the breeze, others are taking them in and preparing to come to anchor, and with an endless variety of rigging, alike picturesque and novel. Most of them are fishing-boats, just returned from their three or four days' voyage to the Spanish side of the strait, or to the opposite coast of Barbary, and are emptying their scaly prizes into baskets, to be sent to the fish-market, close within the gates. A boat is landing from the opposite shore, with a cargo of country people, who are coming out upon the dock. At their head is a stout Andalusian, six feet high at least, and in his most jaunty dress. What a sensation he would create in the streets of one of our own cities! On his head he wears a low-crowned hat, with the brim turned up all round like a scroll, and on one side there are two rose-shaped cockades, of black floss silk, in size and form much like those with which we sometimes ornament the head-stalls of our horses. His blue jacket is covered all over, sleeves, sides, and back, with cotton embroidery, of an infinite variety of gaudy colors, and instead of buttons in front (for the jacket is not intended to be buttoned), there are tags of silk surrounded with red and yellow strips of cloth wrought into the body of the material. His vest is of flaming yellow, and a broad red belt of cotton net-work is tied round his waist. His breeches, which are blue, come down to his knees, and a pair of gaiters, of stiff, dun-colored leather, come up to meet them, buttoned at the top and bottom, and open at the sides, with a profusion of leather strings hanging down and shaking in the breeze. A pair of yellow goat-skin shoes, completes his equipment. He is altogether a fine-looking fellow, notwithstanding his queer toggery. Doubtless many a tender glance was cast at him by the country maidens of Andalusia, as he sallied forth from his native village, and some faithful heart may, at this very moment, be sending up a fervent aspiration that he may return unscathed from the fiery ordeal of the town. A better specimen of the physical man is not often to be found, and he treads the pavement firmly, as if he were conscious of his strength. As he passes along the dock he is met by a Moor, who gazes at his strange dress as if there was nothing in his own worthy of observation. It is amusing to see them look at each other, the jolly Andalusian with a slight smile upon his features, and the Moor preserving the imperturbable gravity characteristic of his race. In form and proportions the infidel is little if at all inferior to the Christian with whom he is exchanging glances. He is about sixty years of age, and his full white beard hangs down low upon his breast. His features are large and symmetrical, his forehead high, and his eyes beam with intelligence. His dress is low, leaving his throat and neck entirely bare. He wears a shapeless tunic of blue cloth, coming down to his ankles, open in front, and with loose sleeves terminating at the elbows. Under it he has a long shirt or gown, of striped muslin, with sleeves extending to the wrist, and a row of pearl buttons on the side. It is confined about the waist by a red silk sash, and opens below, showing a pair of loose white trowsers, which terminate at the knee. His legs are bare, and his feet are thrust into a pair of yellow slippers. His head is covered with a red cap, with a roll of white linen or muslin bound round it, forming a full turban, and a few gray locks fall down from beneath it upon his bare neck. He is in truth a noble looking personage, and with a suitable dress would grace a woolsack or a senate chamber.

In the vast crowd around the city gates there is nothing which will endure a comparison with these two personages, alike remarkable in their way, though there is much that is novel and striking. There is the Spanish caballero, with his slouched hat, and his cloak thrown over one shoulder, standing idly in the throng; the gaditana, with her mantilla over her head, its only covering in storm and sunshine, making her way through the crowd, and always sure of being treated by the rudest of her countrymen with marked respect; the donkey struggling along with its usual over-load of dirt or stone; the enormous ox-cart, almost the only one known in Andalusia, drawn by two splendid oxen, yoked together by the horns in the most primitive manner possible, and in such a way as to lose at least half their power of traction. These, and a variety of other objects equally novel to an American, give a peculiar attraction to the gates of Cadiz. As we entered them our persons were carefully scanned by the eyes of the custom-house officials. A nurse with a bundle in her arms is stopped by one of them for examination. She unrolls it and discloses an infant, and a shout of laughter greets the disconcerted officer. Our baggage is taken into one of the rooms adjoining the gate, and is examined in the most gentlemanly and unexceptionable manner. We testify our satisfaction by a gratuity, and we afterwards found the examinations still less rigid. After passing the gate we enter the fish-market. It is full of fish of an excellent quality, with a mixture of oysters said to be poor, and a few stalls are covered with huge speckled eels, looking like house-adders, and much better calculated to destroy an appetite than to create one. The fish venders are all shouting at the top of their voices, proclaiming the quality of their commodities, and the prices at which they sell them, and converting the market-place and its neighborhood into a very bedlam. The fish stalls fill the street, running along the inner side of the wall. The wall itself is pierced with arched stores, which are occupied by fruiterers, and there is a bountiful display of raisins, dried and preserved fruit of all kinds, apples, and the luscious Tariffa orange, which finds its best market here and at Gibraltar. As you enter the compact part of the city, you are struck with the cleanliness of the streets and the beauty of the dwellings.

It is difficult to find a better-built city than Cadiz in any quarter of the globe. The houses are from three to five stories high, with balconies projecting into the streets, and uniformly whitewashed. The glare of these white walls would be intolerable but for the narrowness of the streets, which excludes the sunbeams and keeps them in perpetual shadow. By far the greater part of the edifices, public as well as private, have been built within the last hundred years. The city is circumscribed in its dimensions by the sea; and the improvements are necessarily made, not by expanding, but by demolishing worthless fabrics and building up new and beautiful ones in their place. Some of the old town remains, with its still narrower streets, its gloomy dwellings, its darkness and its filth, just as it was hundreds of years ago, excepting the altered races that now fill its prison-like habitations. To the proud Mussulman and the high-minded cavalier have succeeded the fisherman, the mule-driver, the thief, the smuggler, the carrier of wood, the drawer of water, and the laborer, earning a scanty subsistence by depredation, or from the contributions of the higher classes, who throng the better portions of the city.

A short walk brought us to the house of Doña Antonia, our landlady. She is said to keep the most comfortable lodging-house in Cadiz, and we certainly found it in all respects excellent. Indeed, she is the mistress of two lodging-houses, both situated in the best parts of the city. Ours was in the Plazuela di San Agustino, about midway between the city gates and the Plaza de la Constitucion, the centre of fashion. An arched entrance of some six feet in width and twenty in length, occupied by an old man making silk braid and fringe, led us into an open court about thirty feet square, around which the apartments were arranged. The court is open to the sky, and the rain, when it falls, is carried off through a horizontal grate of iron in the centre. The house is five stories in height, and on each story there is a gallery with an iron railing, furnishing the means of communicating with the rooms on its four sides. The upper story was devoted by the widow to household purposes. One room contained a washing apparatus, a second the utensils, furniture, and linen not in constant use, a third was a dovecote, and in another there was a large flock of hens, with a very scientific contrivance of nests—and a capital arrangement we found it, for our breakfast table was always supplied with an abundance of eggs, which were sure to be less than a day old. One of our own housekeepers would consider it a very difficult matter to manage an establishment without a back yard of some description or other. There was no such thing here.

The only vacant space was the central paved court below, which was utterly useless, as well as unoccupied, excepting by a huge pair of steelyards to weigh heavy articles for the household, and a pully and tackle to raise them to the stories above. We got on remarkably well, notwithstanding. Our hostess was the widow of an Englishman, who had engrafted upon her some notions of comfort during their connection, which continued long enough to make her the mother of two daughters; and those who have travelled in Spain can well appreciate the luxury of finding any thing which savors of the good order and cleanliness of an English inn or lodging-house. Our beds were good, the tiled floors were covered with matting, there was an abundance of clean towels and capacious wash-basins, and this was almost the only house in Spain where we found them. Our table, too, was excellent, though the cookery was in the Spanish taste: no roast joints or good old Anglo-Saxon puddings, but boiled or baked beef and mutton, with the invariable accompaniment of pork in some shape or other—for no true Spaniard makes a dinner without hog's-meat. In comparison with the hotels and boarding-houses of the United States and Great Britain, those of Spain, even in the best towns, are wretched. It is but recently that they have acquired some rude notions of comfort; yet they are, as we are told, infinitely better than they were even ten years ago. But they are in general cold, meagre, desolate establishments, with poor provision for eating, and for sleeping infinitely worse.

Though Cadiz is a beautiful city, and a delightful residence for a few weeks, it contains few objects of strong interest. The cathedral, always one of the first things to be sought for in a European town, is certainly, in some respects, among the most beautiful in Spain. It is of white marble, and in architecture purely Grecian, and in this it differs totally from every other we saw. Its interior has recently been completed, after more than one hundred and twenty years of labor, but its exterior still remains unfinished, though the workmen are constantly busy upon it. The vaulted roof within is supported by huge Corinthian pillars, and though of the lightest order of architecture, the building is massive and vast, and the general effect is full as imposing as many other equally heavy edifices of a construction better calculated to produce impressions of sublimity and grandeur. It contains few pictures worthy of notice. Indeed, they are in general without merit. There are a few good copies of Murillo, and two or three pretended originals, which do injustice to that great master at the expense of truth.

In the Chapel of the Capuchins there are several unquestionable works of Murillo. Indeed, the picture over the altar has some excellences hardly surpassed by his best efforts. It was, in fact, his last work. He fell from the scaffold, while engaged in painting it, and broke a leg. He was carried tc Seville, his native place, but survived the injury only a few months. This circumstance lends a strong interest to the picture.

But it has great merits of its own. It was not quite finished by Murillo, and when one has learned this fact, it is not difficult to fancy that in some of its details the hand of the great master is wanting. But some of the principal figures have all the beauty and grace which his pencil knew so well how to impart. The Madonna in the centre is fine; the kneeling figure in front of her, said to represent Mary Magdalen, is magnificent; two angels, one on each side, are exquisitely designed and executed; and as a whole, the picture deservedly ranks high as a work of art. There are three other originals of Murillo in the church, one of them, a St. Francis, a picture of distinguished merit. It is indeed a duplicate, by the artist himself, of a picture of great celebrity in the gallery of the Seville museum.

The great beauty of Cadiz is the walk around the walls, a little less than three miles in extent. Ascending the wall at the gates of the city, which open upon the harbor, and turning to the east, you have the view of the shipping, the villages of Puerta St. Maria and Rota, and the country beyond them, bounded by the line of mountains of which we have already spoken. Following the battlements for about three fourths of a mile, you reach the Alameda, the great public walk of the city, with its statues, its shade-trees, and its little beds of shrubbery and flowers. The trees are small, either because they want age, or because in the atmosphere loaded with the saline properties of the sea, which surrounds the city, and which in high gales sends its surf over the parapet, they can not attain a larger growth; and it is, therefore, in the freshness of the evening, when dense shade is unnecessary, that the Alameda is most thronged. It is then that it presents a scene richer in female beauty than any to be found elsewhere. As you enter the principal walk, you find the long range of stone seats on each side filled with the mothers and daughters of the city, almost equally beautiful, looking out from their dark mantillas upon the dense bodies of pedestrians, who pass up and down between them, and hemming them in with ranks as serried as though they had been marshalled for some hostile purpose. The man who passes often through this ordeal of fiery eyes and comes out of it unharmed, must be exceedingly cold or exceedingly fortunate! In symmetry of features, beauty of expression, well-proportioned figure and grace of movement, the gaditana is certainly unsurpassed. She possesses now the same superiority in personal graces over the other women of the South of Europe, which she enjoyed two thousand years ago among the Romans, when the latter were becoming addicted to pleasure and luxurious ease, and preparing, by an imitation of the vices of the countries they had conquered, the downfall of the republic; and she is reputed to be, in her moral attributes, far more strongly characterized by the frailties of imperial Rome than by the stern virtues of the Roman matron of an earlier age.

Passing by the Alameda, you soon reach a broad

space of unoccupied ground, bounded on one side by the city wall, which is elevated but four or five feet above it, and the compact part of the city on the other. Here the military parade and exercise. Farther on, you pass the point on which the light-house stands, running out from the wall far into the waters of the Atlantic. Nearly opposite, on the city side, an immense edifice, once a palace but now a poor-house, meets you, with a high column in front, sustaining an appropriate group of figures, and bearing upon it inscriptions explanatory of its design. This is a recent establishment, made for the purpose of freeing the streets of the city of its mendicant population. It has now some eight hundred inmates, of all ages and both sexes, and it is withal admirably managed. The old men have their separate apartments, the old women theirs, the children theirs, with suitable school-rooms, where they are well instructed, and every thing wears an aspect of comfort and good order. Annexed to it, but separated from it by a high wall, is an asylum for lunatics, of whom there are now about forty under treatment. The establishment, which is highly creditable to the city, is supported by a portion of the taxes levied at the gates on articles imported for the consumption of the inhabitants.

Still following the wall, and looking out on the broad bosom of the Atlantic, almost always thickly spotted with sails, you pass the Chapel of the Capuchins, containing the paintings of Murillo, then the rear of the Cathedral, when you reach the Plaza di Toros, one of those arenas of cruelty and torture in Spain, where all the brutality of the bull-fight is preserved, without any of the chivalric bearing which made it popular with the Moors. A little farther on you pass the gate which opens upon the city defences upon the land side, and in a few minutes more you are on the high wall opposite the harbor. Throughout this walk there is a continued succession of interesting objects, and on the side of the harbor, particularly, the constant arrival and departure of steamers and sail vessels, and the landing of boats at the docks with their motley lading of men and merchandize, perpetually attract and rivet the attention without fatiguing it. The scene is incessantly varying, and for some weeks, at least, is in no danger of being found monotonous. To sojourners of longer standing than ourselves it may prove otherwise.

The history of Cadiz as a city abounds with incident, although there are few monuments within it to mark the eras of change through which it has passed. It boasts an antiquity of which any city might well be proud, if, indeed, there is more cause for exultation in deducing an origin through a long succession of historical associations of good and ill, than in finding it, like the thrifty towns of the new world, in the labor and enterprise of their own citizens, or, at the farthest, of their ancestors a few generations back, entering the wilderness with no other reliance but their own hands, converting its barren and solitary haunts into abodes of civilization, sustaining and ornamenting them with the arts of social life. But without disputing this question with the gaditanos, it suffices to say that they assign the foundation of their city to the year 1200 before the Christian era, making it more than 3000 years old. Certain it is, that it was occupied by the Phenicians long before the foundation of Rome, and subsequently by the Carthaginians at various periods until they were expelled by the Romans. In the year 237 before the Christian era it was taken by Cornelius Scipio; 441 years after Christ by the Goths; by the Moors in 714; and in 1262 it was recovered from the latter by Alonzo the Tenth. In 1596 it was sacked and burned by the English and Dutch, its archives destroyed, and the church pillaged. The open space in front of the town-house is pointed out as the theatre of a bloody contest between the citizens and the forces of the Earl of Essex, the leader of the expedition, whose fiery valor no opposition could resist. Twenty-nine years afterwards, the British made an unsuccessful attempt to take it, and another in 1702, which proved equally fruitless. But the event in the history of the city, on which the inhabitants particularly pride themselves, is the memorable siege it sustained against the forces of Napoleon, from the 5th of February, 1810, until the 24th of August, 1812, more than two years and a half. It was for this persevering resistance that it received from Ferdinand the Seventh the title of The Most Heroic City, which, with the Most Noble and Loyal, titles conferred on it by Charles the Fifth, in 1524, constitutes a sufficient measure of praise to satisfy the most ambitious. During this memorable siege the French threw 15,500 shot and shells into the city, or rather at it, for their batteries were so distant that they produced but little effect. In 1702, the office of the Royal Board of Trade with the Indies was removed from Seville to Cadiz, and from this moment the commercial prosperity of the latter commenced. It became the emporium of the trade with America; its old houses were pulled down and new ones erected, and its streets were perpetually resounding with the din of busy industry. The sound which rose above all others was the clinking of hard dollars. For large transactions they were put up in bags of 500, and passed from hand to hand, month after month, without being counted or even opened. How altered is the aspect of the city! Her magnificent houses, clean streets, and neat balconies remain. But her population has dwindled from 100,000 souls to less than 50,000; her foreign trade is annihilated, and you may tread the streets which were swarming half a century ago with the busy votaries of commerce, without being once jostled.

There are few public institutions in Cadiz which deserve a particular notice. There is one, however, which ought not to be overlooked—the Drawing Academy. It occupies one side of the square of General Mina, and is every evening filled with the city youth receiving gratuitous instruction in drawing, mathematics, architecture, and other kindred branches. It is furnished with the ablest teachers, and its expenses are defrayed, like those of the poor-house, by a portion of the taxes levied at the gates on articles consumed within the city. In a single hall we counted nearly two hundred young men busy with the pencil, and they were but a small part of the whole number. The establishment, though very extensive, is not on a scale of sufficient magnitude to admit all the youth of the city, and the selection of pupils is, therefore, a matter of great interest to parents. The choice is made from the most meritorious, and by far the greater portion are the children of the poor. We saw a number of men and women coarsely clad waiting at the door of the academy at half-past nine in the evening, to conduct their children, the future artists and architects, to their humble lodgings—garrets, perhaps, in the old town, far better fitted for the haunts of thieves than for the abode of honest poverty. Institutions like these are to cities the real patents of nobility. How much more of true honor is there in one such, than in a hundred barren titles conferred by a licentious king or a gouty emperor!

To Cadiz, as a place of permanent residence, there are strong objections. Among the first of these is its almost insulated position. There is but one outlet by land, no walks excepting around the walls, and no drives excepting along the single narrow neck which unites the city with the main body of the island of St. Leon. On this, however, there is an avenue of trees, not large enough to afford much shade, and a very fine broad street for pedestrians, more than a mile in length. At the extremity of the avenue is the city cemetery, consisting of several acres enclosed in high walls. There are five divisions of nearly equal magnitude, separated by walls about fifteen feet in thickness, built up with arched cavities, one above the other, just large enough to receive a coffin, and as close together as possible. Each cavity has its opening, with a stone adjusted to it, and when it has received its deposit, it is closed up and hermetically sealed. The external walls are about eight feet in thickness, and are pierced in the same manner with these narrow chambers, the openings being all in the interior of the cemetery. This city of the dead above ground has nothing attractive in its appearance. On the contrary it is cold, bare, and repulsive. It presents a naked surface of wall covered with funereal inscriptions, without trees or ornament of any description within it. The price of a burial in the wall is about twenty dollars. Those who can not afford to pay are buried in the ground, and the decomposition of the bodies is usually hastened by the addition of quick-lime, in order to make room for their successors. The cemetery is now about forty years old, and it probably contains as many of the remains of the former population of Cadiz as there are living inhabitants. The remains of the ancient city are not far off. The foundations of the houses, and the ruins of the ancient aqueduct, which brought the inhabitants their supply of water from the distant land, are still to be seen at low tide. What the Romans, the Goths, and the Moors left, the sea has buried. And here they stand, these two monuments of the past, the dead and the living city mingling their memorials, and heralding in the fate of the one the future destiny of the other.

The main land in the vicinity of Cadiz is said to be extremely uninviting—a country overrun by herds of cattle and flocks of sheep, guarded by keepers in goat-skin dresses, with here and there a gloomy-looking village. As you go back in the direction of Gibraltar, it becomes more desolate, the hills are covered with forest-trees, and the traveller is fortunate who is not plundered by banditti. So unsettled is the condition of this district, that property sent fifteen or twenty miles into the interior is frequently insured against plunderers. As you approach Gibraltar the people are, if possible, still more lawless. In repeated instances during the present season, the British officers of the garrison have been taken by banditti within ten or twelve miles of the rock, carried into the mountains, and retained until their friends have paid the sums of money demanded for their ransom. This disorganized state of the body politic is, in a great degree, the fruit of bad government. The laws of the kingdom have put an end to all honest industry, and large numbers of the people naturally, if not necessarily, resort to these desperate methods of procuring a livelihood. It is so much easier a life, too, than one of labor, that it needs but a slight apology to continue when once embarked in it. The bandits are not only exceedingly civil, but very cool calculators. They rarely take life—never, indeed, except when they find it necessary in order to put down resistance. They ease you of your money and valuables, and if you can satisfy them that you will need it, they will hand you back a dollar or two to pay your expenses to the next large town. Now and then a man of respectable standing is concerned in these depredations upon travellers, and if he is discovered by the person who has been plundered, the latter is usually deterred from denouncing him by the apprehension of being visited by the summary vengeance of the party thus exposed, or of his companions in guilt. Half a century of freedom from the shackles which a mistaken and corrupt system of policy has imposed on the labor and capital of the kingdom, would redress much of this social derangement and injustice, and make Spain—what she has every natural facility for becoming—the abode of industry, enterprise, wealth, and good order.

CHAPTER XIV.

CITY OF SEVILLE.

Embark in the Steamer for Seville.—The Coast of Andalusia.—Rota.—The Guadalquivir.—St. Lucar.—The Plain of the Guadalquivir.—Distant View of Seville.—Custom-house Visitation.—Lodgings in the Alcazar and in the Calle de Gallegos.—Our Landlady.—The Cathedral.—View from the Giralda.—The Alcazar.—The Exchange.—House of Pilate.—The Ayuntamiento.

Early in April we embarked in the Trajano, one of the steamers which ply between Cadiz and Seville. Nothing could be neater or more comfortable than our little vessel, and her speed, too, was very respectable. We left Cadiz at ten in the morning, and at seven in the evening—nine hours—we reached Seville, a distance of ninety miles. The first twenty we followed the coast, at a distance of three or four miles from it, passing the town of Rota, near Cadiz, and another small village near the mouth of the Guadalquivir, which we entered and ran by the town of St. Lucar, to a large custom-house, a mile or two beyond, where we came to anchor to land and receive passengers. The coast between Cadiz and the Guadalquivir is low and sandy, with nothing to mark it but a line of martello towers, some five or six miles apart, erected to guard against the incursions of the Moors centuries ago, and to communicate the alarm on the approach of hostile fleets. From St. Lucar until you come within ten miles of Seville, the banks of the river are low, and the country for miles on all sides perfectly flat. It is, indeed, a vast plain, through which the stream has worn its devious way, winding, as rivers always do in champaign countries, in all directions, turning first to the right hand and then to the left, and sometimes retracing its track, as though it were in doubt as to its true course to the ocean. This immense level, as far as the eye can reach, is covered with horses and cattle, roaming over it and feeding upon its spontaneous herbage, which the periodical inundations of the river bring out in rank luxuriance. There is something peculiarly striking in this boundless expanse of marsh and meadow, and the enormous aggregate of animal life which it sustains. The scenery of elevated districts—the mountain losing itself in the clouds, the torrent bursting from its summit and plunging thousands of feet into the valley below—inspire exalted conceptions of the majesty and power of the Hand which created them. The boundless plain is the parent of other thoughts, but of thoughts kindred to these. It is the emblem, not of matchless power, but of illimitable time and space. With this level, through which our little steamer is cutting its way, following the narrow channel of water, which at the distance of a few miles seems but a thread, other associations are connected. It is washed by the great river of the Arabs, undeserving as the muddy stream may seem of the name. It has seen the army of Hannibal entering upon its gigantic march, and destined to carry terror to the very gates of Rome. It has seen in turn the forces of Scipio returning from their mission of blood, with the denunciation, "delenda est Carthago," converted from prophecy into historical truth. On this plain the Moor fought for the conquest of fair Andalusia, and here, centuries afterwards, he struggled against the new-born chivalry by which he was defied and overthrown. The herds which are now ranging over it, countless as they seem, are far outnumbered by the armed hosts which have, in different ages, met in deadly conflict and fertilized it with their blood.

As you approach Seville, one of the banks of the river becomes somewhat elevated and striking. Winding around it, a bald, dun-colored cliff faces you, a village running from the river-side up to the level above, with its little parish church or a convent crowning the height, with its long line of blank wall, its turrets and spires, and with such an air of strength and solidity that it seems as well calculated to sustain a warfare with the brute force of the world as with its profanities. The earth has now become clad with trees, and shrubbery, and foliage. You have no longer the broad, unvarying expanse of grass, which covered the plain below. The orange grove, the olive plantation, and the wheat field, are now the principal features in the landscape, all rich and luxuriant, and giving abundant evidence of a warm climate and a genial soil. As you ascend the river, it is the left bank which is elevated. On your right there is a level of some ten miles in width, bounded by an elevation about as high as that which, on the other side, forms the bank of the river. Thousands of years farther back than our brief and scanty records reach, these two elevations may have been the boundaries of the now shrunk and diminished stream. What may have once been a waste of waters, is now teeming with life, with hardly an acre which the hand of industry has not converted to some purpose of ornament or use. In the midst of this fertile plain, on the right bank as you ascend the river (in strictness its left bank), stands the city of Seville—the most interesting city of Spain—the Giralda, once a Moorish tower, and now the spire of the Cathedral, rising three hundred and fifty feet above the surface of the earth, with its bronze statue surmounting it, and visible at the distance of miles from the river and across the plain. Indeed, the body of the Cathedral is seen, as far as the city can be descried, rising above all other edifices, like a gigantic chieftain standing in the midst of his followers, and towering above them all.

At the distance of a mile from the city, you turn a sharp angle in the river and run up along the Alameda, the beautiful public walk, with its double row of trees, beneath which thousands of the inhabitants at nightfall are seen sitting or strolling, glad to escape in summer from the insufferable heat of the town, and in other seasons to enjoy the bracing air, which pours down fresh and cool from the hills in the back-ground.

At Seville you have—what you find in only one or two other commercial towns in Spain—the luxury of landing at a dock, instead of being pitched, bag and baggage, into a small boat, while the vessel lies anchored in the harbor or stream. We went ashore on a plank (a mode of disembarkation which we now for the first time appreciated as it deserves) and our baggage was brought out after us and placed on a broad, capacious dock, well defended by pickets and gates, and with an array of cutlasses to keep off the crowds who beset the entrance. A bevy of custom-house officers were in attendance to examine the baggage, which they did in the most gentlemanly manner, and the one who performed that service for us declined the proffered gratuity by which we desired to testify our thankfulness. For the honor of the Seville custom-house let it be recorded!

The shades of night were falling fast over the city before we entered it, and our first impressions were not the most favorable. We passed through the gate of the Arenal, and turned off into a narrow and not very cleanly street, in order to reach, by the shortest route, the house to which we were destined. We soon found it, and at nine o'clock we were installed in our new lodgings. The house was once part of the Alcazar, the palace of the Moorish kings, and was, in some respects, not an unworthy appendage of that gorgeous edifice.

Our principal room was at least thirty feet by forty, and some twenty-five feet high, with a richly ornamented ceiling, and with one enormous window looking into a public square, and a fine large balcony on the outside. Our bedrooms were not in keeping with this noble apartment. They were small, all opening upon a corridor, with each a thick massive door and a single grated window, admitting a few rays of light to struggle in vain against the darkness within. The corridor compensated, in some degree, for these gloomy sleeping apartments. It was glazed in its whole extent, as though it had been a hothouse, and looked out into a square court, around which were painted in fresco the arms and insignia of the Spanish kings, an epitome of history of themselves, extending hundreds of years back, with inscriptions explanatory of the origin of parts of the edifice, and of the changes they have undergone. An arched passage from the side of the court opposite to us, led into a court farther on, and still larger, with a beautiful canopied entrance wrought in arabesque.

Notwithstanding the associations with which every thing around us was connected, and the remains of the gorgeous taste and the magnificence of the Moors, which we could see at any moment by merely crossing the court below, we could not be reconciled to our prison-like bedrooms, and in two days we removed to another part of the city. We were now in the best lodging-house in Seville, in the Calle de Gallegos, a central part of the city, and, so far as the house itself was concerned, leaving nothing to be desired. The apartments were on the four sides of a square court filled with trees and shrubbery, with a fine marble fountain in the centre, sending out a copious supply of water, and rendering the whole atmosphere fresh and fragrant. It was formerly the residence of the eccentric Frank Hall Standish, an Englishman, well known to the inhabitants of Seville for his taste for the fine arts, to his own countrymen as the author of several literary works, and to Europe as the donor to the Louvre of the paintings which fill the gallery bearing his name. Though not as comfortable in our domestic arrangements as we were with Doña Antonia at Cadiz, we have no cause to complain. Our rooms are excellent. Though not very spacious, they are airy, and front upon the street, which is constantly thronged with Andalusians, making the day brilliant with their picturesque costumes, and the night vocal with their national songs and guitar accompaniments. When we tire of the confinement within doors, and are not engaged in lionizing, we descend to the open corridor below, and listen to the birds, who find their way to the trees in the court, or to the fountain which is perpetually gurgling with the waters of the Carmona aqueduct, built by the Romans more than two thousand years ago. On these occasions we are never alone. Our landlady, who is young and beautiful, is always with us. The corridor is her throne. She sits there from morning to night, near the only entrance to the house, seeing all that comes in and goes out, and giving her orders to the servants with as much judgment, they say, as though every part of the household was constantly under her own inspection. The only bodily exertion she makes is to walk up at night to the top of the first flight of broad and palace-like steps, where her bedroom is situated. Nothing can dislodge her by day. If it is hot, she lets down a thick screen of matting in front of her to keep out the sun. If it is cold, she sends for a shawl, and a *brassero* of charcoal, gathers the former around her breast and shoulders, and putting her feet on the latter, the glowing embers send up currents of hot air and envelop her in congenial warmth. And thus she sits, week after week, in luxurious inertness and ease, laying in a goodly stock of corpulency for her old age, and if our friendly wishes and prayers avail, of health and comfort also.

The most interesting object in Seville is the Cathedral—interesting for its magnitude, its antiquity, its strangely mixed architecture, its paintings, and the gloomy grandeur which reigns within it. On its eastern side stands the Giralda, formerly a Moorish tower. It was built by Geber, or Heber, a Moorish architect, in the year 1000. It terminated at the height of 250 feet, and was surmounted by four immense gilt globes, piled one upon the other. In 1248 Seville was taken from the Moors by San Fernando, and in 1401 the construction of the Cathedral was commenced, partly upon the site of the ancient mosque, portions of which were demolished, and portions incorporated with the present edifice. The Cathedral, as originally planned, was finished in 1507. Fifty-three years afterwards, Fernan Ruiz commenced, and in 1568 completed, the elevation of the tower to the height of 350 feet, adding one hundred feet to the work of Geber. It is square, each side of fifty feet in width, and in the interior an inclined plane carries you, without the slightest fatigue, to the height of 250 feet. Here hang twenty-four bells, eighteen of them with wheels to be rung by ropes from below, and the other six so large that they are fixed, and are rung by striking. A hundred feet higher up stands the Giralda, from which the tower has borrowed its name—a figure in bronze representing Faith, fourteen feet high, and weighing nearly a ton and a half. For the first eighty feet from the ground the tower presents a plain wall, on which there are a few frescoes, painted by Luis de Vargas, and now nearly obliterated. The surface for the next hundred and seventy feet, extending to the belfry, is broken by a variety of ornamental work in arabesque, comprising a number of balconies and some hundred and fifty columns. The hundred feet added by Ruiz is divided into three portions, diminishing in size, the first of Doric architecture, and the second and third of Ionic. In workmanship, the Giralda is a singular medley; but it is striking, if not beautiful. From the belfry there is a noble view. The city lies beneath your feet, with its hundred chapels and parish churches; its ancient wall, built by Julius Cæsar, and seeming so solid that it may live through another space of two thousand years, to be inspected and admired by races as different from us as we are from those by whom its foundations were laid. Looking beyond the city, a fine expanse of country meets the eye on all sides, studded with farmhouses and villages, and shut in by hills, or slight elevations, hardly deserving the name. On this side a long line of wall runs from one of the city gates into the interior, now built up solid, now with opening arches, and becoming more indistinct as it approaches the heights of Carmona some fifteen miles off. This is the Roman aqueduct, as old, at least, as the city wall, and built, perhaps, under the same distinguished auspices. It was partially rebuilt during the reign of Ferdinand and Isabella; but portions of it still serve its original purpose, and the solid cement in which they are laid seems as hard as the tiles which it binds together. It terminates at the Carmona gate, where there is a reservoir, from which a large number of conduits distribute the water through the city. On the opposite side, in the distance, there is the convent and church of Santa Ponce, and hard by a small village. Here lie the ruins of the ancient Italica, a city once far outvying Seville in its splendor and the number of its inhabitants. Here lived Silius, the poet, surnamed Italicus, from his birth-place. Here were born Adrian, Trajan, and Theodosius, among the bravest and most virtuous of the Roman emperors. When

Scipio Africanus had expelled the Carthaginians from Spain, he founded this ancient city, peopling it with his sick and wounded soldiers. From this beginning it became one of the most beautiful towns within the dominions of Rome. While the walls of Seville, the Carmona aqueduct, and numerous other monuments of Roman power and art remain, Italica is nearly obliterated. So total an annihilation of a city of such magnitude, while other works, but a few hundred years more recent, are in such a state of preservation, can hardly be accounted for but upon the hypothesis of some powerful convulsion of nature, burying or destroying in a moment what the slow attrition of time would not have worn away in thousands of years. But it is not wholly effaced. A few feeble attempts at excavation have been made, just sufficient to show that there is enough here to repay any labor that may be expended on it. The walls of private dwellings, and the ornamental work of one or two public edifices have been partially laid bare—among them one which is supposed to have been the palace of Trajan. A broken capital of a column of the purest Corinthian, fragments of statues, and the remains of baths have been thrown out; the foundation of an ancient colonnade has been exposed; Roman coins are frequently dug up by the country people, and in two or three places pavements in mosaic have been uncovered. About half a mile from these ruins is the ancient amphitheatre, the arena for the conflicts of wild beasts and savage men. It is in tolerable preservation. The rows of seats remain, and some of the cells adjoining the arena are nearly entire. It is singular that of ancient Italica this should be the best-defined vestige. Her temples, her architectural decorations, her works of art, have all perished. She lives only in this single monument of her barbarism! As if in mockery of the splendor of the ancient city, a miserable village has grown up where it stood. The materials thrown out by the excavations have been rudely put together, and a few streets of wretched dwellings formed—the abodes of squalidness and poverty.

The objects in and about the Cathedral are not less attractive than those which are seen from the Giralda. On the northern face is an immense court, shut out from the street on two sides by walls which were once a part of the ancient mosque. It is filled with orange trees, and is always fresh and verdant. Another side is formed by the Sagrario, a church connected with the Cathedral, and built a century after it. If it stood alone, it would be considered an immense edifice. It is one hundred and ninety-one feet in length, sixty-four in width, and eighty-three in height, with five lateral chapels on each side of the single nave which forms the body of the church. Its main entrance is from the Cathedral, of which it is an integral part, by a passage supported by Corinthian columns. Both without and within the architecture is Grecian; but it was erected at a time when the taste for meretricious ornament began to prevail, and it abounds in workmanship of the worst taste. The southern face of the Cathedral has an immense unfinished addition of Grecian architecture —one which it is to be hoped may remain unfinished, for it would only serve to hide the noble Gothic of which the original structure is composed.

But it is the interior which is most grand and striking. As you enter it from the eastern door adjoining the Giralda, the effect is inexpressibly fine and imposing. It is dark, but not so much so as to conceal any of its parts. Sixty columns, each forty-three feet in circumference, sustain the vaulted roof. Those which support the cross-vault are one hundred and thirty-four feet in height, and the others ninety-six. By the side of these enormous pillars, the groups of worshippers, who almost always fill the church, seem like insects swarming upon the marble pavement. Dark as the Cathedral appears, its walls are pierced by ninety-three windows of painted glass, through which the rays of light come streaming with the richest colors. Churches more brilliant and highly ornamented in their interior may be found elsewhere, but none which are better fitted to produce powerful impressions upon the mind and the senses. Its vast extent, its majestic Gothic architecture, its perpetual twilight, when all around is brilliant day, never fail to fill the heart with solemnity and awe. Visit it as often as you will, the same feelings rise up, vivid and fresh as when it is first seen. Singular as it may seem, all attempts to add to its effect by artificial means signally fail. During the ceremonies of the Holy Week it was highly ornamented; an immense monument of Grecian architecture, one hundred and twenty feet in height, and constructed nearly two centuries ago, was raised at the foot of the central nave, and on Good Friday the rending of the veil of the temple was represented, accompanied with a discharge of firearms. But instead of rendering the Cathedral more imposing, they did but impair its effect, by sacrificing its simple grandeur to gaudy decorations, and by representations savoring much more strongly of the theatre than of the sacred temple.

In most of the thirty-eight chapels which surround the body of the church, there are to be found objects of interest. Some of the paintings are of the highest order of merit. The St. Antonio of Murillo is one of his most remarkable works, both for beauty of conception and exquisite coloring. Zurbaran, the cotemporary of Murillo, and his equal in the delineation of single figures, though greatly his inferior in grouping, has also contributed some fine pictures. There are paintings by Valdez, another cotemporary of Murillo, by Alonzo Cano, Luis de Vargas, Pedro de Campana, his predecessors, Tobar, his pupil, and many other distinguished artists of the fifteenth, sixteenth, and seventeenth centuries. The sacristy, with its sumptuous altars, its workmanship in gold and silver, and its precious stones —the choir, with its beautiful wood-work, and its two magnificent organs, which, on feast-days, fill the whole body of the church with the finest music—the Hall of the Chapter, with its pictures, its architectural decorations, and its marble pavements, are all worthy of the noble edifice to which they are appendages, and contribute to render it, what it is conceded to be, one of the finest structures in Europe.

The Alcazar, the ancient palace of the Moorish kings, though not the only specimen of the Arabic remaining in Seville, is the most sumptuous, and the one which, in some of its parts, has undergone the least alteration. Its origin is lost in remote antiquity, though it is said to have been built in the twelfth century, some seventy years before the surrender of Seville to King Ferdinand. In the fourteenth century Peter the Cruel repaired and enlarged it, and made it his residence, and various additions and alterations were subsequently made by other sovereigns. It is now neglected, and in some of its parts almost ruinous, but workmen are busy in repairing and in restoring what time or barbarism has effaced. In 1813 the city of Seville was guilty of the atrocity of whitewashing with lime the Ambassador's Hall, and some of the other principal apartments. Since 1833 great efforts have been made to repair the injury. The gilding is replaced without difficulty; but the brilliant colors with which these exquisite arabesques were overspread, come out cold and faint, and it is not probable that they can ever be fully restored. Fortunately the workmanship remains—the rich mosaics, the elaborate carvings, the infinite complexity of the architectural decorations—all proving how far advanced the Arabs were in skill, ingenuity, and even in taste, for some of the apartments are equally chaste and beautiful in design. The Ambassador's Hall is said to be precisely like that of the Alhambra. It is a square, thirty-five feet in width, and sixty-five in height. About thirty feet above the marble floor there is a large balcony on each side, constructed for the purpose of witnessing the entertainments given within it. Of what varied scenes has this hall been the theatre! Here the polished Moslem held his court—here centred most of the learning, the science, and the arts which had survived the decay of letters, and here the embassies of barbarian Europe were received. If in the hands of its original owners it was the scene of cruelty and bloodshed, history has not recorded it. But the annals of its Christian masters are full of the blackest stains. The blood of one of the brothers of Peter the Cruel, slain in his presence and by his command, still discolors the marble pavement below, and the place is pointed out in one of the balconies above where the tyrant stood and directed the fatal blow. In another part of the palace is his bedchamber. It opens upon an extensive garden, filled with the most luxuriant vegetation, with fountains, orange groves, temples, and statuary, and ornamented throughout with Oriental magnificence. But the nature of the tyrant was untamed by all this display of beauty. From this chamber—from the nuptial bed, which stood in a gilded recess—Blanche of Bourbon was spurned, after a single night, and consigned to the imprisonment in which her wretched life was afterwards murderously terminated by the order of her savage master.

The Alcazar is one of the most splendid regal residences in Spain. The gardens are said to be greatly superior to those of the Alhambra, but the edifice is not so magnificent or so vast, nor are its arabesques so well preserved, though persons who have seen both say there is no single apartment in the latter superior in its workmanship and its ornaments to the Ambassador's Hall in the Alcazar.

Among the other public edifices for which Seville is distinguished is the Exchange. In the sixteenth century it was the custom for merchants and shopkeepers, and their agents, to meet daily at the Cathedral to make their bargains and contracts, and to discuss the temporal topics of the day. A worthy bishop, grieved at this desecration of the sacred temple, undertook, though in a less summary method than his divine Master, to drive the money-changers out. He applied to King Philip the Second, representing to him that the Cathedral was converted into a *quasi* exchange, and that he had exerted all his spiritual authority to no purpose to correct the evil, and he concluded by suggesting the construction of a suitable building for the use of the merchants of the kingdom, and for the vast commerce which was then beginning to centre at Seville. On this pious interposition the present Exchange was founded. It stands directly south of the Cathedral, and is only separated from it by a narrow street. It forms a perfect square, each side 200 feet in extent, and two stories in height. It is of Grecian architecture, and perhaps the most faultless structure in Seville. The whole of the second story is occupied by the archives of the Indies, in which are contained and arranged in the neatest and most orderly manner the papers and documents relating to the Spanish possessions in America, from the discovery to the present time. What a fund of interesting information may not these original manuscripts contain, comprising, as they do, the reports of the governors and public agents to the home government, and destined to shed light, if any one shall be found willing to devote a life to them, upon transactions misunderstood or buried in total oblivion! As we walked around the immense hall in which they are deposited, forming three entire sides of the Exchange, and were making some passing remark in relation to them, the old Spaniard who accompanied us said, with a deep-drawn sigh, "This shows what we were once; but now nothing remains to us of America but these papers!" The old man's exclamation carried centuries of history along with it. It is just three centuries and a half since the new world was discovered under the auspices of Spain, at the very moment when she had expelled the Moors from their last stronghold in Granada, and when the elements of her own social order were to be recombined. Under the influence of the vast commerce which it opened, and by means of the treasures which it poured into her bosom, how rapidly did her wealth and power increase! Her fall has been even more rapid. Less than three centuries ago she put afloat the most powerful naval force that the ocean ever bore. Fifty years ago she built twelve ships of the line at the same moment in one of her magnificent dockyards. Her whole domestic naval armament is now reduced to two frigates; she is overwhelmed with debt, her industry is paralyzed, her social organization disturbed, and all the fountains of her prosperity poisoned by the intrigues of selfish men and the action of bad laws. There would have been as much philosophy and more reason in the old Sevillian's lamentation, if it had been made over the internal condition of his country, and not over the abridgment of her dominion in other quarters of the globe.

The House of Pilate, or the palace of the noble family of Medina-Celi i Alcala, has been the source of much more interest and speculation than other objects far more worthy of attention. It is said to have been constructed upon the plan of the house in which Pontius Pilate lived at Jerusalem, and the Sevillian guides pretend to point out a balcony corresponding with that on which the Roman governor stood and sentenced to death the Saviour of mankind. But the tradition is founded upon the fact that a former head of the house, on returning from the Holy Land, and completing the construction of the palace, which was left unfinished by his predecessor, erected a cross of jasper, and from thence traced out between two of the palace gates, a passage equal to the distance which the Saviour walked while bearing his cross. On this foundation alone rests the tradition, which is so universally received in Seville that it is not easy to refute it by the test of contradictory historical facts. But those who visit the palace in pursuit of an imaginary resemblance, will find it in other respects not unworthy of notice. The edifice is striking, in some of its parts magnificent, and is richly ornamented with statuary and arabesques, and with some fine specimens of Gothic architecture.

Seville abounds with edifices of no ordinary beauty. The archbishop's palace east of the Cathedral; the manufactory of tobacco, a royal monopoly, with its mills, its stores, and its immense halls, containing twenty-five hundred women and girls, making cigars and cigarillas; and the Ayuntamiento, or town hall, in the Plaza de la Constitucion, both for their external architecture and their interior arrangements, well deserve to be seen. The latter is, perhaps, the most remarkable as a specimen of a style of architecture which was characteristic of a short period in the history of Spain. A few centuries ago the Gothic was the dominant style. At the beginning of the sixteenth century, some successful attempts were made with the Greco-Romano; but they were succeeded by a fancy for loading not only bases, capitals, and friezes, but columns themselves with ornament. Workers in gold and silver adopted this style almost universally for altars and the interior parts of the churches, and it was for this reason denominated the *plataresco*, a term formed from *plataro*, a silversmith. In the parish churches of St. Stephen and El Salvador, the latter an ancient mosque, there are some curious specimens of this false taste. But the town-hall is the most extraordinary production of the plataresque architects extant. It is overladen, internally and externally, with the most elaborate workmanship. Columns, pedestals, capitals, and friezes covered with figures and ornaments, in which the imagination has literally run wild; surfaces of doors carved into the most fantastic shapes, and not unfrequently of exquisite beauty, both in outline and detail; in short, a profusion of the richest and most exuberant ornament is the characteristic of this singular edifice throughout. Notwithstanding its departure from all the rules of art and the suggestions of good taste, it is a beautiful structure, and as a specimen of a short-lived and vicious style of architecture, it is more valuable than some others far less exceptionable in design.

CHAPTER XV.

CITY OF SEVILLE

Holy Week in Seville.—The Procession on Good Friday.—Easter Sunday.—The Bull-Fight.—Collection of Paintings.—The Museum.—The Caridad.—Rides, Drives, and Walks.—Private Dwellings.

Holy Week in Seville was once said to be next to Holy Week in Rome. It may be so still; but the ceremonies have lost much of the splendor of former years. The clergy in Spain have been stripped of a large portion of their wealth. The churches are poor, and large numbers of the priesthood are in absolute want. We were repeatedly stopped in the Cathedral and solicited, in God's name, to give a trifle to a "pobre sacerdote"—a poor priest. Some of these holy mendicants were in good case, fat, sleek, and shining, as they were said to be in the prosperous day of the Church; but others gave every indication in their persons and dress of needing the charity they asked. As Holy Week approaches, the city becomes filled with visiters—from the towns in the interior, from Cadiz and Gibraltar, with now and then a few stragglers, like ourselves, from the new world. We arrived a few days before the ceremonies commenced, and, that we might lose nothing, we hired a balcony in one of the principal streets, through which the processions were to pass. They continued, with one or two intervals of twenty-four hours, from Palm Sunday to Easter; and they were all much of the same character—a procession of mutes in black and white masks, priests, soldiers, and bands of music, with cars of images representing the Saviour, the Virgin Mary, and the apostles.

The procession on Good Friday was, however, accompanied with much more pomp and circumstance than the others. It was designed to represent the interment of the Saviour, and was got up with more care and expense than had been customary for years. Long before the hour appointed for the movement of the procession, the narrow "Calle de las Sierpes," the principal street in Seville, was thronged with pedestrians—men, women, and children of all orders and ages—peasants from the country in the national costume, beggars in rags, city dames in flaunting robes of silk and satin, with here and there a representative of the fast-anchored isle elbowing his way through the crowd, regardless of the "carrajos" (a word of unspeakable signification) with which he was frequently greeted, and looking on with an air which spoke as plainly as any thing short of language could, that in his opinion it was all humbug. Our balcony was elevated but a few feet above the pavement, and as the two conflicting currents poured in from opposite directions, we could see every movement and every expression in the huge living mass beneath us. In the midst of the confusion the bells of the hundred churches began to ring, making the whole atmosphere vibrate, and overpowering all other sounds. At this signal the procession moved. On it came, with a troupe of equestrians, armed and clad as Roman cavalry, at its head. We could see their white plumes at the distance of a quarter of a mile floating above the heads of the multitude—in a little while their helmets, breastplates, and lances glittering in the sunbems, and then their white horses, buried beneath the richest caparisons. If we judged rightly, on the close inspection which the narrowness of the street enabled us to make, the armor of these modern Romans was forged by no Vulcan's hand. The art of the tinman "stood confessed," not only in their shining breastplates, but in the very points of the long and not very robust lances which they poised with their right hands. But if they were not formidable, they were certainly very showy horsemen, though we apprehend it would not have been an easy matter for Cæsar, or Sertorius, or either of the two Scipios to mistake them for the soldiers by which the plains of ancient Hispania were disputed. But they served the purpose of the pageant as well as better soldiers would have done; and for the crowd, which it was their business to open and disperse in order to make room for the great body of the procession, they were certainly much safer; for if they had been provoked, by the resistance of the multitude, to commit any act of violence, they could not, with the weapons they carried, have succeeded, by any effort, in inflicting a mortal wound. Happily they were not mortified by having their prowess put to the test. The pedestrians, as they advanced, disappeared, as if by magic, in the cross streets, and a number of dignitaries, some of whom were connected with the church and others with the government, followed them, clad in purple velvet and gold, with a train of attendants at their heels. A miniature mountain came next, carried by some twenty men, and representing Mount Calvary, with a cross on its summit, and at the foot of the cross a human skeleton, figurative of Death, standing on a globe, resting his fleshless cheek in despondency upon his right hand, and holding in his left his useless scythe, with a Latin inscription in silver letters below, purporting "that the Cross has triumphed over Death." Around the globe a serpent was coiled, with an apple in his mouth, emblematical of the error of our first parents, and the sorrows which it has brought down on their posterity. This part of the procession was succeeded by a choir of angels, personated by boys gorgeously attired, and not very well personated either, for, saying nothing of Raphael, and Gabriel, and Uriel, the Angel of the Guard was, to all appearance, as little qualified for any high and responsible office, temporal or spiritual, as he could well be. In a word, nothing could be more repugnant to all good sense and good taste than this portion of the exhibition;

and it was not at all improved by the appearance of twelve girls, representing the sybils, clad in the same costly manner as the angels whom they were following, and giving about as imperfect a conception of their archetypes. Then came four of the most distinguished of the saints—Augustin in the costume of his order, Geronimus in a bishop's dress, Ambrosius also attired as a bishop, and Gregory the Great in his pontifical robes. A choir of musicians with an immense concourse of priests followed, and then came the principal pageant—the sepulchral sarcophagus containing a representation of the body of our Saviour, oblong in form, encased in crystal, resting upon a pall of black velvet, and ornamented in the most sumptuous manner. It was certainly a magnificent spectacle, such a one as might well befit an earthly potentate, but greatly at variance, both in history and morals, with the simple life and humble character of the divine Master. The hearse, or rather the bier, which was borne by ecclesiastics in surplices and black stoles, was followed by a fine band of music, and by a corps of Roman foot soldiers, as gaudy in their dress and equipment as the horsemen who led the van, and, to all appearance, about a fair match for them in the field. Next appeared a triumphal car, with the Virgin, the two other Marys, Joseph, and Nicodemus standing upon it, in theatrical postures, and in still more theatrical dresses—dresses much more appropriate for one of the Marys before her repentance than for the Holy Mother. The clergy of the parish churches, the corporation of the city, and the whole military force of Seville, amounting to several thousand men, closed the procession—on the whole, an imposing exhibition, but deformed by puerilities and violations of good taste, and in many respects at war with the spirit and moral elevation of the times. Still the ceremonies seemed to be performed in a spirit of sincere devotion, and not for purposes of ostentatious display; and we could not but honor the design, whatever fault we were disposed to find with the execution.

The part taken by the Church in celebrating the anniversary was concluded on Easter Sunday at noon, the day having been ushered in by several processions between midnight and sunrise, and the grand mass at the Cathedral having been performed with unusual splendor. But so far as the public was concerned, the celebration did not end here. The afternoon was set apart for the national amusement—the bull-fight. It was the first during the present season, and the most celebrated matadors in Andalusia were announced, for weeks before, as having been engaged to take part in it. As our departure was to take place a few days after, we were unwilling to lose the opportunity of witnessing an exhibition of which so much had been said—so much, by most writers at least, in praise of the skill and dexterity of the persons engaged in it, and the interest excited by the dangers of the arena. Accordingly, at four o'clock, we repaired to the amphitheatre, just outside of the city walls. It forms an immense circle, three or four hundred feet in diameter. There are about a dozen rows of seats, rising one above the other, and affording a perfect view of every part of the arena to all the spectators. About half the seats are of stone, with a permanent canopy or roof of wood over them. The others are of wood, resting upon strong framework, and without any covering. When we entered and took our seats, about half the places were occupied. A crowd of men, women, and children were pouring in through the various entrances, and by the hour appointed the amphitheatre presented one unbroken mass of human heads. Not a vacant seat was any where to be seen. It is said there are places for twenty thousand persons. As well as we could judge, there were about twelve thousand present when the spectacle commenced, and it would not have been an easy matter to add, by any process of condensation, over three thousand more to the number. The arena, when we entered the amphitheatre, and for nearly an hour afterwards, was filled with spectators, belonging, as their dress denoted, to the peasantry from the interior and the laboring classes from the city. As the appointed hour approached, a file of alguazils on foot, armed with muskets, passed across the arena, driving the crowd before them into the lobby, or the vacant space between the arena and the seats, through the narrow passes formed for the escape of the picadors and chulos in case of danger. The arena was now clear; but as the alguazils passed through the outlets by which the crowd had been discharged, five mounted picadors, and about the same number of chulos on foot, entered through the principal gate, thrown open to give them admission. They were in the most gaudy and expensive dresses. We had a few days before seen one of these dresses at a tailor's shop, and were assured that the cost was two hundred and fifty dollars—an assurance which we could readily credit while we examined the splendid embroidery in silk and gold with which it was literally covered. After some brief ceremonies of presentation to the city authorities, who were present, they took their stations, the chulos drawn up in a line on the right of the passage through which the bull was to enter, and the picadors on the left. The latter are the only antagonists of the devoted animal until the final stage of the combat. The chulos carry each a scarf of some brilliant color, and their only business is to attract the attention of the bull and draw him off when any of the picadors are in danger. The picador, on the other hand, is armed with a long, stout spear, in the end of which a sharp-pointed spike is inserted. The wooden end of the spear is left purposely blunt, with only about an inch of the spike projecting, so that it may wound and irritate, without entering deeply into the flesh. In order to defend the picador against the horns of the bull, his legs and thighs are encased in thick plates of cork. If the bull strikes them, however violent the blow may be, it is warded harmlessly off by the elastic wood. If the picador is thrown, it is also nearly a perfect protection. The instances are exceedingly rare in which a leg is fractured, although at every spectacle picadors and horses are frequently overturned together. With these defences, the picador is, in truth, in very little danger. But while every care is taken of the life of the picador, not the least regard is paid to the defence of the horses. They are intended to be gored and slain. In the sight of a true lover of the arena, the entertainment would lose much of its zest if it were otherwise. They are, without exception, poor, miserable, broken-down animals, purchased for the occasion, at prices varying from five dollars to twenty. Some of them are so lean and feeble that they seem hardly to have strength enough to carry their riders across the arena. The consequence is, that at every vigorous charge of the bull they are overthrown. To ensure their discomfiture, their eyes are bandaged, so that they are entirely at the mercy of the enraged animal. In the bull-fights of the Moors, the finest horses were employed, and the rider's skill was reinforced by the quick eye, the sagacity, and the speed of the animal which bore him. It is now a degenerate spectacle, with all the cruelty of the ancient without a particle of its chivalry.

The preparations being complete, all eyes are turned to the passage through which the bull is to enter. He has been for about twelve hours shut up in total darkness, with heavy weights upon his neck, the loose parts of his skin about the neck gathered up in folds, perforated, and tied with red ribbon. He is inflamed to madness by these tortures, and the moment he is liberated he rushes into the arena with the fury of a wild beast. He comes on so rapidly that he passes by the picadors and chulos drawn up on either side, without noticing them. He advances to the centre of the arena, glaring with his bloodshot eyes upon the circle of spectators who hem him in on every side, and is rendered still more furious by the glare of light which suddenly bursts upon him. He is a noble animal; his limbs are symmetrical and clean, his body light, his neck and shoulders broad and obviously of immense strength, his head beautifully shaped, and his horns long and curved. The picadors now begin to move from their stations, following the sides of the arena, and passing round so as to meet him in front. The moment he discovers his enemy, he dashes at him. He waits for no assault. The picador whom he has singled out has but just time to turn his horse's head a little outward, and to draw him up near one of the passages, when the bull attacks him. On he bounds at full speed, until he is within reach, when he throws his whole strength into a single impulse, and dashes his horns into the horse's flank. He has received the picador's spear in his shoulder, but it has not even checked him. With his horns plunged deep into the horse's side, he raises him and his rider clear of the ground, and pitches them both against the wooden breastwork of the arena. They come together to the earth. The horse regains his feet, horribly lacerated, and the rider is instantly upon his back again. The poor animal's pain lends him strength for a moment, and he flies across the arena, in spite of the efforts of his rider, dragging his entrails upon the ground, and trampling on them with his hind feet. The instant the bull has overturned his antagonist, one of the chulos advances, unfurling a red scarf and flourishing it in his face. The animal rushes at him, and as the latter glides out of the arena through one of the passages, vents his rage upon the boards which separate him from the object of his pursuit. But he expends only a moment upon this idle warfare. He sees another picador drawn up to receive him, and he attacks him with the same fury as he did the first. The picador's arm is a little stronger than the other's, or he wields his spear with more dexterity, and the bull is partially foiled. But he returns to the charge in an instant, tears open the horse's flank by a successful thrust, and hurls him and his rider to the ground. The chulos are again upon him, dashing their long scarfs into his face, and he turns upon them, leaving the ill-fated horse and rider to regain their feet. He is now engaged for some moments in a warfare with the chulos. As he turns upon one, or rather upon the scarf he carries, another assails him on the opposite side, always turning him off from his object, and gradually wasting his strength. But the picadors have only a brief respite. He discovers a third, and he seems glad to exchange the bewildering attacks of the scarf-bearers for a contest with a more tangible enemy. He rushes on with renewed fury, the spear of the picador enters his shoulder, and then falls powerless from the rider's hand. The infuriated animal breaks down all opposition by his prodigious force. The horse and rider share the fate of the two first. The rider is thrown and the horse is shockingly gored. The latter runs into the centre of the arena, and there stands, his bowels torn out, and his whole frame shivering with pain. The bull, who has been turned aside by the chulos, discovers him, dashes at him, takes him up, and actually carries him several paces on his horns, and then lets him fall heavily to the ground. Had we not witnessed this wonderful effort of strength, we should have considered it incredible. The arena now presents a scene as full of brutality as the most ardent lover of the bull-fight could desire. The horse just overturned is at his last gasp on the ground, and the two others are dragging their entrails about the arena. The bull's neck is streaming with blood, his tongue is protruded from his mouth, and he is standing a moment, regardless of the chulos, who are besetting him, collecting his waning strength for another contest with his enemies. A fourth picador approaches him, and he instantly attacks him. But he is obviously weakened by loss of blood, and by the efforts he has already made. His attacks are less vigorous, and he is more than once turned aside by the spear. He succeeds in wounding the horse; but the rent in the horse's flank is a slight one, and the picador leads him out to have it coarsely sewed up, and then brings him back again for another contest. The bull is now nearly exhausted, and the banderilleros come in, with barbed darts covered with fireworks, which they thrust into him, and he is soon enveloped in smoke and flame. This is the last stage of torture. A trumpet sounds, and the matador enters. In his left hand he holds a red flag, and in his right a straight sword. He is dressed even more expensively than the picadors and chulos, in a richly embroidered jacket, with white breeches and silk stockings. It is the celebrated Montez, the most expert bull-killer in Spain, and he is greeted with thundering plaudits by the spectators. He advances towards the bull, who eyes him warily, as if he were aware that a new and more dangerous antagonist had taken the field against him. But the animal hesitates only a moment. Gathering all his strength, he rushes upon the red flag which the matador holds out on his left side, pointing with his right the fatal sword at the bull's neck. The bull staggers and falls. The sword has entered the spine, and the blood pours in streams from his nose and mouth. Thus ends the first scene—a scene loathsome, disgusting, brutal, and barbarous—a scene only fit to gratify assassins and to create them—managed with some dexterity, it is true, but without a particle of chivalric bearing, and under all its aspects, a stain upon the humanity and the civilization of the age. The moment the bull has received his mortal wound, one of the gates is thrown open, and three mules, harnessed abreast and adorned with flaunting ribbons, are driven in to drag him out. Two others follow, drawing out the dead horse and the half-living one, who has not strength to stand. But this is only the first scene in the Easter Sunday's entertainment—a day commemorative of Him whose divine morality was all founded in gentleness and mercy—a day desecrated by the grossest violation of His doctrines, and the great lesson of His character and life. Seven other bulls are successively brought in to undergo the same tortures, and to encounter the same fate. Before they are all killed, eleven horses are dragged out, dead or dying, from the arena. The matadors, the picadors, the banderilleros, and the chulos all escape uninjured, or, at the most, with some slight sprains. Though there was, perhaps, less applause, and less apparent gratification among the great body of the spectators than we had expected, it is not to be disguised that it is a favorite amusement. About one third were females. Of these, one was an Englishwoman whom we had met in our travels, the only lady of Anglo-Saxon origin present; but before the first bull was killed, she left the ampitheatre, filled with horror and disgust. Of the tendency of these brutal spectacles to blunt the sensibilities, and to prepare the mind to dwell with indifference upon scenes of bloodshed and cruelty, there can be no rational doubt. We believe it to be neither a harsh nor an erroneous judgment to say, that no people with whom the bull-fight is a national amusement, can ever attain a high rank in the scale of civilization. They may have their peculiar virtues; but humanity towards their fellows, or towards the brutes which Providence has placed in their hands, to be governed and used in kindness and in mercy, will not be one. The cruelty with which the civil wars of Spain have been waged of late years—the hands cut off, the eyes put out, the horrible maimings, in modes too wanton and loathsome to be named—are all the legitimate offspring of the lessons of barbarity taught in the arena. Where the matador is a hero and a favorite, and is, as it were, incorporated into the social mass by the force of opinion, the assassin and the bandit may claim, with some color of title, a place there also. At all events, they will not be wanting. There is equal truth and philosophy in the closing stanza of Byron's description of the bull-fight:

> "Such the ungentle sport that oft invites
> The Spanish maid, and cheers the Spanish swain.
> Nurtured in blood betimes, his heart delights
> In vengeance, gloating on another's pain.
> What private feuds the troubled village stain!
> Though now one phalanxed host should meet the foe,
> Enough, alas! in humble homes remain,
> To meditate 'gainst friends the secret blow,
> For some slight cause of wrath, whence life's warm stream must flow."
>
> CHILDE HAROLD, Canto I. 80.

To the lover of the fine arts Seville affords a rich field for enjoyment. It is now the repository, as it was formerly the seat, of the Spanish school in painting. The great works of art which were produced here, are here preserved. Many of the principal collections are in the museum, formerly the Convent de la Merced. The church contains about two hundred pictures, many of them very large, and almost all of great merit. Some of them, indeed, are inimitable. The most remarkable picture in this part of the museum is the St. Thomas of Zurbaran. In boldness of design, powerful effect, and exquisite finish it may justly rank among the highest efforts of genius. There is a magnificent Conception of Murillo immediately over it, and on each side two other pictures of great beauty by the same master; but it suffers nothing by the comparison. In grouping, Zurbaran was exceedingly deficient; but in single figures he is almost unrivalled for power and effect. In looking round upon different parts of the church, his saints are seen standing out from the canvass in bold relief, and with an air of life which few other pictures in the collection possess. There are a number of fine pictures by Alonzo Cano, Juan de Castillo, the two Herreras, Roelas, Varela, Valdez, and many other masters of the Seville school. In a higher part of the museum there is a single hall devoted exclusively to Murillo. It contains eighteen pictures, all bearing the impress of his hand, and some among the most meritorious of his works. Though they are all the production of a single master, it is questionable whether any hall of the same magnitude can be found, in any quarter of the globe, which contains more beauty.

But the most masterly picture of Murillo is in the Church of the Caridad. It represents Moses smiting the rock, and is full of beauty and power. The grouping, the drawing, the coloring, and the execution are equally excellent. This picture alone is sufficient to place the author in the highest rank of historical painters; and though totally different in character, it has all the beauty which distinguishes his Madonnas. The figures of Moses and Aaron in the centre; the crowd pressing to the water, which gushes cool and sparkling from the rock; the animals satiating or trying to satiate their thirst; the children struggling for the first draught from a cup held by their mother; the horse, which is just reaching the newly created fountain, and the beautiful boy, whom he carries on his back, extending his hands as if imploring some one to take him off, are all admirable. A universal expression of eagerness is spread over the whole canvass, alike pervading man and brute. Such it seemed to us; and it is, perhaps, from the same impression on others, that it is called by the Spaniards "la Sed de Murillo"—the Thirst of Murillo. If the water, and the historical circumstances which identify it, were wanting, we are quite sure the observer would instantly be struck with the idea which the painter designed to embody—that the persons delineated are suffering with thirst. There are five other paintings by Murillo in the same church—one of the same size, representing the miracle of the loaves and fishes, inferior to the one described, but still of great merit. Two smaller ones—an Annunciation and the St. John of God—are of exceeding beauty. Each one has an angel, exquisitely drawn and exquisitely colored—in short, such angels as no other man but Murillo has painted—full of earthly beauty and celestial grace.

In contrast with these beautiful pictures are two of great power by Valdez. One represents Death standing over the ruins of the earth. The other is, in all respects, an extraordinary production. It represents an archbishop, and the Knight of Alcantara (the founder of the Caridad), lying in their coffins, in appropriate costumes. The bodies are partially decayed, and in a state of putrefaction. The worms have commenced their work, and are crawling about, penetrating the cheeks and the sockets of the eyes, and making the dead mass animate with their motion. It is a horrible picture, but painted with wonderful truth and power. Murillo is reported to have said, that no man could look at it five minutes steadily without holding his nose.

Besides the paintings in the Cathedral and the two collections just referred to, there is scarcely a parish church which does not contain some works of merit. He who visits Seville without exploring the parish churches, will leave behind him much beauty unseen. In the Church of St. Ildefonso there is a noble painting of the martyrdom of the patron saint, by Roellas. In the Church of St. Isidoro there are two uncommonly sweet pictures by Tobar, the favorite pupil of Murillo, one of St. John, and the other of the Saviour, as youths. Here, too, is a magnificent altar-piece, by Roellas, representing the death of the patron saint, surrounded by old men admirably painted, with the Saviour and the Virgin attended by choirs of angels. The colors seem to have faded. At all events, they are greatly inferior in brilliancy to three other fine pictures by the same artist in the chapel of the University, which contains also some magnificent monuments. It is somewhat singular that we could not find in all Seville a single picture by Velasquez, or, at least, a single one which was indisputably his. And yet he was a native of the city. He who would even see Velasquez, must go to Madrid. What a reflection upon the city that gave him birth! Though he lived many years in Italy, this circumstance will hardly account for the total disappearance of his works here. Murillo lived and died in Spain. He was never out of it. Indeed, his life was passed almost exclusively in Seville, and here are to be found, as they should be, the principal treasures of his genius. To understand him thoroughly, he must be studied in his native city.

The rides and drives around Seville are full of interest. In whatever direction you turn, the roads are excellent, and they lead you through districts of country abounding in fertility and luxuriance. Almost every spot, too, is full of historical association, and has some remnant of the labors of the different races which, in ages far apart, have held dominion over it. The Roman arch, the Gothic tower, and the Moorish tracery-work are perpetually presenting themselves, often where they are least expected, and recalling to mind the ancient lords of the soil. Its present masters are scarcely less interesting than the vestiges of their predecessors. If the term may be applied to the human family, they may be emphatically denominated a picturesque people, not only in costume, but in their rural inprovements, their domestic economy, and their habits of life. The voluminous cloak, with its immense folds gathered up and thrown over one shoulder; the slashed jacket covered with embroidery; the wide-brimmed hat with its peaked crown; the fiery Andalusian horse and his equally fiery rider; the trains of loaded mules upon the highways; the ungraceful dwelling embosomed in the shade of olive trees and vines, with the indispensable noria hard by, turning its great wheel laden with buckets, and bringing up water to irrigate the surrounding levels; the shepherd in his goat-skin suit standing in the midst of his flocks; the laborers stealing into the orange groves, when the sun is high, to thrum the guitar or enjoy a cool siesta; these, and a thousand other kindred objects, give a peculiar character to the scenery of Andalusia, and people it with forms and visions of romance.

The immediate environs of Seville, upon the river

and directly below the city, are full of beauty. Passing out of the gate near the amphitheatre, and turning to the left, you enter a broad walk with three or four rows of shade trees, the river on one side and the walls of the city on the other. You soon reach "la Torre del Oro," the Tower of Gold, a high octagonal edifice of hewn stone, built by the Romans for the protection of the river and the shipping. It was formerly connected with the city wall and the Alcazar, and in the time of Peter the Cruel, he used it as a prison in furtherance of his objects of vengeance and of lust. Immediately after passing the tower, you cross a small creek by a bridge, and enter the beautiful grounds, several acres in extent, between it and the College of St. Elmo, full of trees, and shrubbery, and flowers, with seats for the accommodation of visiters. They are always open to the public, and even at this season, the first of April, when there is no heat to render the city uncomfortable, they are filled with men, women, and children, breathing the pure air, and enjoying its quiet shaded walks. Between these grounds and the river there is a broad avenue with a carriage-way in the centre, and footpaths for pedestrians on each side, separated by rows of shade trees, and extending from the little bridge near la Torre del Oro, three quarters of a mile below the city, directly upon the banks of the river. A more delicious promenade can not be fancied. The Sevillians are not insensible to its beauty. Every evening it is overflowing with them—ladies and gentlemen in their best dresses filling the walks, with long lines of carriages and parties of equestrians moving up and down the broad carriage-way. These, with the boats and vessels constantly in motion upon the river, give an air of brilliancy and animation to the scene which few others possess. Groves of huge forest trees extend far above the amphitheatre in an opposite direction. But they are not a fashionable resort. They are crossed by a thoroughfare from the city to the town of Triana, on the opposite side of the river, by the floating bridge, which from time immemorial has been the connecting link between them, consisting of a most uneven and unworkmanlike platform laid across the bare backs of ten vessels, of all heights and sizes, anchored in the stream with stout iron cables. Higher up, too, the novices belonging to the military bands are every afternoon assembled, the little drummers making horrible attempts at "daddy mammy," and the beginners upon the trumpet and the clarionet cracking their cheeks and the atmosphere at the same time with most diabolical sounds, and causing every man, woman, and child, of any pretension to nerves, to hurry as fast as possible out of sight and hearing. There is a curious gate in this direction, manifestly Roman, and the wall adjoining it is of most singular construction, as well as a broad shelving pavement of flat stone, running down into the water as far as the eye can reach, and having some connection, probably, with the vast commerce of which Seville was the centre a hundred and fifty years ago.

In short, wherever you turn there is something to interest you—something belonging to the past or the present to fix the attention or chain the sight. Yet Seville is by no means a beautiful city. Strip it of its public edifices, its groves, and its works of art, and it would lose almost all its attraction. The streets are very narrow, and the houses are generally antiquated and ungraceful. Yet it contains many private dwellings of great beauty—some, indeed, which are splendid in their exterior, as well as in their interior arrangement and finish. They are built around a square court, with colonnades below and a fountain in the centre. The whole court is filled with plants and statuary, and an iron gate of open-work, through which the passer-by can look and see all that is going on within, shuts it out from the street. To these courts the family descend in hot weather, covering the whole with a canvass awning, under which they sit during the heat of the day, the clear cool water of the fountain and the odor of the flowers and shrubbery filling the air with perpetual freshness and fragrance.

Were it not for the extremes of temperature to which Seville is said to be subject, no city would possess greater advantages as a place of residence. Good houses are always to be found at very moderate rents, the surrounding country abounds not only in the necessaries of life, but in its luxuries—in fruits, game, and fish. In short, every thing necessary to health, comfort, and amusement are to be found in perfection and abundance. But the summers are said to be hot, and the winters cold. The mountains are too distant to diminish the heat, or to break the currents of cold air, which sweep over the plains with resistless force. Still, the winter is the severe season of a very warm climate. Few houses have fireplaces, and they are not often needed. A pan of charcoal, or of hot embers from the kitchen, put into the largest rooms for an hour or two in the morning, renders them comfortable, or at least tolerable, for the day; and even this defence against the cold can not be necessary excepting for a few days in January and February. A large portion of the inhabitants are wholly without fire. They drink nothing but water and wine, and their meals consist of bread and fruit, with now and then a bowl of soup, a fried fish, or a bit of pork, prepared at a cook-shop. Thus they dispense with the use of fire for cooking, and get rid of a serious annoyance in hot weather and close rooms. The wants of the laboring classes are few, and easily supplied. Though their labor brings them little money, it is well compensated in reference to the little they need to support life. In a warm climate, abounding in grain, oranges, olives, and oil, there can but be little positive suffering for the want of the necessaries of subsistence.

It was with sincere regret that we took leave of Seville. We had passed three weeks there, constantly occupied, instructed, and amused; and as the steamer dashed down the Guadalquivir, leaving a forest of masts between us and the bridge of boats, the enchanting Alameda, with the Tower of Gold at one extremity and a beautiful pavilion half buried in shade at the other, shutting out the plain on one side of the river from view, and the immense body of the Cathedral, with the Giralda far o'ertopping it, rising above walls, and towers, and trees, it was with no ordinary degree of pain that we considered how faint a prospect we had of ever renewing a visit so brief as ours had been, and yet so full of enjoyment.

CHAPTER XVI.

GIBRALTAR.

Departure from Cadiz.—The Straits of Gibraltar, and the immense body of Water passing it from the Atlantic.—The Bay and Rock of Gibraltar.—San Roque.—The Coast of Barbary.—Fortifications.—The City, Population, etc.—The Garrison, and the Excavations.—Siege of 1779, '82.—Expense of maintaining the Post.—Departure for Marseilles.

Our sojourn in Cadiz on our return from Seville was only for a few days. We had seen all it contained, and were impatient to pass on to new scenes. On the last day of April we embarked for Gibraltar, in the British steamer Lady Mary Wood, one of the finest steam-vessels we have ever seen. She was large, an admirable sea-boat, exceedingly neat and clean, and furnished with every imaginable convenience for travellers. Every week a vessel of this description touches at Cadiz, on her way from Southampton to Gibraltar. There are also several French and Spanish steamers running between Cadiz and Marseilles, and touching at all the important points between. In order to pass a few days at Gibraltar, we took one of the British vessels, having previously engaged our passage from that city to Marseilles in a Spanish steamer, which was to leave Cadiz a week afterwards, and take us up on her way. It was ten o'clock in the evening when the Lady Mary Wood weighed anchor. The sky was clear, but without a moon; and the walls of the city, which seemed so white and radiant through the heavy mist in which we were enveloped as we entered the harbor six weeks before, were now only visible as a dark, heavy mass, with its upper outline broken by domes and spires, and faintly illuminated by the lights which were flashing across the water from the battlements. The opposite coast was seen with the same indistinctness. Even the shoals, which were the object of so much apprehension as our little vessel bounded by them in the gale which brought us into port, had disappeared in the darkness; and in an hour nothing was to be seen but the distant light of St. Sebastian, rapidly sinking to the horizon. At daylight we were in the Strait of Gibraltar, running within three miles of the Spanish coast, with the opposite shore of Barbary three times as far off. In two hours we passed the little town of Tarifa, a miserable place with some five thousand inhabitants, not worth possessing for any purpose, but still the scene of frequent conflicts, from the time of the Carthaginians to our own day. By the aid of the current we were now sweeping on with prodigious speed to Gibraltar. We were then in the narrowest part of the Strait, which is scarcely nine miles in width at this point, with a depth varying from one to three thousand feet. There is something singular in this immense volume of water pouring perpetually from the broad Atlantic into the Mediterranean, at the rate of several miles an hour. From time immemorial it has been so. Another current is also pouring in from the Black Sea, and yet the Mediterranean has no outlet. What becomes of the great volume of water with which these two feeders have for century after century supplied it, saying nothing of the rivers which empty into it from the African, Asiatic, and European coasts? Can it be wasted by evaporation? It would seem physically impossible. Is the current through the Strait of Gibraltar merely superficial, and is there an undercurrent of equal or greater volume, restoring to the ocean the surplus the Mediterranean receives? The latter is, perhaps, the best opinion, and it is said to have been confirmed by the fact that a vessel which was sunk in the centre of the Strait, was thrown ashore a few days after twelve miles to the westward, while the current of the surface was setting with great force the other way. The perpetual current eastward is a source of serious annoyance to vessels going into the Atlantic. A westwardly wind for a few days always accumulates a large number in the harbor of Gibraltar, as it is totally impossible to beat through the Strait; and when the wind continues unfavorable for two or three weeks, the detentions amount to hundreds.

It was seven o'clock when we entered the Bay of Gibraltar, and certainly a more remarkable object is not to be found than the Rock, on which the town and the fortifications are built. It seems at a distance to stand in the ocean wholly disconnected from the land; but as you approach it, the low, flat tongue which unites it with the Spanish peninsula becomes visible, though neither in form nor in hue does it appear to have any thing in common with the European continent, to which it is thus loosely joined. Its greatest length is two miles and three quarters, and its greatest breadth three quarters of a mile. One of its sides, that which faces the Mediterranean, is nearly perpendicular in its whole extent. The other side rises in a gradual slope about a quarter of a mile, when it becomes abrupt, and continues so until it meets the eastern face in a sharp ridge elevated nearly fifteen hundred feet above the surface of the sea. The northern end of the Rock is also perpendicular. It looks out upon the Spanish territory, and in it the excavations are formed. The southern end consists of two planes, the upper one of which is about four hundred feet above the sea, and from this level it runs up with an abrupt ascent to a point nearly as high as the most elevated part of the Rock, crowned with a ruined tower, which was built by Gen. O'Hara, and bears his name. The southern extremity of the lowest of these planes is known as Europa Point, and it has usually been considered as the southern point of Europe; but Tarifa is now ascertained to be several miles farther south. The upper plane is known as Windmill Hill, from two stone towers formerly used as mills, but now falling into ruins. Slightly elevated above this level is a range of barracks, occupied, while we were at Gibraltar, by the 79th, a splendid regiment of Highlanders. Near the centre of the rock, and apparently at its summit, stands the telegraph, from which approaching vessels are reported to the town below. This is not, however, the highest point. It lies still farther south. Indeed, the telegraph was formerly on a more elevated station; but in consequence of repeated injuries from lightning it was removed, and being now somewhat lower, it suffers less.

The aspect of the Rock as you enter the bay is singularly beautiful. It is of light grey marble, and when the sun shines brightly upon it, it is one of the most brilliant objects in the world. From the northern to the southern extremity, an unbroken line of fortifications runs along the shore, close down to the water's edge; and nature, as if to aid the art of man in rendering it impregnable, has strewn along this face of the Rock a multitude of shoals, which render unsafe the near approach of large vessels. Above the water-batteries, if they may be so termed, rises the town, presenting at the northern extremity the appearance of a compactly built city, and as you look south, of a well-settled suburb, thickly planted with trees, with groves, gardens, and extensive buildings intermingled, flanked by batteries, and overtopped by the lofty Rock, clad in vines and tropical vegetation. Turning back again to the north, the town is seen surmounted by a huge tower, bearing on its face palpable marks of antiquity. This is the ancient Moorish castle, built in the beginning of the eighth century by the General Tarif Ebn Zarca; and it is said to be the earliest vestige of the occupation of the Rock of which there is any living record. Though more than eleven centuries old, it seems still in good preservation, and we are told that it is used to this day as a place of confinement for criminals. Looking across the sandy neck which separates Gibraltar from the Spanish territory, a chain of not very elevated mountains bounds the sight, some twelve or fifteen miles off, and at one third of the distance a lower range of hills circles around the water, with the Spanish town of San Roque on the summit of one of them, and in front the city of Algesiras, on the other side of the bay, where commercial intercourse with this district of Spain centres. The whole view is pretty, but when you turn from the Rock to the other objects around you, they seem comparatively tame and spiritless. The opposite coast of Barbary, however, has, at the distance of about fifteen miles, a strongly marked and imposing aspect. It is still more elevated than Gibraltar, and it presents a face so closely resembling the Rock, that the latter is supposed to have been torn from it by some convulsion of nature, and cast upon this side of the Strait. This opinion is strengthened in the popular belief by the fact that the caves and fissures near the telegraph are inhabited by monkeys, who are often seen sporting in the sunbeams in warm weather—

the only spot in Europe where they are found as fixed residents. But even upon the hypothesis of such a separation from the opposite coast, it is extremely questionable whether in so rude a shock any of the animal life of the Rock would have been spared. Indeed, the very fissures referred to, a thousand feet above the level of the sea, bear strong evidence of having been, at no very remote geological epoch, beneath the water. On a high point of land fifteen miles south of Gibraltar, on the African side, lie the town and fortification of Ceuta, the Botany Bay of Spain. It is the southeastern termination of the Strait, and farther on the view is bounded by the blue waters of the Mediterranean.

As you enter the Bay of Gibraltar and come near the town, the water, as well as the land, bears testimony to the vast physical force by which the post is defended. Several vessels of the largest size always lie anchored off the town. An immense mole, built of rock and of admirable workmanship, runs far out into the bay, with a battery of guns on each side, and bearing the significant name of the Devil's Tongue. On the north side of this mole is the landing-place; and it is always covered with a motley assemblage of men of different nations: the Spaniard with his peaked hat and leather gaiters; the Moorish merchant with his full turban and embroidered cassock; the Jew with his close skull-cap and bag-like coat; the Greek with his full trowsers and jaunty jacket; the filthy Arab crouching upon the ground; the Bohemian with his coarse blanket overcoat and thick boots; in short, men from almost all parts of the globe may be seen here, our own countrymen not excepted, as though this were the World's congress, in which every race had its representative. Amid the motley throng the British sentinel marches up and down his prescribed station, with measured tread, the perfection of military neatness and discipline, and in all that constitutes the soldier, so far as externals go, the very opposite of the arms-bearing portion of the population of Spain. When you have entered the city, the same mixed mass is seen filling the streets, occupying the shops, and mingling in all the business of the place. The resident population amounts to about 15,000 persons, of whom about 10,000 are British subjects. They are, for the most part, temporary residents, engaged in the extensive and diversified traffic which Gibraltar opens with the opposite coast of Barbary, with Spain, and the other countries of the Mediterranean. Not the least important and lucrative part of this traffic, either to the persons engaged in it or to Great Britain, is the smuggling carried on with the interior of Spain. Gibraltar being a free port, merchandise is carried there and deposited in large quantities, for the purpose of being taken out again as opportunities occur, and illicitly introduced within the Spanish lines. Taken as a whole, the population of Gibraltar is as wretched in appearance as it is mixed in character. There are some fifteen hundred Jews, and by far the greater portion are miserably clad and exceedingly foul in their persons. Of the native Christians, some, who are engaged in menial services, are not much before them. The city itself, that part of it at least which is connected with its business, is indifferently built. On the other hand, all that belongs to the place as a military station, is solid, substantial, and not unfrequently in very good taste. The fortifications themselves are built in the very best manner. In masonry nothing can be superior to some of the defences on the water side. The barracks are large, and apparently commodious and airy. The houses occupied by some of the officers of the higher grades are exceedingly pretty, in the cottage style, surrounded by gardens filled with tropical fruits, and with an abundance of shade-trees; and the position of some of them, especially in the direction of Europa Point, where the surface is broken and irregular, is very beautiful and picturesque. The Alameda, occupying nearly a central position between the northern and southern extremities of the Rock, has an area, to all appearance, of some thirty or forty acres. A large portion of it consists of beautiful walks, groves of forest trees and shrubbery, with here and there a fountain or a statue, and with a graveled square on its western side sufficiently capacious for the evolutions of a regiment. On several days in each week two of the military bands are upon these grounds, far enough removed from each other to avoid the intermixture of sounds, and the walks, groves, and square are, on these occasions, always thronged with the population of the city. This is the chief source of public amusement in the place. The officers, and the persons connected with the city government are, with their families, sufficiently numerous for all social purposes; there is a very fine miscellaneous library; the station is near home; it has a mild winter climate; the heat in summer, though great, is not insupportable; and Gibraltar, for the military, must be one of the most desirable stations among the British possessions. But to a stranger there are no objects of attraction, excepting the fortifications, and these are seen in one or two days. The most remarkable are the excavations cut in the perpendicular face of the Rock, looking out upon the neutral ground which separates the Spanish from the British territory. They consist of extensive galleries entirely within the Rock, with port holes cut out so as to enable the guns to bear upon the neutral ground and the causeway which connects the Rock with it. The galleries are wide enough to allow a gun to be drawn through them, and where the cannon are mounted the excavation is enlarged, so as to enable them to be worked with ease. The number of guns in each of these apartments varies from two to six, and they are so distributed that not only the neutral ground, but the road below, on the eastern face of the Rock, is commanded by them. Above these galleries there are numerous batteries in the open air, and the summit of the Rock itself is crowned with cannon and mortars If any military post can be said to be impregnable, certainly this may; and so long as Great Britain retains her naval preponderance on the ocean, it can scarcely pass into other hands, unless by treachery.

With an immense line of fortifications below, and with numerous batteries upon and within the Rock above, it would be supposed that Great Britain would maintain a numerous garrison here. This is not so. It rarely exceeds 3500 men—a force just about equal to that kept up by Spain at the little town of Ceuta, on the Barbary coast. The number of guns mounted and ready for use at Gibraltar is about 1000. A garrison of 12,000 men would not be more than sufficient on a war establishment; but with the means afforded by steam navigation of sending in reinforcements on short notice, one third of the present force would be ample for any emergency that could arise. The efficiency of the galleries as a means of defence has not been tested, and is not likely to be, excepting in the last extremity. That they might be very serviceable in case of an attempt to assault the works on the side of the isthmus is unquestionable. But whether they would bear long and continued discharges from the cannon within them may be doubted. They are cut in the rock with only a slight shell between them and the exterior surface, which is generally perpendicular, and it would not be surprising if, by repeated firing, some of these superficial chambers should give way. The rock, it is true, is of compact limestone; but when the violent concussion produced by the explosion of cannon within a very confined space is considered, sometimes causing the blood to start from the nostrils and ears of the cannoniers, it is not unreasonable to apprehend serious disasters from a long-continued use of these batteries. As auxiliary to the fortifications below, and to be employed in emergencies, they may be of service; and it is in this point of view alone, perhaps, that they are to be regarded as of essential importance. For all other purposes, the batteries in the open air are likely to prove of far greater value.

Gibraltar was taken from the Spaniards in 1704, by the combined forces of the English and Dutch. The garrison consisted of only 150 men, while the assailants had about 2000 land forces, supported by a strong fleet. This important post, which Spain had so feebly prepared for defence, she now made the most desperate efforts to regain. In three months after its capture a strong force was sent against it by France and Spain. The siege commenced on the 11th of October, 1704, and continued until the following March, when the beseigers withdrew, both parties having borne themselves with distinguished gallantry; and in 1713 Gibraltar was formally ceded to Great Britain by treaty. In 1717 a second effort was made by Spain to regain by force of arms her lost possession. The place was besieged by a force of 20,000 men for six months, when further operations were interrupted by an armistice, preliminary to the general peace, which soon followed.

Failing to regain Gibraltar by force, Spain made repeated attempts to procure a retrocession by negotiation; but Great Britain was too sensible of the importance of the post to her, as a maritime power, to yield it, and though some encouragement was given by George the First to Philip the Fifth, the demonstrations of popular feeling against the measure were so strong that the subject was not even brought before Parliament, as the Spanish king had been led to expect from the assurances given to him. In 1779, when Great Britain was involved in hostilities with her American colonies, Spain, united subsequently with France, made a final effort to wrest this important post from her. In June of that year the operations commenced, by cutting off the communication between Spain and Gibraltar by land, and soon after by blockading the harbor with a powerful naval force. For more than six months not a shot was fired from the land, but the Spaniards were industriously employed in strengthening their defences and erecting new works for the contemplated bombardment. During this period the garrison, shut up as it was, suffered the severest privations for want of abundant and healthful food. Thistles, dandelions, and the most common weeds constituted a large portion of their sustenance. On the 12th of January, 1780, the first shot was fired from the Spanish lines, and on the 17th of the same month Admiral Rodney, after having defeated and dispersed the blockading squadron, relieved the fortress with men, provisions, and munitions of war.

During the whole of the year 1780 the Spaniards continued extending their works, and maintained a strict blockade by water. In the early part of the following year (1781), the garrison were again in extreme distress for want of provisions, but in April they were again relieved. The Spaniards, now despairing of reducing the besieged by famine, commenced the bombardment, for which they had made such ample preparations. On the 12th of April the fire was opened from sixty-four pieces of artillery and fifty thirteen-inch mortars. For several days the firing was incessant, and the garrison sustained serious injury; during the month of May the number of rounds daily did not exceed 1000; in June it fell to 500, and in July and August much less. During this time the garrison did not remain idle. In September they fired 700 shot a day, and received about 800 in return. The Spaniards, notwithstanding this incessant firing, continued to push forward their works, and General Elliott, the commander of the garrison, formed the gallant determination of destroying them by a sortie. This design was executed on the 12th of November, 1781. Two thousand men, in the dead of night, sallied from the fortress, surprised the besiegers, drove them from their lines, set fire to all that was combustible, laid trains to the magazines, blew them up, and in less than two hours re-entered the fortress, with a loss of only thirty killed, wounded, and missing. In the history of modern warfare there are few deeds of greater gallantry, performed as it was in the face of a vastly superior force, and few crowned with such triumphant success. In July of the following year the Duke of Crillon took the command of the combined French and Spanish forces, amounting, it is said, to 40,000 men, while the garrison did not much exceed 7000 effectives. In August the Spanish lines were fully repaired, and important additions made to them, entirely crossing the isthmus at a distance of 800 yards from the Rock. On the 8th and 9th of September nearly 8000 shot and shells were fired into the garrison from the Spanish lines, while nine ships of the line and fifteen gun and mortar boats were pouring in their fire from the bay. On the 10th the bombardment was continued at the rate of 4000 shot in the twenty-four hours. On the 12th the combined fleets of France and Spain anchored between the Rock and Algesiras. A more formidable preparation has rarely been seen. Forty-seven sail of the line, ten battering-vessels—novel in their construction, and carrying more than two hundred guns—frigates, gun and mortar boats, and other craft almost without number filled the bay. Forty thousand men were ranged within the Spanish lines, with the Duke of Crillon, one of the most gallant soldiers of his time, in command, and two princes of the royal blood of France, the Duke of Bourbon and the Count D'Artois, fighting under his orders. The Spanish queen herself encouraged the besiegers by her presence. She took her seat on a rock in rear, still known as the Queen's Chair, and declared she would never leave it until the Spanish flag waved over Gibraltar. This declaration having reached the ears of General Elliott, he sent her word that he would relieve her from the inconvenience which was likely to arise from her determination, and accordingly he hoisted the Spanish flag for a few minutes, but with the British ensign over it.

The morning of the 13th of September, 1782, was chosen by the besiegers for their great and final effort. At an early hour the land batteries opened upon the garrison, and the battering vessels were immediately brought into position, and moored within half a mile of the fortifications. All the guns on both sides which could be brought to bear were now in action. More than four hundred pieces of artillery were sending forth their iron missives, carrying death and destruction with them. Until the middle of the day, the guns of the garrison had made no impression upon the battering-ships, so admirably had they been constructed, and their fire, being directed with great skill, had become exceedingly destructive. And now the commander of the garrison resorted to an expedient which he had reserved until the last moment of necessity. The guns opposed to the battering ships were served with hot shot, and for three hours the atmosphere was literally glowing with fire. The ships were frequently seen burning, but by the use of fire-engines the flames were speedily subdued. They could not, however, long withstand the flood of fire which was poured in upon them. At the approach of night two of them were enveloped in flames, at two o'clock on the following morning six others were in the same condition, and by noon the whole ten were destroyed. Two thousand men are supposed to have perished in these ill-fated vessels; and the hopes of the besiegers perished with them. The investment continued five months longer; but the offensive operations were confined to petty annoyances by gun and mortar boats. In February, 1783, the general treaty of peace settled between the contending parties, and the acknowledgment of the independence of the American colonies by Great Britain, terminated the siege.

Thus ended one of the most obstinate and well-conducted contests of either ancient or modern times. The siege continued three years and seven months, and was managed with consummate skill and judgment by the besiegers. Their only error was in neglecting to guard against surprise; but with their vastly superior numbers they could not have anticipated so daring an enterprise as a sortie. On the part of the garrison all was done which skill, gallantry, prudence, perseverance, and unyielding resolution could effect. The amount of ammunition expended is almost incredible. The garrison fired more than 205,000 shot and shells, and expended more than 8000 barrels of gunpowder. The besiegers fired more than 258,000 rounds, without including the battering-ships; and the loss of life on their part was enormous. The entire loss of the garrison during the siege was about 800 killed and 1000 wounded. After the destruction of the battering squadron, it was proposed to attempt to carry the works by storm; but the design was overruled by the Duke of Crillon, as rash and impracticable.

From this time Great Britain has remained in the undisturbed enjoyment of her possession; and so long as she retains her ascendency on the ocean, it is not probable that any attempt will be made to drive her from it; for another could not possibly be made under auspices so favorable as that which so signally failed. Should she lose her supremacy as a naval power, Gibraltar would be of little, if any, value to her. Of itself it commands nothing; not even the Bay of Algesiras.

Though the Rock of Gibraltar is principally of compact primitive limestone or marble, there are some slight variations in its geological structure. On the western side there is a mixture of argillaceous earth, quartz, and breccia of great variety and beauty. In the more elevated parts of the Rock holes are found, filled with quartz and jaspers, worn round, like the holes themselves, by the action of water, and affording the strongest evidence that the whole formation was once beneath the waves. In the fissures and cavities fossil bones are found in great quantities. A large number were examined by Cuvier, who pronounced them to be the remains of domestic animals; and the shells, of which there are many varieties, he found to belong uniformly to fresh-water species.

The expense of maintaining Gibraltar is about $850,000 per annum. Of this amount about $150,000 is paid by the revenue of the place, leaving an annual balance of $700,000 to be paid by the government of Great Britain. The commerce of Great Britain with Gibraltar, and through Gibraltar with Spain, is very considerable; but it is not, of itself, sufficient to indemnify her for the expense of keeping up the establishment. It is only through its advantages as a military post that she can be considered as compensated for her heavy annual disbursements in maintaining it. The whole amount of goods of the manufacture of the United Kingdom and its colonies introduced annually into Gibraltar, does not equal five millions of dollars in value; and so much of this amount as is designed for external consumption, would find its way to the consumers through other channels, if Gibraltar were not in her hands. Still, the profits on her commercial intercourse with the place, deduct something from the annual burden of maintaining it.

CHAPTER XVII.

EASTERN COAST OF SPAIN.

Departure from Gibraltar.—Malaga.—The Cathedral.—Almeria. —The Eastern Coast of Spain.—Mines.—Dampness of the Nights in the Mediterranean. — Aguilas. — Carthagena.— The Docks.—Former Naval Power of Spain.—Her Decline.—The Dinner at Carthagena. — Alicante. —Valencia. —Barcelona. — The public Walks.—The Cathedral.—Ruins of the Hall of the Inquisition. — Insurrection of Barcelona. — Espartero. — Siege and Bombardment of the City from Montjui.

On the evening of the 5th of May we embarked in the Spanish steamer, Premier Gaditano, for Marseilles. It was just before sunset that we got under way—the very hour when fine objects are seen to best advantage. The beams of the sun, falling on them in nearly horizontal lines, and spreading extended shadows over the surfaces of land and water, above which they rise, bring them out with a distinctness which they never possess at other times. Nothing could be more striking than the Rock, as we saw it for the last time, its gray tints fading in the twilight, and standing out strongly from the blue background of the Spanish hills. There was not a breath of air to ruffle the surface of the Mediterranean as we entered it, nor was there any sign of motion beyond our own stout vessel. For several days the Bay of Gibraltar and the surrounding waters had been literally covered with the canvass of ships destined to the Atlantic, but unable to make head against the westerly breeze, which was drawing strongly through the strait. To-day the east wind had set in, and as the sun went down, not one of that vast fleet of traders remained in sight. We entered the Mediterranean alone; but it was not long before a black cloud appeared in the east, then a dark vessel vomiting sparks and smoke, and in a few minutes the Liverpool, a huge steamer from Alexandria, in Egypt, swept by us, having traversed in a week, in nearly its greatest extent, a sea on which, in distant ages, the heroes of classic story were tempest-tost for months, and even years, in vain attempts to reach their homes.

Early the next morning we found ourselves moored in the harbor of Malaga, within a long mole extending far out into the sea, with a lighthouse at the end. At the other extremity, close to the city, a large number of traders were lying, some of them discharging and others receiving freight. Of all the Spanish cities between Gibraltar and the coast of France, Malaga is, perhaps, the least striking. It lies low, though on the right, as you enter the harbor, the land rises into an eminence crowned with a fortress. Over the line of stores and dwellings, which face the water, the turrets of the cathedral are seen, with the roof of the edifice itself, large and massive, but, like almost every cathedral we have found in Spain, unfinished. This was the meeting-house which the mate of the Mexican commended to us so warmly. We could do no less than visit it; and though we had so recently seen others much superior in all respects, it was well worth the examination. The interior is not unlike that of Cadiz, though it falls far short of it in architectural beauty, and in the richness of its materials. The city of Malaga is well built, and presents many evidences of prosperity; but of late its trade has sadly fallen off, especially with the United States, with which it has for many years carried on the most profitable exchanges. They tell us the business streets are comparatively deserted, and they certainly exhibit very little activity. But there are many rich and showy private edifices in the city, particularly on and about the Alameda—a fine, broad square near the water, with avenues of shade-trees, and some not very successful attempts at embellishment, though every thing about it savors of prosperity and wealth. Southwest of the city the country is said to be very fine for several miles. It seems so from a distant view. The whole surface of the earth is clad in dense foliage and vegetation, and at a short distance a range of hills, at the base of which a large village is seen, runs from the water far back into the interior. Malaga is said to be hot in summer; but, lying as it does on the water, the heat must be tempered by the currents of air constantly drawing in from the sea upon the sunburnt plains and hills which surround the city. In winter it is, perhaps, more mild than any other of the Spanish cities, though cold winds sweep over it occasionally from the mountains of Granada, which, to a late period in the spring, remain covered with snow.

Though the arrangement of the Spanish steamers between Cadiz and Marseilles enables one to see all the principal intervening cities, the time allotted to each is so brief as to afford a mere glimpse of them. At Barcelona they stop two days, but at the other cities the extent of the delay is twelve or fourteen hours. Before nightfall we were again under way, running along the coast by moonlight, without a breath of air, and with as little motion as though we had been navigating a river. Thus it remained until midnight, when a strong breeze sprung up, and continued to increase until daylight. We soon afterwards entered the harbor of Almeria, if an open and extensive roadstead may be so called, and came to anchor. But the wind blew with such violence that it was extremely difficult to land. Here we lay all day, not in the most comfortable position; but our steamer was very large, and we were but slightly incommoded by the motion. The city of Almeria, as seen from the water, has nothing particularly attractive. It is a small place, but is walled in, with a somewhat extensive fortification above it, flanked by the turrets of a dilapidated castle on one side, and on the other by a succession of columns and broken arches, which seem to be the ruins of an ancient aqueduct. On the right of the city a long, flat neck of land stretches itself out to a point, with clumps of trees scattered over it, and with other indications of fertility and cultivation. On the southwest all is rudeness and sterility. The shore rises abruptly into steep, ragged cliffs, without a trace of vegetation, with here and there a solitary castle or tower surmounting its lofty peaks, and a road leading to them cut into the solid mass of the rock, and walled up, to prevent the loaded donkeys and carriages which pass over it, from being precipitated into the waters below. Nothing can be more barren and rugged than the whole eastern coast of Spain until you reach Barcelona, with the exception of the Bay of Valencia, and a few small patches of green in other places. As far back as you can see, there is a continued succession of rocky hills, almost invariably without trees. Yet upon this rude coast, worthless as it seems, there is a constant series of strongholds. At the distance of every eight or ten miles, a tower, standing high above the water, looks down upon you as you pass, with nothing worth defending within the compass of the eye. Sometimes these singular and picturesque defences take the form of enormous castles, built upon such steep eminences that they seem to be alike inaccessible to friend and foe. In the times of the Carthaginians, the Romans, and the Moors, they may have had their use; but the progress of civilization has rendered them utterly worthless. They serve only to give an aspect of romance to a coast which would, without them, be wholly devoid of interest. We were not often so near the shore as to enable us to distinguish the geological character of this vast extent of rocky coast. From Malaga it appeared to consist of the older series. From the effect of the sunbeams upon some of these enormous masses, reflected in rays of silvery light, it was obvious that they were of micaceous schist. In the neighborhood of Alicante, on the other hand, the Portland stone, and other formations of the tertiary series, prevail. Between Almeria and Carthagena, a few miles back from the sea, the country abounds in gold and silver mines. They were extensively worked in the days of the Carthaginians and Romans, but for hundreds of years they had been totally neglected. Of late the current of speculation has been setting strongly towards them; and in the years 1835 and 1836, there was nothing more wild and reckless in the United States, than the operations in these ancient mines within the last two years in Spain. They have often changed hands at enormous advances in price; companies have been formed to purchase and work them; shares have been sold at the most extravagant rates; and, what is more rational, they have been opened and worked successfully, though not so profitably as to repay the outlay of those who have invested at high prices. We had on board our steamer a singular instance of the change of fortune growing out of these speculations, in the person of a gentleman who had for years been living in extreme indigence, lacking even the common comforts of life. He was the owner of one of these apparently worthless hills. An ancient mine was discovered in it, and was purchased of him the year before by a company of wealthy individuals, who reopened and were then working it. The agent of the company, a highly intelligent and gentlemanly Spaniard, was on board, and he assured me that he had paid the purchaser three thousand dollars a few days before, as a quarterly instalment of the annual interest on the purchase money. Here was an income of twelve thousand dollars a year derived from one of these sales. That this whole district is rich in mineral treasure—particularly in gold, silver, and lead—is unquestionable; and they may, perhaps, at no distant day, be destined to compensate for the diminished supply of the precious metals from South America. But this can not happen to any appreciable extent, until Spain, by the adoption of a more liberal policy in respect to the application of capital and labor, shall secure to industry its legitimate rewards.

Fortunately, the wind fairly blew itself out before night, and we left Almeria at sunset with a light breeze, which died away in turn before midnight, and the water was soon calm again. Nothing is more delightful than these excursions along the Spanish coast when the weather is fine. You steam by night, and by day enter some fine old town, full of interest, and explore it while the steamer is getting ready for the continuance of her voyage. If the moon is out, the nights are enchanting, running, as you do, close under the land, with the light and shadow moulding the rugged cliffs which line it into a thousand fantastic shapes, and the remains of past ages constantly bursting upon the sight, and calling up visions of romance and chivalry. The only drawback to one's pleasure is the dampness of the nights. The dew falls so rapidly, particularly in and near the Gulf of Lyons, that in the course of a few hours it gathers into pools and runs in streams across the deck. Beautiful as the climate is, it is exceedingly trying to mariners. A British officer assured us that more invalids were sent home from the Mediterranean with pulmonary affections than from any other portion of the foreign naval service of Great Britain; and it is, perhaps, owing as much to the dampness of the nights, as to the frequent and sudden variations of temperature on a sheet of water shut in by Alpine snows on one side, and bounded by burning sands on the other.

The morning after we left Almeria we entered the little port of Aguilas. It is an outlet to some of the mines a few miles back, and the operations in them have given a stimulus to the place within a year or two. It is very small, and is likely to remain so. It is doubtful whether it is destined ever to rise much above the dignity of a landing-place. It is shut in on both sides by high rocks, and nestles prettily enough between them, close down upon the shore. On the left, as you face the land, there is a noble cliff several hundred feet high, and a well-built castle or fort surmounting it. This is obviously a modern structure, and is quite a sufficient preparation for the little place it defends.

We were delayed but a few hours at Aguilas, and at least an hour before noon we were entering the port of Carthagena. This is by far the finest harbor on the eastern coast of Spain. At the distance of about two miles from the city you enter the mouth of the harbor, defended on both sides by high hills. On the left, a succession of fortresses defends the passage. The opposite side also has its share of batteries and breastworks, though the channel is more distant from it, and it is not so strongly fortified. As you pass the entrance, the harbor expands into a capacious bay, and affords excellent anchorage for shipping. The city, as you approach it, is very striking. A strong wall covers its entire front, and above it ranges of fine public edifices and private dwellings are seen, varied by the spires of churches and the arms of windmills. High above the town, and rising almost from the wall, is the citadel, with an ancient castle, said to have been built by the Carthaginians, and which certainly has nothing in its appearance to call the tradition in question. It is as antiquated and uncouth in its aspect as need be. North of the citadel, across a portion of the bay, there is another eminence, with a very extensive fortress upon its summit. In short, in whatever direction you turn, the shores of the bay are lined with military works, making it one of the best defended harbors in the world.

Carthagena was one of the three great naval depots of Spain in the days of her commercial prosperity. The docks still remain. They are in the form of an immense oblong, covering several acres, and with water sufficient to float vessels of the largest size. Around them are the public stores, vast in extent, and admirably arranged. But they are, like the docks, rapidly decaying. They were formerly filled with naval stores, spars, and every thing necessary to equip a fleet. But they are now mere shells, containing a few models and broken instruments of naval warfare. In one of them we saw also a few hundred muskets, the only contents of these vast repositories which are of any value. What eloquent testimony do these ruins bear to the rapid decline of Spanish greatness! There is no instance in the history of mankind, in which a people, without being overwhelmed by foreign conquest, have fallen so suddenly from great power to consummate weakness. There is, it is true, much in the rise, progress, and fall of her colonial possessions to account for it. When the Americas were discovered, she had but just expelled the Moors, and had her domestic organization to complete and establish upon a solid basis. The impulse which her American colonies gave to her commerce, facilitated the object. She became united, rich, and powerful. But the very fountains of her wealth proved the elements of her downfall. It seems to be in the order of Providence that national opulence shall be but the harbinger of national weakness. The very industry which is severely and assiduously tasked to procure the necessaries of life, is in itself one of the first elements of strength. The accumulation of wealth, or the easy methods of acquiring it, which render men, as it were, independent of the Scriptural denunciation of earning their bread in the sweat of their face, and enable them to lay aside their habits of laborious application, are the great agents in the work of demoralization. Luxury, ease, and their kindred vices speedily complete what the suspension of honest toil has commenced. The loss of her American provinces would, of itself, not be sufficient to account for the rapid downfall of the power of Spain. It must be sought for in a great degree in the decline of her domestic industry, one of the first fruits of her excessive opulence, and in the bad habits and bad passions, which centuries of luxury have introduced into her social economy, sullying her fame, and impairing her strength by intestine dissensions and wars. Much as there is to find fault with in the present characteristics of the Spanish nation, it is difficult to traverse these immense storehouses, or walk around these docks, still splendid in their ruins, without a mixture of regret with the pain any such spectacle is calculated to produce, or without feeling at heart a wish that she may rise again from her abasement, and take her former rank among the great powers of the earth.

The external appearance of Carthagena is decidedly more agreeable than its interior. The streets are narrow, and the buildings almost uniformly old and semi-barbarous in taste. We have seen no city which is so decidedly antiquated under all its aspects. At the same time it is far from being uninteresting, and, indeed, it is perhaps more truly Spanish than any of the towns we have visited, except Seville.

As it was about noon when we reached the city, no one of us, excepting myself, was disposed to land, and, being a stranger, I joined a party of Spanish ladies and gentlemen in exploring the place. We stopped first at an hotel, if a very ordinary tavern, and almost the only decent one in Carthagena, could be so called, and having ordered dinner at three o'clock, we commenced our explorations. We first visited the hospital, a very clean and apparently well-managed establishment; then the cathedral, an ordinary edifice, with little within it to compensate for want of interest in the building itself, and having made a hasty tour of the principal streets, and reserved the docks for the afternoon, we reached the tavern at the hour appointed for dinner. Our party consisted of fourteen, five ladies and nine gentlemen, and we were speedily seated at table, with nothing upon it but bread, wine, and olives. Our landlady had not been as punctual as ourselves, and while dinner is preparing, I avail myself of the opportunity of taking a glance at my fellow-travellers. Directly opposite to me are three beautiful

Spanish girls from the neighborhood of Valencia, who are just completing the tour of Spain. They were a few days after us in Seville, on their way from Madrid to Cadiz, and on our embarkation at Gibraltar we found them on board. Three fairer sisters it is not easy to find in any country. They are well formed, and have symmetrical features, with countenances full of expression, and they speak the Spanish language with the most soft and musical tones of voice. At the mention of a Spanish beauty, dark, piercing eyes, black hair, and a skin of the shade of the olive instinctively suggest themselves. These young ladies are of a totally different race. Their hair is auburn, their complexions fair, and their eyes blue. If the truth could be known, the fair-haired hordes from the north who poured down upon Spain fourteen hundred years ago, and held dominion over it for three centuries, might undoubtedly lay claim to a large portion of the blood of these bright-skinned damsels. Their father is the only companion of their voyage. He is a sturdy, good-natured-looking man of fifty-five, and, according to an account which the eldest of the three gave me a few evenings ago on the deck of the steamer, as we were running along under the rocky coast, with a flood of moonlight pouring down upon castle and watch-tower, and adding fresh interest to her earnest and eloquent narration, he has borne himself with distinguished gallantry in some of the intestine conflicts by which his country has been scourged in latter years. He sits between two of them at table, and a very gentlemanly young Spaniard, by special favor, separates one of them from the third. On the right of the youngest, who is the fairest also, sits a Spanish officer, a veteran manifestly, of some sixty years of age, remarkably courteous in his manner, and full of good humor and boyish glee. He is paying assiduous court to the damsel, who is but just turned of fifteen; but she has all the self-possession of a woman, and she receives his compliments and attentions with a degree of ceremonious civility which is admirable. Gibraltar itself is obviously not more thoroughly impregnable than she; but he keeps up as brisk a fire upon her as though he was sure of a surrender. By way of enforcing his suit, he now and then selects from the dish one of the finest olives and presents it to her on his own fork. She receives it, takes the olive with her lips, and hands the fork back. This, it would seem, is not a very unusual mark of courtesy among familiar acquaintances. A young gentleman who sits next to the officer, and who is determined not to leave him in undisturbed possession of the field, leans across his plate and offers a similar compliment, and she receives it with the same formal courtesy. While this trial of strength is going on between the two candidates for her favor, let us look at our own side of the table. On my right is the Spanish gentleman who has grown suddenly rich by the mining mania. No man could bear prosperity better. He is kind, unassuming, and pleasing in his manners. But fortune, while filling his purse, is severely afflicting his person. He is rapidly losing his eyesight, though scarcely turned of thirty-five, but he has happily a devoted wife, who sits next to him, and attends assiduously to all his wants. On my left there is another married couple; and near them two other gentlemen, as full of joviality as the officer, complete our number. We have now been sitting half an hour at table, talking and eating bread and olives, and the dinner is not yet come. The landlady has been called repeatedly, and urged in the most vociferous manner not to keep us longer fasting. The officer and the two gentlemen on my left, who are wags, are the most earnest in their solicitations. They rise to their feet when she comes in, clasp their hands, declare that we are in the last stages of starvation, and entreat her, if she has a particle of humanity, to send in the dinner. In the midst of this mock-pathetic some well-directed jest sets the whole table in a roar. The landlady is not at all disconcerted; she parries the jokes, joins in the laughter, and has pledged her sacred honor at least a dozen times that the soup will be in the next minute. At last it appears, and the whole apartment echoes to the shouts with which it is received. A flood of compliments is poured out upon the landlady, and the burden of it all is that she is a very pattern of punctuality. The courses now follow each other in rapid succession —fish, beef, mutton, omelettes, puddings, pastry, and fruit. A more bountiful or well-cooked dinner one could not well desire; and certainly no banquet could be more highly seasoned with hilarity and good humor. The officer, as the wine bottle at his side becomes low, grows more fervid and eloquent; the flashes of wit from all parts of the table are more brilliant; the forks, with choice bits from each others' plates, are handed to the ladies; and with all the uproar and noise the gentlemen never lose their courtesy, or the ladies their dignity and self-possession. A more light-hearted party I never saw assembled, and from the few opportunities I have had of seeing Spaniards in groups, I am satisfied that their distinguishing characteristics are gayety and unceremoniousness, and not, as I had always been taught to believe, stateliness and gravity.

The dinner being ended we called for the bill, but were told by the landlady that it was paid. A few of us remonstrated and insisted on defraying our share of the expense; but the gentleman of the gold mine, to whom we had traced this interference with our rights, coolly remarked that he was at home, that we were, most of us, from other parts of the kingdom, and that when one is in a foreign country or province he is bound to submit to the masters. The reasoning was unanswerable, and we agreed unanimously to consider the dinner our first, as it would probably be our last, installment of the profits of the Spanish mines.

At eight o'clock we were again upon the water, with another bright night, stealing slowly but steadily along under the sea-beaten cliffs, and with the same wild and romantic objects, which have been constantly before us since we left Malaga. At eight o'clock the next morning we were at Alicante. The harbor is open and partially defended, like that of Malaga, by a mole, with a lighthouse at the outer extremity. The view of the town itself is exceedingly pretty. It presents a very fine show of edifices, and on the right there is a high hill—an immense mass of oolite—surmounted by an extensive fortification. The city circles around it, and runs partly up the ascent, as if to get as close to its protector as possible. The internal appearance of Alicante is far superior to that of Carthagena. The houses are less antiquated and in better taste. Still there are few objects of interest. There is a collection of several hundred pictures belonging to a Spanish nobleman, in a very fine palace in the heart of the city; but with the exception of some paintings of birds, it has few of merit. The Cathedral, one of the first things to be seen in a Spanish city, is very unattractive, both externally and internally—somewhat massive, but simple without beauty. A Frenchman who was with us justly observed, that it was only remarkable for the solidity of its walls. There are in and about Alicante a large number of furnaces in active operation, smelting metals. We visited one established about a year ago, by an association of English gentlemen. It is on a large scale, with many fine buildings, and it is said that it yields a profitable return on the investment of capital. It is engaged in smelting silver ore, which is transported from the neighborhood of Aguilas. The amount of pure silver produced by the association during the last year was about four hundred thousand dollars. Our time was limited, but we saw the ore going through some of the first processes. The ore yields about eight per cent. of silver and about twenty-five per cent. of lead. The coal used in the operations is all brought from England, and pays a heavy impost at the port of entry—a serious drawback upon the profits of the company, but not so great as to discourage them from enlarging their works, which are already very extensive.

Our next stopping-place was the Bay of Valencia, one of the most beautiful in Spain. We reached it at about six o'clock on the morning after we left Alicante, entering its bright and sparkling waters shortly after daybreak. The sun was soon out, lighting up the opposite shores of the bay with extraordinary brilliancy, dissipating the thin mists which hung over the land, and bringing into view the numberless groves and farmhouses which lie thickly scattered over the level surface. The sea was still calm, and the whole scene was of that quiet repose which is so characteristic of a spring morning in higher latitudes, and which accorded so well with the objects around us—with the vast plain spread out before us, covered with rural beauty and luxuriance, and enclosed on all sides with a range of hills, which rose up at a distance of about ten miles, as if to shut it out from the influences of the ruder districts, which lie farther back. At seven o'clock we were on shore, and four of us having taken a light carriage drawn by a single horse, and in form much like one of our covered meat-carts, though of finer materials and finish, we set out for the city, about two miles distant. The drive is exceedingly beautiful. You pass the entire distance through avenues of immense trees, with branches so lofty that you have a perfect view of the country beneath them. The soil, as far as you can see, is cultivated like a garden, and farmhouses are thickly scattered over it, without enclosures, the different farms and gardens being separated from each other only by paths or light hedges. As we approached Valencia, groves and public walks extended along the river, with a profusion of ornamental shrubbery, and rendering the environs of the city altogether more beautiful than any thing we have seen in Spain. We crossed the river, which washes the eastern face of the town, by a fine, substantial bridge of stone. The channel was nearly dry ; but in wet seasons it is a large stream, and surrounds the city wall with a broad sheet of water. After breakfasting at a very excellent hotel, we passed hastily through the streets, visited the Cathedral, the market-place, and the University, and at two o'clock were again on board the steamer. Of all the towns we have seen in Spain, Valencia is decidedly the most beautiful. It has few objects of attraction to the lover of the arts ; but in other respects, as a place of residence for a few months, it has many advantages over the cities of Andalusia. The streets are generally clean, the houses large and well-built, the greatest profusion of fruits is to be found at all seasons, the surrounding country is highly improved and ornamented, and there are carriages without number, which may be hired for a few pence an hour to conduct you through this exquisite scenery. The Cathedral is a fine-looking edifice, and from the tower you have a magnificent prospect. The city lies beneath you, and to the base of the mountains on three sides, and to the shores of the Mediterranean on the other, there is a perfectly level surface, rich with vegetation, spotted with farm-houses, villages, and spires, and forming the most gorgeous exhibition of rural wealth and beauty we have seen. The market-place is a large oblong square, with ancient edifices of curious architecture about it, and with a most bountiful display of oranges, strawberries, apricots, and other fruits, through its centre and along its sides. The University building is new, and in good taste. It has a large scientific and miscellaneous library, and about 2200 students are receiving instruction within its walls. With only four hours at our disposal, we could see but little; but cursory as our glimpse of the city was, it was sufficient to make us regret that we had not arranged to pass at least a month in it. Besides, of the large cities, it is the last truly Spanish town as you go northward on the coast of the Mediterranean. Here the national costume is preserved, differing somewhat from that of other provinces, but still national. The ornamented jacket and the

Spanish hat are still seen, but with them there is an article of dress unknown to the southern districts of Spain—a mantle, usually of light ground and dark stripes, thrown over the shoulders and gathered around the body. It is worn by the lower orders, and has a singularly picturesque effect.

Though we were on board at two o'clock, as we were desired to be by the captain when we landed, it was five before we were in motion. We had parted with our three Spanish girls and their respectable father, the owner of the gold mine, and with the officer, who, it seems, was stationed at Valencia. On board, the latter had worn a plain blue jacket, and a forage cap, somewhat the worse for the service it had rendered, looking much more like a member of the invalid corps on short allowance than an officer in active service on full pay. As we were entering the University, a magnificently dressed personage, with chapeau de bras and ostrich feathers, and a pair of gold epaulettes, walked rapidly up to us, extending his hand in token of recognition. It was the officer—though it was not until we had taken a long look that we identified him. He had gone to his quarters, equipped himself in his best, and was on his way to the hotel to make a last assault upon the heart of the youngest of the sisters. Our lives upon it, the ostrich feathers and the epaulettes, attractive as they are to the eyes of the fair sex, will avail him nothing. She is reserved for a more youthful conqueror. But if we mistake not the signs of the times, our veteran friend will, at no distant period, have an opportunity of winning laurels in a more congenial service, and of finding consolation in the favor of Mars for the defeat he is destined to sustain at the hands of Venus.

At five o'clock in the afternoon on the following day we entered the port of Barcelona, a fine harbor, though neither so spacious nor so secure as that of Carthagena. The southeasterly wind blows into it, but the waves are broken by an eminence on one side, on which stands the castle of Montjui, and by an extensive mole on the other, running half a mile out from the point, where the greater part of the shipping usually lies. We landed near the extremity of this mole, on the inner side, within a few yards of the lighthouse, and hastened into the city to procure lodgings for the day and two nights we were to remain here. The two great hotels were filled with lodgers; not a single room was to be found in either; and after looking at two miserable taverns, dark, filthy, and suspicious in their appearance, we returned to the steamer for the night.

The next day we took a carriage and drove through the city, visiting its principal objects of attraction. It is remarkably well built, and portions of it are exceedingly beautiful, with public and private buildings in excellent taste. The rambla, a fine public walk, filled with shade-trees, runs through the city near its centre. On this wide avenue are the two principal hotels—indeed, the only ones in which one can find comfortable accommodations. Not far distant from it is the Cathedral. It is of immense size, and its exterior is entirely unfinished. On one side only can you see any marks of the noble Gothic, after which it was planned. But the interior compensates for its external defects. It is a most finished specimen of Gothic architecture, with all the elaborate workmanship characteristic of that style, and yet so well proportioned in all its parts, as to give it an air of majestic simplicity, at once beautiful and imposing. With the exception of the Cathedral at Seville, we have found no church in Spain so striking. Near by it are the ruins of the Hall of the Inquisition. Its foundations remain, and some of the partition walls—a monument to the horrible superstition of which it was the instrument. Seville once boasted that she was the first city in which the Holy Office performed its bloody rites; but of the building, in which its sessions were held, there is hardly a trace to be found, and the lapse of half a century has left it without a defender in the country which was the chosen theatre of its barbarities. Such has been the rapid diffusion of moral and intellectual light!

The circumstance which will first strike a stranger in Barcelona, coming from the south of Spain, is nearly the entire absence of the national costume. The general aspect of the city is Spanish—the narrow streets, lofty houses, and the physiognomy of the people. But their dress has nothing characteristic. It partakes more of the French and English than of that of Spain:

and the streets lack, in a great degree, the picturesque effect which in more southern cities they borrow from the prevailing costume. In other respects, Barcelona has the appearance of a French or English town. It is a highly manufacturing place. The laboring of the steam-engine is heard as you pass through the streets, and clouds of smoke hover constantly over the city, bearing testimony to the extensive application of steam-power to practical uses.

The country around it is highly cultivated and embellished. For miles along the shores of the Mediterranean, both above and below Barcelona, there is a constant succession of villages, and the intermediate spaces are filled with farms and farmhouses. A mile or two back there is a range of hills, along the base of which, and, indeed, high up their sides, pleasure-grounds and country-seats are scattered, forming a magnificent background to the picture of rural beauty spread out before it. It is in direct contrast with the whole coast from Valencia to Malaga; and yet it has the castles and the towers which render the latter so striking, though here they stand amid rich masses of vegetation, instead of crowning barren rocks and sea-girt cliffs, with no trace of man around them. And it must be confessed that they lose much of their romance when they rise up in the midst of cultivated fields, and are hemmed in on all sides by the evidences of human industry, and art, and civilization. But as you approach the boundaries of France, the coast again becomes rugged and inhospitable. The castle and the tower stand alone upon the summit of the rock, or on the mountain's side, with no sign of life but the eagle or the sea-bird sailing about them. This is the true region of romance. Here the imagination can soar unshackled, and find no uncongenial vestiges of humanity to call it back to the sober realities of an age of statistics, and steam, and philosophical truth.

The recent disturbances in Barcelona are a subject of deep interest, not only as concerns the past, but from the probable connection they have with the future; for it is not to be disguised that they have made a serious impression upon the people of other portions of Spain as well as Catalonia. To enter at length into the causes in which they had their origin would not be consistent with the cursory nature of these sketches. Suffice it to say, that they are not only connected with the general divisions of party in Spain, but they are also, in a great degree, local in their char acter. While Spain has enforced a rigid system of exclusion, or of impositions tantamount to an exclusion, against most articles of foreign manufacture, that system has been, in respect to certain fabrics, relaxed in relation to Catalonia, of which Barcelona is the great commercial town. Barcelona, being also a highly manufacturing place, justly complained that the general system applied to other portions of the kingdom ought, on every consideration of impartial justice, to be enforced in respect to her, and that a relaxation of it in her case was doubly pernicious and unequal from the large capital she had embarked in manufacturing. But this was not the only cause of complaint. The high duties on articles not absolutely prohibited had given rise, as we have before stated, to a contraband trade, which had grown into a regular branch of commerce, numbering among those concerned in it persons high in rank, as well as the very custom-house officers charged with its suppression. From these causes, and others of a general character, Barcelona had been for a long time in a state of strong disaffection to the government.

The open outbreak commenced on the 13th of November, 1842, although for several days before there had been indications of a meditated movement. Armed groups of people were now seen in the streets, inflammatory speeches were heard, and some arrests were made by the police—among the persons arrested the editors of the Republican, a popular press. On the morning of the 14th these disturbances increased; the streets were thronged with malcontents; a crowd of people surrounded the jail, and demanded the release of the prisoners; the garrison was put under arms, and the military force was employed to defend the prison. Early in the afternoon the troops took their position in the rambla; and a large body of the militia or national guard occupied the Square of the Constitution, with every indication of supporting the government forces. Before night they were dismissed, with orders not to reassemble unless required by the proper authority. But at an early hour of the night they came together again in detached parties, organized themselves, posted sentinels, and prepared for a contest. At eight o'clock on the morning of the 15th the troops were fired upon by the populace, aided by the militia in detached bodies. This was the signal for a general movement. The troops, wherever they appeared in the narrow streets, were assailed with missiles of every description. Chairs, bureaus, stones, and tiles were hurled down upon them from the windows and roofs of the houses, while a galling fire was kept up from barricades in the streets. The whole city seemed to have taken arms against the government forces, and the neighboring villages and towns, alarmed by the discharge of cannon and ringing of bells, sent in reinforcements to aid their city brethren. At sunset the troops, commanded by Generals Van Halen, Zabala, and Zurbano, had withdrawn from the field of combat, and occupied the Castle of Montjui, the cita del, and two other positions in and near the city. Their loss during the day exceeded two hundred in killed and wounded, according to the official report, though it is generally believed to have been much greater. The loss of the insurgents was comparatively trifling. They were defended by barricades, and sheltered by the houses, which they occupied, and from which they poured a deadly fire upon the troops without being endangered themselves.

On the morning of the 16th a popular directory or junta was announced, though in what manner elected remains unexplained. The president was John Manuel Carsy, a Valencian, known only as the editor of a journal, and the seven members, and the secretary, were persons of little consideration. Though this first act on the part of the victorious city was exceedingly unfortunate, and was calculated to destroy confidence in the progress of the movement, the insurgents continued, nevertheless, to be successful.

On the 16th hostilities were renewed, and on the 17th, in the morning, the citadel was found deserted; in the course of the day the other positions in the city were surrendered, and the troops retired to Montjui and Sarria. The city was now completely victorious, but it was soon threatened with a bombardment, and the confusion which the threat created was augmented by the want of energy in the junta. On the 24th the prisoners taken by the insurrectionists, amounting to 2500, were allowed to retire unarmed. They immediately repaired to Montjui, and made a strong addition to the garrison. The junta in the mean time organized a regular force, and committed the great error of appointing to the command a Belgian, a foreigner, and a stranger to the local interests out of which the popular movement had principally sprung. Nor was the insurrection at Barcelona supported by corresponding movements in other parts of the kingdom, as it might have been, if it had been directed with proper energy and wisdom. On the 28th, after a reign of twelve days, the junta was dissolved by the national militia, and another was created; but the latter was never assembled; and on the 29th, ten individuals of character and talent were chosen, and took upon themselves the administration of the city, in a state of hopeless disorder and confusion. On the same day the arrival of Espartero, the Regent of Spain, was announced by a salute from Montjui, and Duranda, the new general of the city forces, took refuge on board a French man-of-war brig lying in the harbor. The new junta now labored with zeal and energy to put an end to the insurrectionary movement. The regular force levied by their predecessors was discharged, and the defence of the city was given up to the national militia. A commission was dispatched to the general-in-chief expressing an earnest desire to bring hostilities to a close. On consultation with the Regent and the minister of war, the committee was informed that nothing short of a disbandment of the national militia would be satisfactory, and that unless this demand was complied with, the city would be bombarded. The Regent refused to hold any communication with the committee, or even to receive the bishop, who went to him in the capacity of a pacificator. Such was the posture of affairs on the 1st of December. The city authorities had voluntarily liberated 2500 of the government forces, who had surrendered or been captured by the people; had dissolved the first junta; elected a new one friendly to a pacification; the new junta had disbanded the regular force raised by their predecessors; and they offered to open their gates to the Regent, and surrender the city to him. These propositions were declined, excepting on the hard and unnecessary condition that the national militia should give up their arms. This demand was the signal of new confusion in the city.

The junta friendly to a pacification was declared dissolved, and on the 2d of December a new one created, composed of obscure individuals; even the president was known only as an itinerant vender of perfumery about the coffee-houses. The next day, the 3d of December, was designated for the bombardment, unless the demands of the Regent were complied with. The city was deserted by most of those who could leave it, or who had not some sinister motive in remaining. Its population of 150,000 was reduced full two thirds. The citadel was nearly deserted by the militia. The city was literally disarmed by confusion and anarchy. In every point of view the bombardment, with which it was threatened, was useless, revengeful, and barbarous. At half-past five on the morning of the 3d, notice was again given that the fire would commence in six hours. A scene of indescribable disorder ensued. Multitudes of men, women, and children rushed to the city gates, to escape from the impending storm; the shipping in the harbor was filled with the fugitives; and cries of alarm and terror were heard on all sides. The fatal hour, half-past eleven, arrived; and a flood of flame and smoke burst from the castle of Montjui! Shells and round-shot filled the air, bearing terror and destruction to the devoted city; old men, women, and children rushed to the churches, and to buildings which were reported to be fire-proof, for an asylum; and the bursting of shells, the groans of the wounded, and the shrieks of the terrified, mingled with the crackling of houses set on fire by the burning missiles. "Many edifices," says an eloquent narrator of the events of this fatal day, "are in flames. There an old house has fallen to the ground. That wretched woman, who is rushing through the street with disheveled hair, and imploring mercy in frenzied accents, is a mother, whom a capricious destiny has spared to lament the fate of a tender infant, left in the cradle and buried beneath the ruins. That pallid youth, with agonized look, and with a priest at his side, is going to receive the last sigh of his mother, who is too infirm to flee, and who is sinking with terror and affright. Here, in the midst of a group of men, stands a girl, weeping, and imploring them: they are demanding a larger sum of money than she possesses to carry her father, who has been for many years a cripple, and who is stretched upon a litter, to a bomb-proof shop belonging to a worthy artisan, who receives and shelters all that present themselves. But see! they are suddenly buried in dust: the terrific noise which accompanies it is from the falling roof of that house, which has come in one mass to the ground. The litter is crushed, the harmless cripple and his flock-bed are buried beneath the falling tiles and the exploding shells. The daughter has sunk senseless among the fragments of burning rafters, her face bespattered with blood: can it be the blood of her father? Alas! let us fly from the scene of horror. We can not pass through this narrow street: there are two houses burning, and the flames are borne by the wind to the opposite side. Here, a knot of wretchedly-clad but well-armed men, with the physiognomy of savages, block up the way: they are fierce and relentless—they watch when the laws sleep—they are hoping and waiting for the sequel—they will soon rush fearlessly through the flames, and riot in pillage and the worst excesses of crime. Some pretend to give assistance; but when the fire lessens, they will strip the owner of the house of all the flames have spared. Let us leave these horrid scenes. And yet we can not escape the agonizing shrieks of a multitude of innocents, shut up and expecting death at every instant. They are the tenants of the orphan asylum. Near by are the girls of the house of charity. Merciful Heaven! are these unfortunate children among the guilty? Yes, all! Do you not hear the thunders of Montjui proclaiming their guilt? Equally deserving of vengeance are the tenants of the military hospital, who die lacerated to-day by projectiles cast by the very power in whose defence they fought and bled yesterday. Guilty are the sick, the mad, the infirm, in the civil hospitals and in other charitable asylums; guilty the living thousands of the house of charity—all, all are guilty! Neither men nor their actions are punished here. It is against a condemned precinct that the thunderbolt is hurled; that precinct is marked out by the city walls; and all that is within it must bear the anathema of destruction—an anathema fulminated by a justice of iron, and recorded in letters of blood."

Such was the justice visited upon Barcelona! a city defenceless, and incapable of resistance! The fire continued, without intermission, until midnight, more than twelve hours, and the next day the troops took quiet possession of the town. During the bombardment, seven hundred and eighty shells, ninety-six grenades, and one hundred and thirty-eight cannon-balls were thrown into the city. Four hundred and sixty-two houses were destroyed or injured, and the loss of property is estimated at a quarter of a million of dollars. The conduct of the Regent throughout was most extraordinary. It is manifest that he went to Barcelona to take vengeance—not to allay discontent or subdue hostility by moderation and wisdom, the great virtues of a sovereign, and the more essential in one who is but a temporary representative of sovereignty. He was in the neighborhood of Barcelona from the 29th of November to the 3d of December, the day of the bombardment; and he remained from the 4th, the day the troops reoccupied the city, until the 22d, and yet he did not once set his foot within it. To the innocent and the guilty alike he manifested himself only in the thunders of Montjui. His offence is not against Spain only: it is an offence against the enlightened humanity of the age, and, soon or late, the retribution it deserves will fall upon him. The ruined city was speedily repaired; a thousand men were immediately at work upon it, and all traces of the devastation are obliterated; but a deep wound remains—one which no time will heal. Though tranquillity reigns, though five months have elapsed since the reoccupation without outbreak, or without any external sign of discontent, the government is now, at the very moment I am writing, in a state of disorganization in the city. A public prosecution was brought, a few days ago, against a citizen of Barcelona, for publishing a severe criticism on the late events; and every member of the jury summoned to try him has secretly withdrawn from the city, in order to defeat every attempt to enforce the law against him. There can be no better evidence of a latent and wide-spread spirit of disaffection and hostility to the government—a spirit which may, ere long, break out into new and more serious insurrections.*

CHAPTER XVIII.

VOYAGE TO LEGHORN.

Departure from Barcelona.—Smuggling.—Steam-power.—The Boundary between France and Spain.—An American Sloop of War.—Arrival at Marseilles.—The Harbor and the City.—Departure from Marseilles.—The Coast of Italy.—Genoa, the Harbor and City.—Arrival at Leghorn.—Watermen.

On the evening of the second day after our arrival at Barcelona we were on board of the steamer at an early hour. She was lying a few rods from the landing-place, moored under shelter of the mole. The custom-house officers had been on board during the afternoon, and had made a show of examining every part of the vessel for articles not specified in the ship's papers. We were there during the latter part of their examination, while they were searching the main cabin, and had ocular proof of the closeness of the scrutiny. Just after sunset the captain went on shore, and the mate, whether by design or not it is not for us to decide, was also out of the way. In a few minutes a large boat came up under the stern, and the waiters proceeded to hand out through the windows a great number of packages, most of them taken from the very closets which had been opened by the custom-house officers a few hours before. One of these officials was on deck when the boat was taking in its lading; and he was seen to walk up and look over the vessel's stern and then retire to another quarter, so open and barefaced are these violations of the revenue laws! There can be no better comment on the impolicy and injustice of the restrictive system of Spain, than the general disregard in which it is held, and the wide-spread corruption which it has introduced.

Early in the morning on the third day after our arrival we were again under way, passing out of the harbor with the Castle of Montjui on our right and the lighthouse on our left. Another steamer left the city at the same time for Cadiz, and a third was preparing to start for the Balearic Isles. The great motive-power of the age is now everywhere seen, annulling distance, overcoming physical impediments, and assimilating moral diversities. In the narrowness of our views we have regarded it principally as an instrument of physical and intellectual advancement. In the sight of a philosophic forecast, it ought, perhaps, to be considered, first of all, as the great agent of political revolution and improvement—as the lever by which the restrictive system is to be upheaved from its foundations, and overturned to rise no more. When the products of the remotest districts of the earth can in a few days be laid at the door of those whose health or comfort requires them, the arm of exclusion will be extended in vain between them and the objects of their wants. There may be many a fierce conflict between the million and the privileged few who have grown wealthy and powerful by unequal constitutions and laws; but in every such conflict the victory in the end will side with the vast numerical majority, in which resides the preponderance of physical power. It is the great felicity of all popular movements that the privileged classes are compelled, in the effort to maintain their unjust advantages in the apportionment of social and political rights, to resort to brute force—the very agent in which the masses have themselves the superiority. For this very reason the latter must always triumph, when they move united, and with the determination of accomplishing their object. The few bayonets which the single despot or the privileged orders can bring against them are as naught in the great aggregate of a nation's strength.

During the entire day on which we left Barcelona, we were running along close to the shore. As the sun went down, the vessel's head was turned off in the direction of Marseilles, across the Gulf of Lyons. Two mountains, scarcely a mile apart, rose up astern, high above the surrounding land. Each had a castle on its summit. The boundary line of France and Spain runs between these two outposts of national jealousy and power. Here two great kingdoms meet; and agreeably to the established order, they meet in an attitude of hostility. Far to the west of these hills a magnificent line of the Pyrenees was seen, while the beams of the setting sun cast a light tint of gold upon their deep blue masses. This was our last glimpse of Spain. France, too, which we had just seen, and some of our party for the first time, was also sinking in the distance as we entered upon that stormy sheet of water, the Gulf of Lyons, hardly less boisterous than the opposite Bay of Biscay on the Atlantic side, with the hope of again seeing the French coast with the rising sun. But rough as the gulf usually is, it was calm and unruffled for us. Not a breath of air was felt during the night, and, as we had hoped, the sun rose and disclosed to us the coast between Marseilles and the mouth of the Rhone. In two hours we were at the entrance of the outer harbor of Marseilles. A Greek frigate was sailing out of it with a light breeze, which rose with the sun. As we approached the inner harbor, a beautiful sloop of war was lying at anchor. A more fairy or graceful vessel the ocean never bore. Her hull was perfectly black, her dark outline was finely expressed upon the misty land beyond, and with her long yards spread out, she seemed like a sea-bird resting upon the waves, and ready at any instant to take her flight. For miles we had admired her fine proportions, as much surpassing the fleet of traders about her, and even the Greek frigate which was passing by, as the high-bred racer exceeds the cart-horse. But as we came near, how did our hearts swell with pleasure and pride, as we saw the star-spangled banner floating over her—that glorious emblem, sacred to freedom; the standard of the fatherland to which we turn, in all our wanderings, as the centre of our associations of the past, and our hopes of the future. In the keeping of the gallant vessel over which it now waves, no stain shall sully it. She seems in all her lineaments like one of the youthful champions of a chivalric age, who may be beaten down by force of numbers, but who yields not to an equal antagonist.

The harbor of Marseilles is one of the most singular, as well as one of the most secure, in the world. Its entrance is not more than a hundred yards wide, and within it there is space for fifteen hundred ships. The narrow opening, through which they pass, is flanked on both sides by solid rock, rising high above the water, and covered with strong fortifications. It is, in fact, wholly impregnable to attacks from the water. The harbor itself is a mere basin, without outlet; and the consequence is, that the water within, the Mediterranean being without a regular tide, is stagnant, and usually exceedingly offensive to the smell. Various projects have been formed to make an artificial opening, by means of which the water could be readily changed, as a strong wind either in the direction of the entrance or the outlet would create a current through the basin. The winds in the Gulf of Lyons are frequent, violent, and often of long continuance. While we were at Marseilles, there was a heavy gale for three days blowing directly into the harbor, and yet the entrance is so narrow that there was scarcely any agitation of the water a hundred yards within it, although directly outside two or three coasting vessels were wrecked, with a loss of life in each instance. About eight hundred vessels were lying in the harbor, among them four government steamers, which ply regularly between Marseilles and Constantinople, and the southern and eastern ports of the Mediterranean, carrying the mails and passengers. They are beautiful vessels, and are kept in the most admirable order. We were on board one of them, intending to take passage to Leghorn; but finding they did not touch at Genoa, we took a Neapolitan steamer, quite as large, and equally commodious.

Marseilles has few attractions. It is purely a commercial town, and the traveler will lose nothing by hurrying through it as rapidly as possible. If he is an invalid, the more haste he makes the better; for there is no city in the south of France in which such cold, penetrating winds prevail. We were there after the middle of May; and for the first time for a year we were compelled to have a fire in our apartment. On the third day the wind abated, and we embarked in the steamer Herculaneum, for Genoa and Leghorn, a short time before sunset. The night was dark, and we saw only the steep, rocky coast near Marseilles. But the next morning at sunrise we were running along under the western shore of the Gulf of Lyons. We saw Italy for the first time, and the view brought with it no disappointment, elevated as our expectations had been. The land rises gradually to the height of mountains, and from the water's edge to the highest peak it is a rich mass of vegetation, in which the vine and the olive are conspicuous, dotted with villages, castles, and villas. Though much of the same character as the Spanish coast near Barcelona, it is far superior in luxuriance and beauty. For miles you see the same rich, ornamented, and thickly settled country, and it was not until we shot across the bay beyond the sight of the land, that the scene changed. About two o'clock in the afternoon, the city of Genoa, in the centre of its amphitheatre of hills, covered with fortifications, was before us. It reminded us strongly of Funchal, though the scenery is far less bold and striking. In the magnificence of the city, the palaces planted upon hills above the lower town, and the extent of the defences, which frown upon you from every height, Genoa is far superior. The harbor, too, is excellent. As you enter it an extensive mole stretches out on the right, while on the left another of less extent approaches it, forming a narrow passage; and a lighthouse, several hundred feet above the water, guides vessels into it with unerring certainty both by night and by day. The part of the city immediately in contact with the basin is not very inviting, though the principal hotels stand close upon the water. Some of them have been palaces in their day, and in their architecture are much more worthy of their former offices than of the uses to which they are now devoted. At a short distance from the water you enter the finest streets, with edifices of great height on both sides, filled with merchandize, jewelry, and articles of traffic. Others are literally streets of palaces, many of them of great architectural beauty, though in some, if not in most instances, bearing evident marks of neglect and dilapidation. There are still, however, a large number of wealthy families, and they are said to live with great economy within doors, for the purpose of maintaining the external show of splendid dwellings and equipages. The environs of Genoa are exceedingly beautiful. From the edge of the town the villas and gardens extend, across the intermediate spaces, to the base of the mountains, and high up their sloping sides. The same rich and luxuriant vegetation which greeted us, as we caught the first glimpse of Italy, reigns here in full exuberance. From all appearances Genoa must be a delightful summer residence. Though the amphitheatre of hills may collect the rays of the sun, and give them the additional force of concentration, the cool breezes from the surrounding elevations and from the sea must perpetually counteract the effects of the heat, and produce a moderate temperature. In winter the same local causes must render the climate wet and chilly: the hills, instead of being just high enough to shelter it from the rude and piercing blasts of the north, are so lofty as to be of themselves the cause of the propagation both of cold and moisture.

Genoa was, by the fiat of the Holy Alliance, annexed to the kingdom of Sardinia—an arrangement repugnant to reason and to all considerations of fitness, excepting such as are connected with the chimerical idea of the political balance of power in Europe. Its republican predilections are all averse from the association, and it is regarded with no friendly eye by the sovereign. The very intercourse with strangers is clogged with restrictions. We were passengers in a steamer running from Marseilles to Malta, and touching at the intermediate ports. We were bound to Leghorn. We had no business in Genoa. We stopped there merely because the steamer stopped to discharge and receive passengers and freight. Yet when we arrived, we were not allowed to go on shore for several hours; and, as a preliminary, we were paraded at the gangway in files, like a band of convicts, and counted, in order that no fraud might be practiced upon his Sardinian majesty. We were then allowed to land, but for this privilege we were compelled to pay three francs, or about sixty cents a head, to the government. The true policy of every country is to encourage visitors from others, if for no better reason, with a view to the expenditure they make. But it is said the intercourse of Genoa with strangers is viewed with suspicion; and it seems difficult on any other supposition to account for so illiberal a measure as a tax upon persons landing for a few hours from a steamer to see the city.

We left Genoa at sunset, and at sunrise the next morning we were in Leghorn. Here we staid but a few hours, reserving to a future day our examination of the few objects of interest it contains; but these few hours were long enough to convince us that the accounts we had heard of the impositions of the watermen, and the retainers of the public houses, were well founded.

There is a large class in the city who live mainly by services to strangers, and they become more exorbitant as the business becomes more lucrative. Every addition to the tens of thousands who annually crowd into Italy, whets the appetite for extortion. But the watermen at Leghorn are not only extortionate—they are exceedingly impudent; and the sooner the traveler gets out of their hands the better for his comfort. We had the good fortune of passing the ordeal of the docks unharmed, but not without paying a high price for the acquaintance we made with the gentry, who seem, in spite of the police, to have absolute possession of them.

Leghorn is a free port, and every thing one needs can be found in the greatest profusion, and at the cheapest rates. Clothes, manufactured goods of all countries, pictures, statuary, and, in short, every thing that nature or art produces, can be purchased at prices scarcely exceeding those which the same articles obtain at the place of production.

CHAPTER XIX.

JOURNEY TO FLORENCE.

Pisa.—Its former Power.—Count Ugolino.—The Duomo.—The Baptistery.—The Campo Santo, and the Leaning Tower.—The Lungarno.

IMMEDIATELY after breakfast we took a carriage and hurried on to Pisa, about fifteen miles distant, passing through a level and well-cultivated district, at the distance of some two or three miles from the sea. The Arno divides the city into two not very equal parts. It is here a fine stream, and its banks are flanked by streets of well-built and handsome edifices. The general aspect of the city is cheerful, and it ranks next to Rome as a winter residence in Italy for invalids. There is very little remaining in it to remind the visiter of its former greatness. Six centuries ago it was one of the most powerful commercial states in Europe. It had taken Sardinia from the Saracens, and conquered the Balearic Isles; it possessed Corsica, Elba, and numerous other islands; and had made various commercial establishments in the Levant. Its decline commenced in 1284. Its fleet was destroyed at the battle of Meloria, by the Genoese, under Oberto Doria, and its commander, Morosini, taken prisoner, a few galleys only, under Count Ugolino, escaping by flight. The tower in which this treacherous nobleman was starved to death, with his four children and grandchildren, the "Torre della Fame," as it was called, was recently visible; and, as is said by Sismondi, his is almost the only instance in history in which the punishment of a tyrant was so barbarous as to overbalance the odium of his crimes, and to render him an object of compassion rather than of hatred. Revolting as it was in itself, the genius of Dante has rendered it still more so by the language in which he has clothed the description of it, in the 33d canto of his Inferno. No one can read the account he puts into the mouth of Ugolino of the few last days of suffering which he and his children endured, without losing sight of the traitor in the barbarity of his punishment. With what horrid circumstances is the tale told!—his children, seeing him biting his own hands in agony, imploring him to take theirs, and assuring him that it will grieve them less than the spectacle of his suffering—"To you," they say, "we owe this miserable flesh—tear it from us, and let it nourish the life to which we owe ours"—his youngest son falling at his feet in the last moments of agony, asking him for hopeless aid, and then dying; the other three sinking, one by one, under their torment; and himself left alone, blind with weakness, for three days groping among their lifeless bodies, calling them by name, and then yielding to famine the little which grief had left. The whole tale is more horrid than any which history has recorded. A learned Pisan has written a quarto volume to purge his fellow-citizens of the reproach of revenging themselves in so savage a manner upon their victim; but history, as well as poetry, has fixed the stain upon them too deeply to be wiped away, though they have suffered all vestiges of the tower in which he perished to be obliterated.

The Duomo, the Baptistery, the Campo Santo, and the Leaning Tower bear ample testimony to the former wealth and splendor of Pisa. They form a group, in which nearly all the interest that belongs to the city centres. The Duomo, or Cathedral, was commenced in 1063, and finished in 1113, and it is one of the most beautiful structures of the middle ages, far surpassing in architectural taste every other ecclesiastical edifice of the same period. Indeed, very few cathedrals of any age are to be found which are so striking or beautiful in their interior. Portions of its exterior are hardly less imposing; and as a specimen of the Romanesque style it is, perhaps, unsurpassed. It is also rich in specimens of art, especially in bronzes and paintings, numbering among the former some highly meritorious works of John of Bologna, and among the latter some very fine pictures by Andrea del Sarto.

The Baptistery is nearly two centuries later than the Duomo. It is circular in form, surmounted by a dome and cupola, and is, in all respects, a worthy companion to the Cathedral. Its diameter is 100 feet, and its entire height about 180. It has been so often copied, and is so widely disseminated in alabaster, that, with this knowledge of its dimensions, a very just conception of its exterior may be obtained by those who have never seen it. But the interior must be seen to be properly appreciated, especially the pulpit, by Nicolo Pisano, with its extraordinary and elaborate workmanship.

The Campo Santo was founded near the close of the twelfth century, by Archbishop Ubaldo, who brought from Mount Calvary the earth with which it is filled. The present enclosure was commenced a century later, and finished near the close of the fifteenth. It is over 400 feet long, nearly 140 wide, and nearly 50 in height. It abounds in sepulchral monuments, sarcophagi, and statues, and in paintings in fresco by Giotto and other artists, representing, for the most part, Scriptural subjects. Few of these paintings possess any extraordinary merit; but the Campo Santo itself, its historical associations, the remnants of antiquity contained in it, extending as far back as the era of the Roman empire, its sepulchral monuments of emperors, nobles, and the distinguished men of the Republic of Pisa, ecclesiastics, warriors, civilians, artists, promiscuously intermingled, have an interest no other cemetery possesses. A portion of the pavement consists of marble slabs, bearing funereal mementoes of the Pisans who are buried beneath. The number of families who had the right of interment is said to have been about six hundred. The slabs, worn by passing feet, are gradually losing their value as memorials. Some of the carvings are totally effaced; and in a few centuries more these last vestiges of the extinct families they represent, will, like the republic they adorned, have perished forever.

The Leaning Tower, though last in the series, is by no means the least in point of attraction. It is a beautiful structure in itself, and its position, thrown, as it is, far out of the perpendicular, gives it an accidental interest, equalled only by the towers of Bologna, which are inclined in the same manner, but not to the same extent. It is an appendage to the Duomo, standing a few rods from it, and containing, like many other towers of the same age, separated from the main edifice, the Cathedral bells. It is 178 feet high and 50 feet in diameter, and in form a perfect cylinder of eight stories of columns sustaining arches, with open galleries within. It was commenced late in the twelfth century and finished about the middle of the fourteenth. The ascent is by 330 steps to the belfry, which contains seven bells, the largest weighing nearly six tons. From the open gallery on this story there is a beautiful view of the city of Pisa, and the surrounding country, with Leghorn and the Mediterranean in the distance.

The chief interest attached to this tower is its inclination, which exceeds that of every other in Italy. It inclines towards the Arno, which divides the city in two parts, and is twelve feet six inches out of the perpendicular. The base is fifty feet eleven inches in diameter, and the centre of gravity is, therefore, far within it. Great differences of opinion have prevailed in respect to this peculiarity. Some have supposed the tower was built in this manner to gratify a grotesque fancy; but the better opinion is, that it was caused by the nature of the soil. This is not only the most rational conclusion, but it is confirmed by the fact that both the Duomo and the Baptistery exhibit the same peculiarity, doubtless from defective foundations. Scarcely a single portion of the exterior of the Duomo is vertical, and at the west end there was a subsidence of nearly three feet when the edifice was in a course of construction. It is generally supposed that the inclination of the tower became apparent soon after it was commenced, and that there are evidences of the attempts of the architects to restore the perpendicular of the superstructure, by making the two sides of unequal height. But this conjecture is not confirmed by the measurements. On the contrary, they prove it unfounded. The lower story has the same dimensions on the overhanging side and its opposite, though a portion of the former is below the surface of the ground. It is thirty-four feet ten inches in height. The second story is nineteen feet ten inches high on the overhanging side, and nineteen feet nine inches on the opposite. This very slight difference could hardly have been otherwise than accidental. The third story is nineteen feet five inches high on the overhanging side, and nineteen feet eight and a half inches on the opposite; and the fourth story nineteen feet on the overhanging side, and nineteen feet one inch on the opposite. In both these cases the difference of height would have been reversed, if the object had been to regain the perpendicular. The fifth story affords some color to the supposition we are combatting. It is eighteen feet four inches high on the overhanging side, and seventeen feet nine and a half inches on the opposite—a difference of six and a half inches, nearly double the difference in the third story in the opposite direction. The sixth and seventh stories are of like elevation on both sides. But the upper or eighth story, in which the bells hang, is only twenty-three feet seven inches on the overhanging side, while it is twenty-four feet six inches on the opposite, making a difference of eleven inches. Thus it will be perceived that the greater number of variations in the height of the stories on the opposite sides of the tower are directly at variance with the supposition that they were designed to recover the vertical position of the superimposed portions of the structure. It is certainly difficult to account for these variations, especially that in the eighth story or belfry, where its effect is to increase the inclination of the story itself, and the apparent inclination of the whole edifice.

The Lungarno, the common name in this as well as other Italian cities similarly situated, for the street formed by the two banks of the Arno, has a large number of very fine edifices; three bridges cross the river;

the neighborhood is beautiful; and in its most frequented parts the city has an aspect of cheerfulness and of life, which must make it an agreeable residence in winter. It has the reputation of being favorable to pulmonary diseases, and it is a place of common resort for invalids. But the climate of Rome is in all respects preferable, and the only superiority of Pisa must be in its comparative cheapness, surrounded as it is by a fruitful country and less frequented by visiters.

After a hasty visit to the beautiful Santa Maria della Spina, our day's labor closed; and the next morning we continued our journey to Florence, passing through a charming country, highly cultivated, and shaded by trees festooned with vines, with here and there a town or village of cheerful aspect.

CHAPTER XX.

FLORENCE.

The City divided by the Arno.—Population.—Extent.—Gardens.—The Cascine.—Wealth and Simple Habits of the Ancient Florentines.—Degeneracy of the Modern.—Poggio Imperiale.—Our Summer Residence.—Temperature.—Sunset Effects.—Galileo's Tower. — Paintings and Statuary. — Palaces and Churches.—History of Florence.—Advice to Invalids.—Winter in Italy.

THE city of Florence lies directly upon the river Arno, which severs it into two unequal parts. At least two thirds of the population are upon the north side, but the objects of interest are somewhat more equally divided between the two portions of the city. On the north side are the Palazzo Vecchio, the great gallery of the Uffizi, the Duomo, the churches of St. Lorenzo and Santa Croce, the fortress of St. John the Baptist, built by the first duke of the Medici family for his personal security, the Strozzi and Riccardi palaces, the last built by Cosmo, son of John the founder of the Medici family, and a variety of other monuments connected with the history of Florence. On the other side are the Pitti palace, the residence of the Grand Duke, and the gallery connected with it, the magnificent Boboli gardens adjoining, the Museum of Natural

History, several fine churches, and the beautiful gardens of the Torregiani family. Many of the finest hotels are upon the banks of the Arno, and from them the remotest part of the city is reached in a few minutes. It had within the walls, in 1840, a population of 102,148 souls, and all comprised within a space of perhaps six square miles. The compact part of the city is hardly at any one point in contact with the walls. Within them, on all sides, gardens spread themselves out, often comprising eight or ten acres in a body, filled with trees and shrubbery, and making the atmosphere of the city fresh and fragrant. At least two square miles of the surface comprehended within the walls are covered with gardens. These, with the broad bed of the Arno, through which there is, either one way or the other, a perpetual current of air, render the city, in the hottest weather, tolerable, if not more so than most others under the burning sun of Italy. The streets are also kept cool by the great height of the houses, which throw the pavements in constant shade. Still, the city has the reputation of being very hot in summer, and it is so; but it has within a short distance a number of cool retreats. On the western side, along the banks of the Arno, there are the Cascine, an immense extent of pleasure grounds and pasturage belonging to the Grand Duke. Cascina is literally a cow's park or pasture, and though a part of it is still devoted to grazing, a name more appropriate to its present uses might be found. A large portion of it is covered with trees, and you may drive through it for miles in dense shade without being molested by a single ray of the sun. It is the fashionable resort of the Florentines in the evening. About sunset the carriages begin to pour out of the Porta el Prato, and from that time until dark there is a perpetual stream of coaches, horsemen, and pedestrians seeking the refreshing shade. Among them some of the Grand Duke's carriages are almost always seen, with mounted outriders in cocked hats and drab-colored livery. Many of the equipages of the nobility and gentry are exceedingly stylish, and in showy liveries they far outstrip the Grand Duke, but in the beauty of their horses they fall as much behind him. The aspect of the Cascine at nightfall, when filled with the city population, is exceedingly gay and brilliant; and the throng is as mixed in character as it could well be. The coach of the nobleman or the foreign ambassador, with two or three chasseurs in full uniform standing behind it, is often followed by a common hack, driven by a man in his shirt sleeves, or, perhaps, by an outlandish two-wheeled carriage, into which a countryman has crowded his wife and children, and brought them out to catch a glimpse of the splendor of the court. The woods, the fields, and the footpaths are free to all classes, and all are free to be represented in these evening gatherings. A more orderly population is rarely seen. The only disturbance of which we heard, during the four months and a half we passed in Florence, was a horsewhipping which one gentleman inflicted on another (neither of them Florentines by-the-by), and which he chose to administer here for the sake of the publicity of the thing.

A very considerable portion of the Cascine is devoted to grazing. The Grand Duke has his farmhouses and farmers, and his cattle, and the city markets are daily supplied with his milk and butter. It is needless to say that the fields are in the best condition, the cattle of the finest breeds, and all the products of the dairy of most excellent quality. As you drive through the grounds, coveys of partridges and pheasants spring up before you, and hares run across your path, and dash into the nearest thicket. They are rarely molested, and they are almost as tame as domesticated animals. During the summer, a favorite dog, belonging to a noble lady, broke loose from the servant, who had him in charge, and killed two pheasants. The game-keeper, who was near by, shot him dead on the spot. The lady complained to the Grand Duke, and demanded the punishment of the game-keeper; but the Grand Duke, while condoling with her on account of her misfortune, refused to punish him, as he had only performed his duty. The lady swore vengeance; but the day of poisons and assassinations has gone by in Italy, at least in high life, and the injury will doubtless go unavenged.

One of the greatest advantages of the Cascine is, that they are in actual contact with the city walls. A drive of fifteen minutes brings you to them from any part of the city. As you enter them, you have on one side the banks of the Arno, along which you may ride or drive for about two miles; then, turning to your right, you come out upon an open lawn, skirted on one side by thick forest trees, which shut out the sun, and, on the other, a noble range of mountains bounds the view, with the classic remains of Fiesole crowning a nearer height. The whole view is rich and beautiful, and as the sun goes down, the hill tops, bathed in purple, stand out from the clear blue sky with a brilliancy which no other land can rival. Some of the sunset effects are most extraordinary for the combination and intenseness of color. I have seen the mountains of deep violet, and the sky above them of the richest gold, crimson, and sea-green. This did not occur more than twice during the summer, and the appearance was so singular, that I involuntarily closed my eyes to see, on opening them again, whether there was not some optical illusion in it. But the colors still remained as bright as before, gradually fading away as the sun fell below the horizon.

Near the middle of the Cascine is a ducal palace, designed by Manetti. There is an open square before it, and here the coaches and equestrians usually stop a few moments, and fill up the vacant space with a brilliant array of equipages. The Florentines have a strong propensity for show in carriages, horses, and dress; though, in this respect, they only participate in the general frailty of the times. In the days of the Republic, and these were, in every sense of the word, the best days of Florence, the inhabitants were remarkable for the simplicity of their habits. The richest merchants were often the most plainly clad, and the fairest dames were content with the close scarlet robe, girded about the waist, which was the costume of their sex. Yet with all this simplicity Florence had accomplished the greatest public enterprises without, and was carrying on within some of the most expensive works, which adorn the city at the present time. The magnificent Cathedral was in progress; the three central bridges, which span the Arno, were built; the foundations of the tower of Giotto, the Campanile, had been laid—a work remarkable for its rich and well-executed embellishments, and its singular design—the windows, or openings in its sides, increasing in size as they approach the top, thus reversing the usual effect of distance and aerial perspective; the Baptistery had been furnished with its three wonderful gates of bronze, which Michael Angelo said deserved to be the gates of Paradise; and the great ambition of the Republic was to distinguish itself, in the only way in which republics can properly be lavish of their wealth, by the grandeur and beauty of its public edifices. At this very period, the beginning of the fourteenth century, Florence produced the richest manufactures of wool and silk. The nobles and ladies of every court in Europe shone in her articles of finery, while she herself, though abounding in wealth, abstained from all show and luxury, and was intent only on enlarging her commerce, nourishing her internal industry, and leaving monuments of her taste to after ages. What a change has the lapse of five centuries wrought in her social and political character! She lives passively under a monarchical form of government, absolute in itself, though administered, it is true, with moderation. She is doing little or nothing for the fine arts; she is, in respect to them, reposing on the achievements of past ages. The Grand Duke, who is himself the embodiment of her political power, is finishing the mausoleum of the Medici, and meditates completing the western end of the Duomo, which still wants the marble facing of the rest of the edifice. This is the extent of the movement in progress in the embellishment of the city. Her people are now as much distinguished for show as they formerly were for simplicity. Indeed, the higher classes have some habits which are characteristic of the worst stages of luxurious indolence and ease, and which are not in the best taste on the score of manners. It is no uncommon thing to see a lady, in an open barouche, half sitting and half lying back, with her feet raised and deposited on the front seat. What a torrent of disgust and virtuous indignation would such an exhibition have called forth in the Trollopes, the Marryatts, and the Basil Halls, if it had been seen in America! No better evidence would have been desired of the idleness and indelicacy of the American ladies. But in classic Italy it passes unnoticed, or, perhaps, even as the unceremonious ease of high refinement. The dog mania, or at least the mania for useless dogs, seems to rage with extraordinary malignancy. We have more than once seen a magnificent coach, with two chasseurs behind, in splendid uniforms, epaulettes and all, going out to give an airing to a dog, who was the only inside passenger, and who occupied the back seat as complacently as though he had been the master of the establishment. While the health of this bloated and over-fed beast was thus attended to, the children were probably breathing the close air of the nursery in the city. Nor are these unusual exhibitions. You can scarcely walk out of town without meeting a footman in livery leading out a dog to take the country air. These follies are certainly not confined to Florence. They exist wherever there is overgrown wealth perpetuated by descent, where the hereditary rich grow degenerate by inaction, and where social distinctions are so strongly marked that the needy retainer of the great is more honored, though he be but a dog-tender, than the independent ploughman, who earns his bread "in the sweat of his face."

On the southern side of the Arno, as you pass out of the Porta S. Pier Gattolini, commonly called the Porta Romana, you enter a beautiful avenue, with two rows of ancient trees on each side, leading to a royal lodge at the top of a hill, which rises gradually from the level of the city. The avenue is precisely a Tuscan mile in length (equal to 1808 English yards), though it is so perfectly straight, and the ascent so uniform, that it seems not half that distance. The lodge, or Poggio Imperiale, at the head of the avenue is, in fact, a magnificent palace, built by the Baroncelli family, but purchased in 1602 by Maria Maddalena, of Austria, wife of Cosmo the Second, since which time it has been the property of the royal family of Tuscany. It is the most magnificent of the Grand Duke's villas, but it has during the present summer been unoccupied. Some half a dozen times, perhaps, his carriages have been standing before it, and we have as often seen some of the family walking in the garden, which is prettily laid out, and adorned with a large quantity of poor statuary. Our own villa adjoins the Grand Duke's grounds, and one of our favorite walks in the afternoon is under his olive trees and vines.

We had been but a few days in Florence before we became convinced of the necessity of finding a residence in the pure air of the country, if we hoped to pass the summer comfortably, and we were so fortunate as to obtain the Villa di Monteturli, belonging to the Marquis D'Elci, and usually known as the Villa D'Elci. All things considered, it is, perhaps, the very best situation in the neighborhood of Florence. It is very near the head of the avenue which terminates at the Poggio Imperiale, and in the hottest weather one may walk nearly the entire distance to and from the city in perfect shade. It stands on the summit of an eminence, from which the ground descends on all sides, so that it is fanned by every breeze that blows, and it commands, in every direction, a beautiful view of the adjacent country, covered with villas, farmhouses, and fields green with the olive, the vine, and the mulberry. It has, in the central court, an excellent well of water, which is always a matter of the first importance, and in Florence particularly, where this great necessary of life is not in general of the best quality. The villa itself has all the requisites for a hot climate. It is, first of all, spacious; and no one can live in comfort in the south of Italy in summer, without large and airy rooms. It is built around a square court, is over one hundred feet in length, and nearly one hundred feet in breadth, is two stories high, and has in each story a complete suite of apartments for a family, with a kitchen, and all other necessaries for housekeeping. On the lower floor it has a billiard table, which enables us to exercise within doors when the sun is too hot to go out. In the whole establishment there are about thirty rooms, and there are extensive grounds around it, belonging to the estate of the D'Elci family—fields, through which you may ramble and inhale the odor of green grass and of the fresh earth as it is turned up by the plough. The house is completely furnished throughout with every article that comfort or luxury requires, except linen and silver, which we provide ourselves; and for all these conveniences we pay but forty-six Tuscan dollars a month—a little more than ten pounds sterling, or about forty-seven Spanish dollars. We hire it only for four months, and we pay more in proportion than we should if we took it for a longer period. It might probably be hired for a year for three hundred Tuscan dollars. Reasonable as this is, we have heard of villas in the neighborhood, less spacious, of course, which have been hired for twenty dollars a month. The other necessary expenses of housekeeping in Florence are as cheap as rents. Servants' wages are low, provisions are moderate in price, and fruits and vegetables are abundant, and cost little. We have certainly never lived in any place where a family may enjoy so many comforts and luxuries for so little money. Though strangers, we have had no reason to find fault with any of those with whom we have had transactions in money, or to suppose that they have taken any unjust advantage of us. The contadino, or farmer, who has supplied us with milk, wine, and oil, the servant who has marketed for us, and, in short, every native of the country who has been in any manner connected with us, has been courteous and kind, and, as we believe, honest and conscientious. We have heard much of the bad conduct and dishonesty of servants towards foreigners, but we have been so fortunate as to escape it entirely ourselves, and we are strongly inclined to believe that it is in most cases brought on by infirmities of temper, or total inattention on the part of strangers to their own affairs. The head of an establishment, who keeps a vigilant eye upon its daily expenditures, is no more likely to be cheated in Italy than elsewhere, and he must be very deficient in attention if the frauds committed upon him are continued long without detection. The only time we saw our landlord, the Marquis D'Elci, was when we made the bargain for the villa. Our subsequent transactions, such as receiving and surrendering the possession, paying rent, and settling for broken crockery, etc., were all made with a very gentlemanly agent, and every thing was arranged on the most fair and liberal terms. The same praise is due to another landlord of ours, at No. 1886 Via Maggio, in the city, near the Arno, where we took rooms for a few weeks in the fall, after giving up the villa, and while we were preparing to go to Rome.

Nothing could be more delightful than a summer residence at the Villa D'Elci. The season was said to be unusually cool, and it must have been so, unless the climate of Florence and its environs is grossly slandered. The temperature of the entire month of June was low for the summer of a moderate climate. The thermometer more than once stood at 56° Fahr. two hours after sunrise, rising to 70° in the middle of the day. In July it was once as high as 86°, and once as high as 84° at two o'clock, P. M., the period, ordinarily, of the greatest heat. In August it rose to 86° twice, and to 87° once, and this was the highest temperature of the season. There is something inexpressively balmy and soothing in the air—something which is to be felt rather than described. The sun is hot; but even when the temperature is not high, and when one is in shade, every thing around appears to radiate sensible heat. There is a peculiar softness in the air independently of its temperature, which, in its effects upon the senses, differs as widely from ours as a soft-water bath differs from one of hard water. We are, as it were, perpetually bathed in this warm, genial atmosphere, and soothed into serenity and languor. There is nothing positively enervating in it, but we feel disposed to be quiet and revel undisturbed in the luxury of our own sensations. It is difficult to decide which we enjoyed most, the mornings or the evenings at the villa. For three or four hours after sunrise we were either walking or seated in the shade, looking out upon the beautiful landscape, covered with the richest vegetation and picturesque edifices, convents, villas, farm-houses, olive orchards, and vineyards promiscuously intermingled, and bounded by a distant line of the Appenines, on the tops of which patches of snow were visible, until we were far advanced in July, lighting up the misty blue of their high and waving outlines. In the evening, as the sun went down, they became of deep purple, and when some of the sunset effects, to which I have before alluded, became visible in the sky above them, they constituted altogether a picture of rich and varied beauty, which nothing could equal. On another side we had a glimpse of Florence, several hundred feet below us, its spires, and the magnificent dome of the Cathedral finely relieved by a nearer range of mountains, and by the classical height of Fiesole, itself one of the most striking objects in the environs of the city. Still farther on, back of the Grand Duke's villa, is Galileo's Tower, a square, rude belvedere, covered with ivy, and surmounting a farmhouse. From this tower he made those observations on the planetary bodies, and drew those deductions from their motions, which shed so much light on the true theory of the solar system, and rendered his name immortal. Farther on, but concealed from our view by an intervening hill and grove, is the house in which he was imprisoned, by the tribunal of the Inquisition, on account of the new views of astronomical science which he unfolded—an imprisonment from which he was only liberated to insist, in spite of all the blind superstition and ignorance of the age, that the earth turned on its axis notwithstanding. An inscription over the door of this house commemorates the circumstance which has rendered it illustrious. Back of the villa, towards the southeast, there is a beautiful range of hills at a distance of about four miles, covered with farmhouses and cultivated fields, and crowned by a church with a lofty tower. In fact, wherever you turn, exquisite scenes of rural beauty present themselves, rich, varied, and perpetually changing their outlines as the sun rises or descends, and casts his shadows in opposite directions. This is the season for seeing Italy and enjoying it. There is no greater error than to suppose that any just

Galileo's Tower.

conception of the climate or the scenery can be formed in winter, the season at which strangers usually visit it. Cities may be explored, and their treasures of art investigated. But of the rural beauty of the country scarcely a trace can be seen excepting in spring, summer, or autumn. In winter the trees are stripped and bare, the luxuriant foliage of the vines totally disappears, and the whole aspect of things is cold, barren, and uninviting. The atmosphere may be clear and brilliant, but it has none of the warm and hazy glow, which is peculiarly Italian. In short, I am not aware of any advantage which the country in Italy has in winter over the more northerly regions of Europe, excepting a more moderate temperature.

Florence possesses some advantages over every other city in Italy as a place for a permanent or temporary residence. Every thing is abundant and remarkably cheap. Fruits come in endless succession, and almost endless variety, from April to November, and they cost nearly nothing. Bread, meats, groceries, and, in short, all the necessaries of life, as well as its luxuries, can be obtained at moderate prices, and for $400 a year a large and well-furnished house can be obtained. Several years ago it was the centre of fashion for visiters, and every thing was comparatively dear. Some twenty thousand strangers winter in Italy, and wherever they congregate in great numbers, their presence is manifest in the increased prices of lodgings.

Rome and Naples are now the chief places of resort, and they are comparatively dear.

To the lover of the arts the two great public galleries, the Uffizi and that of the Pitti palace, afford a perpetual source of instruction and enjoyment. The Tribune, with the Medicean Venus and the other well-known masterpieces in painting and statuary, is unsurpassed for artistic treasure. Nowhere is there to be found so much grace and beauty in so limited a space. The Venus alone would give this magnificent apartment a superiority over any other devoted to exhibitions of art. It is by universal admission the most faultless specimen of sculpture either of ancient or modern times. Yet it does not embody the most exalted conceptions of female beauty and grace. It lacks the refinement and purity of expression which give to the female character its highest attraction. She is a terrestrial, and not a celestial Venus: and such must have been the conception of the artist. In all that is calculated to charm the senses by a display of voluptuous beauty and fascinating grace, this statue is unquestionably unsurpassed, nor is it at all likely to be equaled by modern art.

The Apollino, the Dancing Faun, the Wrestlers, and the Slave whetting his Knife, are fit companions for the Venus as works of art. In variety, skill, genius, and beauty, this little collection of statuary is unrivaled.

The pictures in the same apartment are of the same

high order of merit. The magnificent portrait of Julius the Second, the Fornarina, the Holy Family, and others by Raphael, the Virgin of Michael Angelo, the two Venuses of Titian, and a large number of other pictures by the great Italian masters, complete the treasures of this noble apartment.

The Tribune is but the beginning of this great collection—the richest and the most varied in the world. It would be the work of months to examine, even superficially, every object it contains. The vestibules, corridors, and the immense suite of apartments running off in opposite directions from the Tribune, are crowded to overflowing with pictures and statuary, in which the different Italian schools and the distinguished masters of all countries and ages are represented. This noble gallery, as well as that of the Pitti palace, is open to visiters at all times, without charge, and artists are afforded every possible facility for copying the works it contains.

The collection derives its name from the building in which it is contained. It was built under Cosmo the First, for the convenience of the public offices (Ufizzi). Vasari constructed the principal edifice in the sixteenth century, and the corridor, which was designed to connect, by a private passage, the Palazzo Vecchio, adjoining the Ufizzi, with the Pitti palace, on the other side of the Arno. The Tribune was built by Buontalenti at a later period.

The Palazzo Vecchio (the old palace) standing on

the right of the Ufizzi, and on the eastern side of the Piazza del Gran Duca, is one of the most striking edifices in Florence, not only for its extent, but for its quaint and lofty tower, rising above all others, and constituting a landmark in every view of the city from the surrounding elevations. It was built in the thirteenth century as a residence for the gonfaloniere, or mayor, and the principal magistrates of the city. In the sixteenth century it was occupied for several years by Cosmo the First, and it is now devoted to the use of the public offices. It has an intimate connection with the history of Florence, and in the great hall, one of the finest in the world for its height and the grandeur of its architecture, some of the principal events in the reign of Cosmo the First are represented in fresco, by Vasari. The bronze equestrian statue of Cosmo, by John of Bologna, stands in the Grand Duke's square (the Piazza del Gran Duca) opposite—a noble work, though when one has seen the equestrian statue of Marcus Aurelius on the Capitoline Hill, at Rome, the impression made by this is greatly impaired. Cosmo was the founder of the dynasty of the Medici. For a century before, and two centuries after him, his family held the destinies of Florence in their hands. They found it, as we have described it, industrious, powerful, frugal, and rich in commercial enterprise; they left it rapidly sinking into the inferiority it has since reached. During the last century Tuscany has undergone several transformations in its government, but without much advantage, so far as the people are concerned, excepting during the brief ascendency of Napoleon. Criminal trials were made public, roads were improved, and various improvements were introduced in the economical administration of the kingdom, the salutary influence of which the Grand Duchy feels to this day. Nor is the truth disguised. In a small historical account of Florence, recently published, dedicated to the present Grand Duke, the obligations which Tuscany owes to Napoleon in these respects are frankly acknowledged. No man is less likely to look with disfavor on a candid statement of facts, even when connected with the temporary banishment of his own family, than the Grand Duke. He is a noble specimen of simplicity and purity of character, and he is as just and conscientious as he is simple and pure. In his manners and habits he is perfectly free from ostentation, though one of the wealthiest sovereigns in Europe. We frequently met him during the summer, walking in the neighborhood of our villa, leading one of his children by the hand, with no other attendant but a single domestic following him at a distance. The people of Florence sometimes complain that he has not enough of the show which a sovereign ought to maintain. The government is absolute, but it is administered with great impartiality. Indeed, from some slight research into the laws of Tuscany—those especially which relate to its agriculture—they seemed to me to be framed with a more careful regard to the interests of the working classes than to those of the landed proprietors. The people appear to be contented with their condition. They have reason to be so. Their taxes are very light, and they have every possible security for property, personal liberty, and life. If they were to change their form of government by forcible means, it would not be on account of any practical inconvenience or wrong, but from the natural desire every man feels to have a part in the regulation of the political system to which he is subject.

The Grand Duke's square, the Loggia di Lanzi, and the spaces surrounding the Palazzo Vecchio are full of statuary. The Fountain of Neptune, by Ammanato; the David, by Michael Angelo, by no means a great work for so great an artist; the magnificent Perseus, by Cellini; the Rape of the Sabines, by John of Bologna, are conspicuous among the treasures of this noble square.

The gallery of the Pitti palace, on the eastern side of the Arno, is less extensive than that of the Ufizzi, but it has many pictures and statues of great beauty. It is the residence of the Grand Duke and his family; but the gallery is, nevertheless, always open like the other, excepting on Sundays, to the public. The gallery forms a suite of splendid apartments, designated as the Halls of Venus, Apollo, Mars, Jupiter, etc., constructed and embellished in a style of regal magnificence. In the second of these apartments there is a Virgin and Child, by Murillo, a pleasing picture, but not one of his best; the third contains the celebrated Madonna della Seggiola, one of the most exquisitely beautiful of Raphael's paintings; and in the Hall of Flora stands Canova's Venus, which was considered not unworthy to replace the Venus de Medici in the Tribune, when the latter was taken to Paris by Napoleon. It suffers from a stain in the marble, and also, as a model of the goddess of beauty, by being draped. Many of the paintings in this collection will bear a favorable comparison with the most meritorious by the same masters in the Ufizzi. They are more than four hundred in number, and in respect to variety, as well as artistic merit, this gallery, notwithstanding the near neighborhood of the other, can not fail to be ranked among the most attractive in Europe.

The Pitti palace was built by Luca Pitti, in the fifteenth century. Luca was an enemy of the Medici, and a rival of the Strozzi families, and fell into disgrace by a conspiracy against the former. The palace was left unfinished, and was sold by his descendants to the wife of Cosmo the First. The Boboli Gardens, adjoining, were laid out by her, and they constitute one of the great attractions of Florence. The ground rises from the level of the palace below to an elevation commanding a beautiful view of the city. Nothing can be more enchanting than these gardens in summer. Though within the city walls, a perpetual freshness reigns throughout. The groves of forest trees intersected by graveled walks; the arbors buried in shade; the lawns always verdant; the marble statuary scattered in boundless profusion, glistening in the sunbeams, where they stand out from the surrounding trees and shrubbery, or lighting up the deep shadow of the foliage, in which they are embosomed, the perpetual quietude, broken only by the sound of voices, give a peculiar charm to these beautiful grounds. They make the city even in the hottest weather, an agreeable residence. In the freshness of the evening, when the sun gets low, the physical strength, wasted by the summer heat, is soon repaired by the invigorating influence of their cool and peaceful shades. Multitudes resort to them, but they are of so great an extent that they are never disagreeably thronged. The gardens of the Torregiani family are also exceedingly beautiful, and they are usually open to the public; but they are comparatively limited in extent, and they lie low and close to the city walls. The elevation to which the Boboli Gardens rise, gives them additional coolness, and they have to invalids an advantage over the Cascine, which lie upon the bank of the Arno, and are, for this reason, not always free from dampness. To complete the attraction of this locality the Grand Duke's band plays every morning at nine o'clock in front of the palace. It is composed of a large number of musicians, well trained and skilled in their art. Sometimes an entire opera is performed, and their music is always listened to by a large number of auditors.

Besides the two great galleries of the Ufizzi and the

Pitti palace there are many private galleries well stocked with pictures, and the churches contain numerous specimens of painting and sculpture from the Italian masters. The principal churches, the Duomo, Santa Croce, San Lorenzo, Santa Maria Novella, and the Annunziata, are almost unsurpassed for the objects of interest they contain. They constitute, in fact, one of the chief attractions to the lover of the arts as well as to the student of history.

The Duomo is one of the finest cathedrals in Italy. It is 454 feet in length, and its height to the top of the cross 386 feet. The dome, which is octagonal in form, exceeds that of St. Peter's in circumference. The Campanile, standing on the east side, rises to the height of 275 feet; and the beautiful Baptistery on the south completes the group—inferior in interest to that of Pisa, but surpassing it in some of its architectural embellishments.

Santa Croce and San Lorenzo are the two churches which abound most in objects of interest and in historical associations—the former as the principal mausoleum of the ancient Florentine families, and the latter as that of the Medici. The former is filled with noble monuments, commemorating alike the illustrious dead to whom they were erected and the immortal sculptors by whose hands they were carved. Before the church, in the square which bears its name, the foundations of the democracy of Florence were laid, in the middle of the thirteenth century, and the great political truth, too little respected in modern times, was practically asserted, that all the powers of government are derived from the popular will.

With the most uninviting exterior San Lorenzo contains more attraction than any other church in Florence. Near the altar stands the monument of Cosmo, the father of his country, and in the old sacristy the sarcophagus of John, his father. In the new sacristy are the monuments of Lorenzo and Julian. The building and the monuments were designed for each other, and the effect of both is improved by this unity of purpose. The monuments are among the noblest works of Michael Angelo. The allegorical representations of Day and Night are wonderful conceptions. They may be criticised as exaggerations, but they are bold, grand, and unique, like their great author—as a sculptor and painter, alike unrivaled and unimitated. He touched nothing without leaving on it the impress of his mighty genius ; his works may not be without faults, but in spite of all imperfections, they surpass in grandeur the masterpieces of all others in the same departments of art. His unfinished works may be known by the marks of his chisel. No other sculptor could make by a single stroke so deep an impression in the solid marble. His hand, like his mind, seems to have been armed with superhuman force.

The Laurentian Library, the noblest living monument of the Medici family, and the Medicean Chapel, constitute parts of the church—the former rich beyond comparison in its manuscripts, and the latter equally so in tasteless extravagance of ornament in precious stones.

The Annunziata is celebrated for the Madonna del Sacco, in fresco, by Andrea del Sarto, unhappily faded and partially obliterated, but exceedingly beautiful, and for many other fine frescoes, easel paintings, and bassi relievi; and Santa Maria Novella for its cloisters, frescoes, and arabesques. The square, on one side of which the latter stands, has an obelisk in its centre supported by tortoises, the work of John of Bologna. Here the festivities of the Florentines are celebrated, some in the modern taste, and some in imitation of the ancients. The chariot race on the anniversary of St. John the Baptist, the patron saint of Florence, can not well be surpassed as a burlesque of the Greeks and Romans. No man who venerates the classics should witness it. He can never read a description of this trial of equestrian skill in ancient verse, without having all the poetic illusion dissipated by a remembrance of the bungling Florentine imitation—the annual race around the obelisk and the tortoises on the 24th of June.

The fireworks on the preceding evening are of a higher order of merit. They are, in truth, very fine. They take place on the Ponte alla Carraja; and between this and the Santa Trinita, the most graceful bridge in the world, there is also a miniature sea fight, which belongs to the same category as the chariot race.

To an invalid Florence, as will have been seen, offers

numerous attractions and advantages. The city is compact; its chief objects of interest lie within a narrow compass, and the freshness of the country may be enjoyed even within the walls. The mind may be constantly attracted and turned away from the infirmities of the body without fatiguing either. If an excursion into the interior is desirable in hot weather, there are the delightful baths of Lucca, at the distance of a day's drive, where the cool air of the mountains may be enjoyed in perfection; or the charming vale of Vallombrosa may be reached at less than half the distance, and a quiet day or two may be passed among the hospitable friars. Fiesole, towering high above the surrounding country, is but an hour from the city, and here the purest air may be breathed in the midst of cyclopean remains thousands of years old. Indeed, on all sides some elevation may be found, where in an hour one may look down upon the city, and enjoy a delicious atmosphere, and a moderate temperature. A family designing to pass a year or two in Italy, might advantageously make Florence their headquarters, going to the more northern districts in midsummer, and to Rome and Naples in midwinter. To American invalids, the most interesting question is, in what manner it can be most safely and conveniently reached. To those who leave the United States in the spring, the best route is through France. But to those who embark in the fall, this route should by all means be avoided. The autumn of France is the reverse of ours. It is raw and wet.

The cases are numerous in which invalids, passing through France on their way to Italy, in November, have contracted colds, from which they never recovered. It is far better to go to England, and leave it immediately by the Oriental line of steamers from Southampton to Oporto, Lisbon, Cadiz, Gibraltar, and Malta. From Malta there is a line of steamers to Naples, touching at some of the ports in Sicily. A better mode still is to avoid England, and winter in Madeira, or go by a Marseilles packet to Gibraltar, where an Oriental steamer may be taken to Malta. In this way an invalid improves his climate from the very hour he leaves New York, and avoids the great peril of passing through France at a season always doubtful, if not inclement. Good vessels can be obtained from New York to Madeira in October, and there are always opportunities of going from Madeira to Lisbon, Cadiz, or Gibraltar, with tolerable accommodations. The passage rarely exceeds a week from Funchal to either of the three places last named, and they are all on the regular route of the Oriental steamers. On leaving Madeira late in the spring, the route from Gibraltar to Marseilles by the Spanish steamers, and from Marseilles to Leghorn by the Sardinian or Neapolitan, is preferable. A cursory view may thus be had of the cities on the eastern coast of Spain, and Florence may be reached at the season when it is clad in the richest verdure, and made balmy and fragrant by the most luxuriant vegetation.

To the student of history, Florence possesses an extraordinary interest, in the fact that its rise and fall are comparatively recent, and that there are living monuments to mark all the great changes through which it has passed. There is scarcely a public edifice or a private palace which does not commemorate some event in its history. Florence may be regarded as the geographical centre of the cluster of fiery little Italian republics which sprang up on the ruins of the feudal system, and involved the whole of southern and central Europe in their feuds. The struggles of her own factions became nearly as extensive in the combinations to which they led, and paved the way to the destruction of her liberties. Her streets, squares, private palaces, public edifices and monuments are memorials of these conflicts in some of their phases. The history of the Medici and the other distinguished Florentine families may here be studied with the great advantage which these living records afford. To enjoy Florence its historic details should be familiar to the observer before he commences his examinations. With this preparation there are few cities in Europe which can be explored with an interest so deep or sustained.

September is usually a delightful month in Florence. The temperature at mid-day is about 18° Reaumur or 72° Fahrenheit; and the beauty of the atmosphere and the autumnal vegetation draws one out, in spite of one's self, into the open air. On the 1st of October the Appennines were again covered with snow, and now and then a cold blast from them swept over the valley of the Arno, pinching the vegetation and covering the earth with showers of falling leaves. We regarded this as the proper signal for another remove to the south, and on the 16th (precisely a year after we sailed from New York) we turned our faces towards Rome.

Biographies.

	Retail
BLAKE'S BIOGRAPHICAL DICTIONARY. Royal 8vo, -	5 00
LIVES OF THE PRESIDENTS. 8vo; sheep, - - - -	2 50
FLEETWOOD'S LIFE OF CHRIST. Complete edition; illustrated; extra, - - - - - - - - - - - - - -	2 50
BANCROFT'S LIFE OF GEORGE WASHINGTON. New edition; one vol., 12mo; cloth, gilt, - - - - - - - - -	1 25
LIFE AND CAMPAIGNS OF NAPOLEON BONAPARTE. New edition, illustrated; one vol., 12mo; cloth, gilt, - - - - -	1 25
LIVES OF THE HEROES OF THE REVOLUTION; comprising the lives of Washington, and his generals and officers who distinguished themselves in the war of Independence. Illustrated; one vol., 12mo; cloth, gilt, - - - - - - - - - - -	1 25
LIFE OF CHRIST AND HIS APOSTLES. By Rev. John Fleetwood, D D. Illustrated with numerous engravings; one vol., 12mo; cloth, gilt, - - - - - - - - - - - - -	1 25
PILGRIM'S PROGRESS; with Notes, and a Life of the Author. By Rev. Thomas Scott. A new edition, illustrated; one vol., 12mo; cloth, gilt, - - - - - - - - - - - - - -	1 25

ILLUSTRATED LIBRARY.

THE LIFE OF FRANCIS MARION. By W. G. Simms. With numerous illustrations; 400 pages, 12mo; cloth or half roan, -	1 13
THE LIFE OF CAPT. JOHN SMITH, of Virginia. By W. G. Simms. With numerous illustrations; 400 pages, 12mo; cloth or half roan, - - - - - - - - - - - - - - -	1 13
THE LIFE OF GENERAL ISRAEL PUTNAM. By W. Cutter. With numerous illustrations; 400 pages, 12mo; cloth or half roan, - - - - - - - - - - - - - - -	1 13
INCIDENTS IN AMERICAN HISTORY. By J. W. Barber. With numerous illustrations; 400 pages, 12mo; cloth or half roan, -	1 13
THE SIGNERS OF THE DECLARATION OF INDEPENDENCE, Biographical Sketches of the Lives of. By B. J. Lossing. With numerous illustrations; 400 pages, 12mo; cloth or half roan, -	1 13
THE LIFE OF BENJAMIN FRANKLIN. By O. L. Holley. With numerous illustrations; 400 pages, 12mo; cloth or half roan, -	1 25
THE LIFE OF GENERAL LAFAYETTE. By W. Cutter. With numerous illustrations; 400 pages, 12mo; cloth or half roan. -	1 13
THE LIFE OF GENERAL GREENE. By W. G. Simms. With numerous illustrations; 400 pages, 12mo; cloth or half roan, -	1 13

THE LIFE OF JAMES K. POLK. By J. S. Jenkins. 12mo; cloth, - - - - - - - - - - - - - - - -	1 25
THE LIFE OF JOHN C. CALHOUN. By J. S. Jenkins. 12mo; cloth, - - - - - - - - - - - - - - -	1 25
THE LIFE OF SIR W. RALEIGH. Illustrated; 18mo; cloth,	50
THE LIFE AND RELIGION OF MOHAMMED. By Rev. J. L. Merrick. 12mo; cloth, - - - - - - - -	1 50

	Retail
THE LIFE OF NAPOLEON. Illustrated; 12mo; cloth,	1 25
LIFE OF MRS. S. B. JUDSON, - - - - - - -	75
SPARKS' AMERICAN BIOGRAPHY. 2d series; 15 vols., -	1 00
ROBERTSON'S CHARLES THE FIFTH. 8vo; sheep, -	1 75
DR. JOHNSON'S LIFE AND WORKS. Two vols., 8vo; sheep,	3 00
ABBOTT'S (J.) ALEXANDER THE GREAT. 18mo; muslin,	60
" ALFRED THE GREAT. 18mo; muslin, -	60
" CHARLES THE FIRST. 18mo; muslin, -	60
" CHARLES THE SECOND. 18mo, muslin, -	60
" DARIUS, KING OF PERSIA. 18mo; muslin,	60
" QUEEN ELIZABETH. 18mo; muslin, - -	60
" HANNIBAL THE CARTHAGINIAN. 18mo,	60
" JULIUS CÆSAR. 18mo; muslin, - - -	60
" MARIA ANTOINETTE. 18mo; muslin, -	60
" MARY, QUEEN OF SCOTS. 18mo; muslin,	60
" RICHARD THE FIRST. 18mo; muslin, -	60
" RICHARD THE THIRD. 18mo; muslin, -	60
" WILLIAM THE CONQUEROR. 18mo, -	60
" XERXES THE GREAT. 18mo; muslin, -	60
*** Either of the above, muslin, gilt edges,	75
" SUMMER IN SCOTLAND. 12mo; muslin,	1 00
" (J. C. S.) KINGS AND QUEENS. 12mo, -	1 00

Popular Medicine.

MEDICAL INFORMATION FOR THE PEOPLE, AND TRUE GUIDE TO HEALTH; to which is added a practical Essay on Sexual Diseases. By C. D. Hammond, M.D., member of the Eclectic School. 100 illustrations; 524 pages, 12mo. Just published. This is one of the most compact and valuable books of the kind. The best sources in the language have been consulted in its compilation, -	1 50
Do. Do. Do., family edition, - - - - - - -	1 50
GUNN'S DOMESTIC MEDICINE, or Poor Man's Friend; in plain language. New edition, 118th thousand; 890 pages, 8vo; sheep,	3 00
BUCHAN'S FAMILY PHYSICIAN. 8vo; sheep, - - -	2 50
BEACH'S AMERICAN ECLECTIC PRACTICE AND FAMILY PHYSICIAN. Nearly 200 illustrations; one vol, 8vo., 800 pages; sheep, - - - - - - - - - - - - - - - - -	5 00
BEACH'S MIDWIFERY, on reformed principles. Numerous colored engravings, - - - - - - - - - - - - -	6 00
BEACH'S ANATOMY AND PHYSIOLOGY. Numerous colored engravings, - - - - - - - - - - - -	3 00

Miscellaneous.

	Retail
THE MECHANIC'S TEXT BOOK, AND ENGINEER'S PRACTICAL GUIDE; containing a concise treatise of the nature and application of mechanical forces. By Thomas Kelt. One vol., 12mo; cloth, gilt,	1 23
DICK'S WORKS. Eleven vols. in two. New edition; 8vo; sheep,	4 50
BUNYAN'S COMPLETE WORKS. New edition, illustrated; 760 pages, 8vo. (Sold only by agents.)	3 00
MEMOIRS AND SKETCHES OF TRAVEL AMONG THE NORTHERN AND SOUTHERN INDIANS. By Col. T. L. M'Kinney. Illustrated; 8vo; sheep,	2 50
TRAVELS AND ADVENTURES IN CALIFORNIA AND OREGON; a history of the Gold Regions. By T. J. Farnham. Maps and illustrations; 8vo,	2 50
CYCLOPÆDIA OF MORAL AND RELIGIOUS ANECDOTES. By Rev. K. Arvine. 3000 facts, etc., etc. 450 pages, 8vo; morocco, extra,	2 75
UNITED STATES EXPLORING EXPEDITIONS. Voyage of the United States squadron, commanded by Capt. Charles Wilkes; discoveries made by Admiral D'Urville, Captain Ross, and Lieutenant Lynch. By John S. Jenkins, author of Life of Silas Wright, History of the War in Mexico, etc., etc. Illustrated; 8vo,	2 25
MACKENZIE'S FIVE THOUSAND RECEIPTS. Sheep,	1 25
BOLLES' PHONOGRAPHIC PRONOUNCING DICTIONARY. 100,000 words; royal 8vo,	3 50
PILGRIM'S PROGRESS, AND TRAVELS OF THE UNGODLY. Scott's notes. Large type, illustrated; 8vo; sheep,	1 50
Do. Do. Do., imitation morocco, gilt,	2 00
NEW CLERK'S ASSISTANT, by Jenkins. 4th edition,	2 25
FREMONT'S EXPEDITION TO OREGON. New edition,	1 25
SCRIPTURE GEOGRAPHY, OR A COMPANION TO THE BIBLE. By T. T. Smiley, D.D. Maps, etc.,	1 12
DARING EXPLOITS AND PERILOUS ADVENTURES. Numerous engravings; 500 pages, 12mo; arabesque,	1 25
GENERALS OF THE LAST WAR. Illustrated,	1 25
SIGNS OF THE TIMES, PAST, PRESENT, AND FUTURE; comprising a vindication of Capital Punishment. By the Rev. Lebbeus Armstrong,	75
BUTTERWORTH'S CONCORDANCE. 8vo; sheep,	1 25
CALMET'S DICTIONARY OF THE BIBLE. Maps and numerous illustrations; royal 8vo,	4 00
THE LIBRARY OF NATURAL HISTORY; compiled from the best writers. 400 illustrations; royal 8vo,	3 00
LADIES' DOMESTIC GUIDE, AND FRUGAL HOUSEWIFE. By Mrs. L. G. Abell. 659 receipts,	25
BARHYDT'S INDUSTRIAL EXCHANGES AND SOCIAL REMEDIES. 240 pages, 12mo; cloth.	75

	Retail
WHYTE'S HISTORY OF THE WORLD, with a continuation to the present time. Finely illustrated; 550 pages, 8vo; emb. roan,	2 50
DOWLING'S HISTORY OF ROMANISM, brought down to the present time, with a memoir and portrait of Pope Pius IX.; fifty engravings,	3 00
D'AUBIGNE'S HISTORY OF THE REFORMATION. New edition, 644 pages; illuminations and cuts,	2 25
PENINSULAR WAR, by Napier. 800 pages, royal 8vo; cloth,	3 00
REMARKABLE EVENTS IN THE HISTORY OF AMERICA. By J. Frost. Illustrated; two vols., 700 pages; embossed roan,	5 50
ROLLINS' ANCIENT HISTORY. Maps, etc.; four vols., 12mo; arabesque,	4 00
HISTORY OF IRELAND, by M'Geoghehan. 629 pages, 8vo,	2 50
HISTORICAL CABINET,	1 25
HISTORY OF THE BAPTIST DENOMINATION, by Benedict,	3 50
JOSEPHUS. Family edition; over 1100 pages, 8vo; roan, arabesque gilt,	2 75
MEXICAN WAR, including the Treaty of Peace. By H. Mansfield. Numerous engravings; 300 pages, 12mo,	1 25
HUME'S HISTORY OF ENGLAND, from the Invasion of Julius Cæsar to the abdication of James the Second, 1688. With a complete index to the whole work. Boston Library edition. Six vols, 12mo; cloth, per vol.,	63
MACAULAY'S HISTORY OF ENGLAND; being a continuation of Hume to the present time. Uniform with the above. 12mo; cloth, per vol.,	63
GIBBON'S HISTORY OF THE DECLINE AND FALL OF THE ROMAN EMPIRE. With Notes by Rev H. H. Milman, and a complete Index to the whole work. Uniform with Hume and Macaulay. Cloth, per vol.,	63
LAMARTINE'S HISTORY OF THE FRENCH REVOLUTION OF 1848. One vol., 12mo; cloth,	75
HUME AND SMOLLETT'S HISTORY OF ENGLAND; continued to the accession of Queen Victoria. Abridged, with numerous illustrations; one vol., 12mo; cloth, gilt,	1 25
BANCROFT'S HISTORY OF THE UNITED STATES. Three vols., 8vo; cloth,	6 00
CHAMBERS' CYCLOPÆDIA OF HISTORY. Illustrated; two vols., 8vo,	5 00
RUSSELL AND JONES' MODERN EUROPE. Four vols., 8vo; sheep,	5 00
ROBERTSON'S AMERICA. 8vo; sheep,	1 75
HILDRETH'S HISTORY OF THE UNITED STATES. Three vols., 8vo; cloth, gilt tops,	6 00
BOOK OF CHRISTIAN MARTYRS. By R. Thomas. 600 pages, 12mo,	1 75

Standard Poets in Uniform Style.

	Retail.
BURN'S POETICAL WORKS; with Life, Glossary, and Notes,	1 25
COWPER'S COMPLETE POETICAL WORKS; with Life. A new edition; one vol., 12mo, with portrait; cloth, gilt,	1 25
POPE'S POETICAL WORKS. New edition, with a life of the author. One vol., 12mo, with portrait; cloth, gilt,	1 25
BYRON'S POETICAL WORKS; with a sketch of his Life. One vol., 12mo, embellished with steel portrait; cloth, gilt,	1 25
MOORE'S POETICAL WORKS. An entire new edition; one vol., 12mo, with portrait; cloth, gilt,	1 25
SCOTT'S POETICAL WORKS; with Life. A new edition; one vol., 12mo, with portrait; cloth, gilt,	1 25
THOMSON AND POLLOK; containing the Seasons and Course of Time. A new edition; one vol., 12mo; cloth, gilt,	1 25
TUPPER'S POETICAL WORKS; containing Proverbial Philosophy, Thousand Lines, and Hactenus, complete, with portrait; 12mo; muslin, gilt,	1 25
THE POEMS OF OSSIAN. A new edition, containing ten steel engravings; 12mo; muslin, gilt,	1 25
CROLY'S SELECT BRITISH POETS. A new edition, containing four steel engravings; 12mo; muslin, gilt,	1 25
MILTON AND YOUNG; containing Paradise Lost and Night Thoughts. A new edition; one vol., 12mo, with portrait; cloth, gilt,	1 25
LIFE, GEMS, AND BEAUTIES OF SHAKSPEARE. By Rev. William Dodd. Illustrated with six fine engravings and a portrait. One vol., 12mo; cloth, gilt,	1 25
HEMANS' POETICAL WORKS. An entire new edition, illustrated with steel engravings. One vol., 12mo; cloth, gilt,	1 25
HOWITT, COOK, AND LANDON'S POETICAL WORKS. A new edition; one vol., 12mo; cloth, gilt,	1 25
KIRK WHITE'S POETICAL WORKS, MEMOIRS, AND REMAINS. By Rev. John Todd. Embellished with a portrait,	1 25
WORDSWORTH'S POETICAL WORKS. An entire new edition, with a portrait; 12mo; cloth,	1 25
CAMPBELL'S POETICAL WORKS; with a memoir and portrait. An entire new edition; one vol., 12mo; cloth,	1 25

All the above series may be had in cloth, full gilt sides and edges, for 37 cents per vol. extra.

History.

A HISTORY OF THE UNITED STATES OF AMERICA, embracing the Mexican War. By C. B. Taylor. Numerous engravings; 700 pages; embossed roan,	1 75
1776; or, History of the War of Independence,	2 00

www.ingramcontent.com/pod-product-compliance
Lightning Source LLC
LaVergne TN
LVHW020117110826
845151LV00001B/191

* 9 7 8 1 4 2 5 5 4 2 5 6 6 *